Another Bite at the Apple

A Guide to Section 2255 Motions for Federal Prisoners

Janice L. Bergmann

ABA Defending Liberty Pursuing Justice
Criminal Justice Section

Cover design by ABA Publishing.

Printed in the United States of America.

12 11 10 09 08   5 4 3 2 1

Library of Congress Cataloging-in-Publication Data

Bergmann, Janice.

Another bite at the apple : a guide to section 2255 motions for federal prisoners / by Janice Bergmann. — 1st ed.

p. cm.

ISBN 978-1-60442-268-9

1. Habeas corpus—United States. 2. Post-conviction remedies—United States. I. Title.

KF9011.B47 2008

345.73'056—dc22

2008049719

Discounts are available for books ordered in bulk. Special consideration is given to state bars, CLE programs, and other bar-related organizations. Inquire at Book Publishing, ABA Publishing, American Bar Association, 321 North Clark Street, Chicago, Illinois 60654-7598.

www.ababooks.org

Summary of Contents

Table of Contents

Introduction and Acknowledgments

This book focuses on the special procedures and concerns that arise when a prisoner moves to "vacate, set aside, or correct" a federal conviction or sentence under 28 U.S.C. § 2255. Section 2255 proceedings became significantly more complex with the enactment of the Antiterrorism and Effective Death Penalty Act (AEDPA) in April 1996, and federal courts continue to struggle with the interpretation of the AEDPA's provisions. This book tries to raise the various legal and practical questions that may be encountered in section 2255 proceedings, including those posed by the AEDPA, but because this area of law remains in flux, some of these questions have no clear answers. This book should therefore be considered the beginning, not the end, of one's education about section 2255.[1]

A note on those matters on which this book does *not* focus. First, except where relevant to section 2255 practice, this book does *not* discuss the procedures governing federal habeas corpus petitions challenging a *state* conviction or sentence under 28 U.S.C. § 2254.[2] Second, even though an ever-increasing number of federal death penalty prosecutions have made section 2255 an important remedy in capital cases, this book is intended primarily to assist in the litigation of *noncapital* section 2255 proceedings. Finally, two areas critical to successful section 2255 litigation are not addressed in any detail. This book contains little discussion of substantive law. Rather, it is directed primarily at describing section 2255 *procedure*. This book also makes little mention of the methodology for investigating the facts to support a movant's claims for relief. Again, it discusses only the procedures for presenting those facts to the court.

The seeds of this book can be traced to a conversation I had far too long ago with Assistant Federal Public Defender Paul Rashkind, who is

1. For those seeking a substantially more in-depth discussion of the subjects contained in this book, Professors Liebman and Hertz's excellent two-volume treatise, *Federal Habeas Corpus Practice and Procedure* (5th ed. 2005), which is published by the Lexis Law Company and updated annually, is indispensable.

2. That said, because of the identity between the habeas corpus and section 2255 remedies, section 2255 jurisprudence often mimics that governing state prisoner habeas corpus proceedings under section 2254. As a result, this book intermingles section 2255 and habeas corpus authority when the courts have interpreted the standards or procedures being discussed in concert with one another.

my supervisor and, at the time, was a member of the Book Publishing Committee for the Criminal Justice Section of the American Bar Association. I had just spoken at a national seminar for Federal Public Defenders about section 2255 practice, and was lamenting the lack of resource materials addressing postconviction remedies for federal prisoners. Paul's response was to suggest that I write a book on section 2255, and do it for the ABA. I hope it helps in some small way to fill the void.

This book would never have come to be without the institutional support provided by the wonderful Kathleen Williams, the Federal Defender for the Southern District of Florida, as well as Paul and my many other FPD colleagues, nor without the patience, thoughtful guidance, and assistance of the publications staff at the ABA, my personal editor Carol Freeman, the Committee, and of course, my amazing family. Thanks to them all.

Janice L. Bergmann
November 2008

Part I:

An Overview of Section 2255 Proceedings

CHAPTER 1

An Introduction to Section 2255

Contents

I. An Introduction to Section 2255

§ 1.01. Section 2255 was enacted to address practical difficulties with habeas corpus.

Although today the writ of habeas corpus is a federal remedy primarily used by *state* prisoners to challenge their conviction or sentence, habeas corpus was also the primary postconviction remedy for *federal* prisoners until 1948, when Congress adopted 28 U.S.C. § 2255. Congress intended section 2255 to supersede habeas corpus as the means by which federal prisoners could challenge the lawfulness of their incarceration, but nonetheless "afford federal prisoners a remedy identical in scope to federal habeas corpus." *Davis v. United States*, 417 U.S. 333, 343, 94 S. Ct. 2298, 2304, 41 L. Ed. 2d 109 (1974). The current text of section 2255 can be found in the Appendix contained in Chapter 20.[1]

Section 2255 was enacted for *procedural* reasons—to divert federal prisoner petitions into the district in which the federai prisoner was originally sentenced. *See Boumediene v. Bush*, ___ U.S. ___, 128 S. Ct. 2229, 2264, 171 L. Ed. 2d 41 (2008); *United States v. Hayman*, 342 U.S. 205, 219, 72 S. Ct. 263, 272, 96 L. Ed. 2d 232 (1952). Prior to the enactment of section 2255, great practical difficulties were caused by the fact that a habeas corpus proceeding must be brought in the district of confinement. As an increasing number of habeas corpus petitions were filed by federal prisoners, those few district courts with major federal prisons within their jurisdiction were required to handle an inordinate number of habeas

1. On January 7, 2008, Congress amended section 2255 by designating its eight previously undesignated paragraphs as subsections (a) through (h), respectively. This amendment was technical only. *See* Pub. L. 110-177, Title V, § 511, 121 Stat. 2545 (Jan. 7, 2008).

corpus proceedings—and to do so relying on the record of a distant sentencing court. *Id.*, 342 U.S. at 212–14, 72 S. Ct. at 268–69. Moreover, if a hearing was ordered, the witnesses often had to be brought great distances to the district of confinement. *Id.*, 342 U.S. at 213–14, 72 S. Ct. at 268–70. Section 2255, which requires a motion to be filed in the sentencing court, largely alleviated these problems by spreading the burden of federal prisoner collateral proceedings evenly over the entire federal court system.

§ 1.02. Section 2255 is used to attack a federal conviction or sentence.

Section 2255 is a very broad remedy. It allows a federal prisoner to move to "vacate, set aside or correct" a federal sentence upon the ground that

> the sentence was imposed in violation of the Constitution or laws of the United States, or that the court was without jurisdiction to impose such sentence, or that the sentence was in excess of the maximum authorized by law, or is otherwise subject to collateral attack.

28 U.S.C. § 2255(a). The nature and scope of the section 2255 remedy and its relationship to other federal postconviction remedies are discussed in detail in Chapters 3 and 7.

§ 1.03. Section 2255 proceedings are unusual.

A section 2255 proceeding has been described as "a further step in the movant's criminal case."[2] Nonetheless, many experienced federal criminal practitioners will find it unfamiliar territory. Like the writ of habeas corpus from which it sprang, a section 2255 proceeding is a hybrid: a quasi-civil litigation of issues of substantive criminal law. For this reason, many of the tools of civil litigation are available in section 2255 proceedings, including discovery, motion practice, and summary adjudications. And because of its quasi-civil nature, the criminal defendant becomes the "movant"—akin to a plaintiff in a civil action—and as such, must be proactive rather than reactive. Moreover, like habeas corpus, a section 2255 proceeding is a "collateral" attack on a conviction and sentence, allowing a federal district court something akin to appellate review in a criminal case, even though the prior judgment may already have been affirmed on direct appeal. Finally, restrictions on the right to relief under section 2255

2. Advisory Committee Note to Rule 1, Rules Governing § 2255 Proceedings.

may implicate the constitutional guarantee prohibiting the suspension of the writ of habeas corpus.[3]

Despite their similarities, however, practitioners comfortable in the arcane world of habeas corpus procedure may also find section 2255 practice confusing. Section 2255 and state prisoner habeas corpus proceedings differ in important ways:

1. Comity and federalism concerns, which play a major role when a federal court is reviewing a state prisoner's conviction or sentence, are irrelevant when the United States is the respondent.
2. Unlike state prisoner habeas cases—where the federal court reviews a cold record of the prior proceedings to evaluate the actions of faceless state court judges—section 2255 requires the district judge to review his or her *own* actions and allows the judge to rely upon his or her own recollection of prior events and the parties involved.
3. Different rules apply. Section 2255 proceedings have their own set of rules, which are similar but not identical to the rules applicable to state prisoner habeas corpus cases. *Compare* Rules Governing Section 2255 Proceedings, 28 U.S.C. fol. § 2255,[4] *with* Rules Governing Section 2254 Cases, 28 U.S.C. fol. § 2254. And because a section 2255 proceeding is *both* a continuation of the movant's criminal case *and* a quasi-civil action like habeas corpus, some of the Federal Rules of Criminal Procedure *and* some of the Federal Rules of Civil Procedure apply, whereas only the Civil Rules apply in state prisoner habeas cases.
4. Although Congress greatly complicated the procedural rules for both habeas corpus and section 2255 cases when it enacted the Antiterrorism and Effective Death Penalty Act of 1996 (AEDPA), Pub. L. 104-132, 110 Stat. 1214 (1996), it did so in slightly different ways for each.[5]

II. An Overview of Section 2255 Proceedings

Although few section 2255 cases can be called "typical," and numerous permutations exist, section 2255 proceedings usually unfold as follows.

---

3. The Suspension Clause states: "The Privilege of the Writ of Habeas Corpus shall not be suspended, unless when in Cases of Rebellion or Invasion the public Safety may require it." U.S. Const. Art. 1, § 9, cl. 2.

4. The text of the Rules Governing Section 2255 Proceedings can be found in the Appendix contained in the Appendix.

5. The AEDPA's impact on section 2255 proceedings is discussed in Chapter 2.

§ 1.04. Timing of section 2255 proceedings.

In general, section 2255 proceedings should not begin until the federal criminal proceedings are completed. Thus, in the usual case, it is not until a person has been tried, convicted, and sentenced, and not until direct appeal proceedings have been completed—including, where applicable, through *certiorari* to the United States Supreme Court—that a section 2255 motion should be filed. *See* Chapter 4.

Once the federal conviction and sentence become final upon the conclusion of direct review, an eye must be kept on the statute of limitations "clock" applicable to section 2255 proceedings. In the vast majority of cases, a section 2255 motion must be filed within one year from the date on which the conviction became final, or all right to relief will be lost forever. *See* Chapter 5.

§ 1.05. Preparation and filing of a section 2255 motion.

Section 2255 proceedings commence with the filing of a section 2255 motion by a person in custody pursuant to a federal conviction and sentence. The motion must be filed in the same federal district court where the movant was convicted and sentenced, and it will likely be considered by the same federal judge who oversaw the movant's federal criminal proceedings. *See* Chapters 6 and 12.

In addition to being filed in a timely manner, it is very important that an initial section 2255 motion contain all of the movant's potential claims for relief. *See* Chapter 7. Any attempt to amend a motion to add a new claim after the limitations period has run will likely be deemed untimely and therefore not allowed. *See* Chapters 5 and 12. Or, an attempted amendment of the motion may be construed as a second or successive motion, and it is nearly impossible to obtain relief on such motions. *See* Chapter 19.

§ 1.06. Responsive pleadings and summary proceedings.

With a complete and timely motion now pending before the federal district court, the court[6] will review the motion to ensure that it is not frivolous, and if it is not, will order the government to file a response. *See* Chapter 13. The response may assert the panoply of procedural defenses provided the government in section 2255 proceedings. *See* Chapters 5–11. The movant may then file a reply. *See* Chapter 13.

6. In many districts, the motion will be referred to a United States magistrate judge for consideration. *See* Chapter 14, *infra*.

§ 1.07. Fact-development procedures.

To develop the facts to support the claims presented in the motion, the movant may move to expand the record or, upon a showing of good cause, obtain discovery. In some cases, the district court will hold an evidentiary hearing on one or more of the movant's claims, either because a hearing is mandatory, or in the court's discretion. *See* Chapter 15.

§ 1.08. The district court's decision and postjudgment proceedings.

The district court will then render a decision. *See* Chapter 16. Following the district court's decision, either the movant, the government, or both, may file postjudgment motions asking the district court to reconsider its decision. A victorious movant may seek release pending appeal. *See* Chapter 17.

§ 1.09. Appellate proceedings.

After district court proceedings are complete, either the movant, the government, or both, may appeal to the United States Court of Appeals with jurisdiction over the appeal. A movant cannot appeal without first obtaining a certificate of appealability, either from the district court or the court of appeals. *See* Chapter 18. Once proceedings in the court of appeals are complete, *certiorari* review may be sought from the United States Supreme Court.

§ 1.10. Second or successive motions.

In very specific and very rare circumstances, the court of appeals may grant a federal prisoner permission to file a second or successive section 2255 motion. Because the filing of a second or successive motion is allowed in very, very few cases, it is imperative that *all* potential claims for relief be included in the movant's first section 2255 motion. *See* Chapter 19.

CHAPTER 2

The Antiterrorism and Effective Death Penalty Act of 1996

Contents

Introduction

§ 2.01. The AEDPA significantly changed section 2255 practice.

In a rose garden ceremony on the afternoon of April 24, 1996, President Clinton signed into law the Antiterrorism and Effective Death Penalty Act of 1996 (AEDPA), Pub. L. 104-132, 110 Stat. 1214 (1996). The AEDPA made significant changes to the statutes and rules governing section 2255 practice.[1] Although more than a decade has passed since the AEDPA's enactment, questions remain regarding the interpretation and application of its various provisions. This is in large part because the AEDPA is less than a masterpiece of clarity: "[I]n a world of silk purses and pigs' ears, the Act is not a silk purse of the art of statutory drafting." *Lindh v. Murphy*, 521 U.S. 320, 336, 117 S. Ct. 2059, 2068, 138 L. Ed. 2d 481 (1997).

The AEDPA altered section 2255 proceedings by (1) imposing a new one-year statute of limitations for filing a motion, (2) requiring a "certificate of appealability" to appeal the denial of relief, and (3) greatly restricting the ability to obtain relief on a second or successive motion. These provisions are introduced briefly in the rest of this chapter and discussed in greater detail in Chapters 5, 18, and 19, respectively.

1. The AEDPA also made numerous changes to federal habeas corpus practice for state prisoners under 28 U.S.C. § 2254. Many of the changes to section 2255 worked by the AEDPA parallel changes the AEDPA made to state prisoner habeas corpus proceedings, and the courts have often interpreted these parallel provisions in an identical fashion. As a result, this book intermingles section 2255 and habeas corpus authority when the courts have interpreted the standards or procedures being discussed in concert with one another.

§ 2.02. In general, the AEDPA applies to any motion filed after April 24, 1996.

"[G]enerally," the AEDPA's provisions affecting section 2255 motions apply to any motion filed "after the Act became effective" on April 24, 1996, *Lindh*, 521 U.S. at 336, 117 S. Ct. at 2068, unless "a retroactive effect would thereby result," *In re Hanserd*, 123 F.3d 922, 934 n.22 (6th Cir. 1997).

I. The One-Year Statute of Limitations

§ 2.03. Before the AEDPA, a section 2255 motion could be made "at any time."

Prior to the AEDPA, section 2255 provided that a motion could be made "at any time." 28 U.S.C. § 2255 (1994). Indeed, the only pre-AEDPA timeliness requirement was that an application for section 2255 relief be filed without prejudicial delay. *See Lonchar v. Thomas*, 517 U.S. 314, 316, 116 S. Ct. 1293, 1295, 134 L. Ed. 2d 440 (1996).

§ 2.04. A one-year statute of limitations now applies.

In a dramatic change, the AEDPA amended section 2255 to establish "a 1-year period of limitation" applicable to section 2255 motions. § 2255(f). In most cases, the one-year limitations period runs from "the date on which the judgment of conviction becomes final." § 2255(f)(1). In other cases, the one-year period runs from some later date: either the date on which an unconstitutional governmental action impeding the filing of a motion was removed, § 2255(f)(2); or, the date on which a new right was recognized by the Supreme Court, if that right has been made retroactively applicable to collateral cases, § 2255(f)(3); or, the date on which the fact supporting the claims presented in the motion "could have been discovered through the exercise of due diligence," § 2255(f)(4). The statute of limitations is discussed in greater detail in Chapter 5.

II. Certificates of Appealability

§ 2.05. A certificate of appealability is now required to perfect an appeal.

Prior to the AEDPA, a prisoner's appeal from a district court order denying section 2255 relief was perfected simply by timely filing a notice of appeal. *See* 28 U.S.C. § 2253 (1995); Fed. R. App. P. 22(b) (1995). This is no longer true. Now, a section 2255 movant seeking to perfect an appeal must both timely file a notice of appeal *and* secure a "certificate of appealability"

(COA). *See* 28 U.S.C. § 2253(c); Fed. R. App. P. 22(b). To obtain a COA, a prisoner must make a "substantial showing of the denial of a constitutional right" with respect to each issue sought to be raised on appeal. § 2253(c)(2) & (3). Certificates of appealability are discussed in greater detail in Chapter 18.

III. Second or Successive Motions

§ 2.06. It is now nearly impossible to obtain relief on a second or successive motion.

As discussed briefly here and in more detail in Chapter 19, the AEDPA changed both the substantive standard governing when section 2255 relief may be granted on a second or successive motion and the procedures governing such motions. It was very difficult to obtain relief on a second or successive motion under the pre-AEDPA standard.[2] The provisions enacted by the AEDPA, however, have made it nearly impossible. As a result, it is *essential* that section 2255 movants include in their *first* motion *all* potential claims for relief.

§ 2.07. The AEDPA altered the standards governing relief on second or successive motions.

Post-AEDPA, a second or successive section 2255 motion will be dismissed unless certain very specific and rare circumstances exist. Relief is available only if the motion contains a claim that (1) is based on newly discovered evidence which demonstrates clearly and convincingly that no reasonable fact-finder would have convicted the movant of the underlying offense, or (2) "relies on a new rule of constitutional law, made retroactive to cases on collateral review by the Supreme Court, that was previously unavailable." *See* § 2255(h)(1) & (h)(2). These are, needless to say, extremely difficult standards to meet.

§ 2.08. The AEDPA altered the procedures for second or successive motions.

The AEDPA also created an elaborate pre-filing procedure—a so-called "gatekeeping" mechanism—that requires federal prisoners to receive

2. Pre-AEDPA, a federal prisoner who wished to bring a new claim in a second or successive section 2255 motion had to demonstrate either cause for failing to raise the issue in the prior motion and prejudice therefrom, or that he was actually innocent. *See* McCleskey v. Zant, 499 U.S. 467, 494–95, 111 S. Ct. 1454, 1470, 113 L. Ed. 2d 517 (1991); In re *Hanserd*, 123 F.3d 922, 928. (6th cir. 1997)

permission to file a second or successive section 2255 motion from the court of appeals before being able to proceed on the motion in the district court. The court of appeals may authorize the filing of a second or successive motion only upon a *prima facie* showing that the motion meets the AEDPA's new substantive standard. The decision by the court of appeals to allow or disallow the filing of a second or successive motion is not appealable, and may not be the subject of a petition for rehearing nor a petition for writ of *certiorari*. *See* 28 U.S.C. § 2244(b)(3).

CHAPTER 3

Relationship of Section 2255 to Other Federal Postconviction Remedies

Contents

Introduction

§ 3.01. Postconviction remedies other than section 2255 should be used in some circumstances.

As described in Chapter 1, Congress enacted section 2255 as a broad post-conviction remedy for federal prisoners. But Congress did not intend section 2255 to be the *exclusive* postconviction remedy for federal prisoners in all circumstances.

Section 2255 itself states that a federal prisoner may resort to the traditional habeas corpus remedy codified at 28 U.S.C. § 2241 when it "appears that the remedy by [section 2255] motion is inadequate or ineffective to test the legality of his detention." § 2255(e). Moreover, if both the section 2255 and section 2241 remedies are unavailable, there are circumstances where the common-law writ of *coram nobis* may be used to collaterally attack a federal conviction and sentence. *See United States v. Morgan*, 346 U.S. 502, 510–11, 74 S. Ct. 247, 252, 98 L. Ed. 2d 248 (1954). Other post-conviction remedies, such as a new trial motion under Federal Rule of Criminal Procedure 33, or a motion to modify sentence under 18 U.S.C.

§ 3582(c), may also be appropriate in circumstances where a section 2255 motion is not.

This chapter discusses the relationship of section 2255 to other federal postconviction remedies.[1]

§ 3.02. Must the claims be filed under section 2255, or is another remedy appropriate?

It is critical to determine whether the claims at issue must be raised in a section 2255 motion or whether resort to another postconviction remedy is appropriate. Procedures differ depending on which remedy is pursued. Importantly, many of the changes to section 2255 practice worked by the Antiterrorism and Effective Death Penalty Act of 1996 (AEDPA)[2] do not apply to other postconviction remedies.

But beware: one may not style a section 2255 motion as a pleading seeking relief under some other postconviction remedy in an attempt to avoid application of the AEDPA. Courts will disregard mislabeled filings and determine whether the application is, in fact, a section 2255 motion when considering the availability of relief:

> Any motion filed in the district court that imposed the sentence, and substantively within the scope of [§ 2255(a)], *is* a motion under § 2255, no matter what title the prisoner plasters on the cover. Call it a motion for a new trial, arrest of judgment, mandamus, prohibition, coram nobis, coram vobis, audita querela, certiorari, capias, habeas corpus, ejectment, quare impedit, bill of review, writ of error, or an application for a Get-Out-Of-Jail Card; the name makes no difference. It is substance that controls.

Melton v. United States, 359 F.3d 855, 857 (7th Cir. 2004) (internal citation omitted) (emphasis in original).

If the pleading is found to be a section 2255 motion even though not styled as such, the movant may lose the ability to obtain relief as a result of the motion's failure to comply with the AEDPA's procedural restrictions.

1. As it is a *post*conviction remedy, section 2255 cannot be used to challenge *pretrial* detention. The Bail Reform Act, 18 U.S.C. § 3141 *et seq.*, is the most appropriate means by which a person under federal indictment can challenge his pretrial detention. *See* United States v. Pepito, 861 F.2d 1006, 1009 (7th Cir. 1987); Fassler v. United States, 858 F.2d 1016, 1018–19 (5th Cir. 1988) *(per curiam)*. This book does not discuss the remedies available to federal prisoners seeking to attack their pretrial detention.

2. Chapter 2 discusses the AEDPA in greater detail.

See, e.g., *United States v. Lloyd*, 398 F.3d 978, 979–80 (7th Cir. 2005) (construing request for sentence reduction under 18 U.S.C. § 3582(c) as a successive section 2255 motion, and denying motion for its failure to meet requirements for such motions); *United States v. Adams*, 372 F.3d 132, 135–36 (2d Cir. 2004) (construing 28 U.S.C. § 2241 petition as successive section 2255 motion and concluding that motion is barred by requirements for such motions); *Poe v. United States*, 468 F.3d 473, 476–77 (7th Cir. 2006) (district court properly dismissed pleading as wrongly filed under 28 U.S.C. § 2241, even though section 2255 motion could no longer be filed on time); *Matus-Leva v. United States*, 287 F.3d 758, 761 (9th Cir. 2002) (noting that if court were to construe *coram nobis* petition as a section 2255 motion, section 2255 motion would be time-barred). To avoid this trap, keep in mind the differences between section 2255 and other post-conviction remedies.

I. The Nature of the Section 2255 Remedy

§ 3.03. Use section 2255 to attack the validity of a conviction or sentence.

Challenges to a federal prisoner's underlying conviction and sentence are properly raised in a section 2255 motion. Section 2255 provides that prisoners may move to "vacate, set aside, or correct" a federal sentence on the grounds that "the sentence was imposed in violation of the Constitution or laws of the United States, or that the court was without jurisdiction to impose such sentence, or that the sentence was in excess of the maximum authorized by law, or is otherwise subject to collateral attack." 28 U.S.C. § 2255(a). *See also id.*, § 2255(b) ("the judgment was rendered without jurisdiction, or that the sentence imposed was not authorized by law or otherwise open to collateral attack, or that there has been such a denial or infringement of the constitutional rights of the prisoner as to render the judgment vulnerable to collateral attack.").

As described in detail in Chapter 7, section 2255 provides a remedy for a wide range of claims. In general, any claim that falls substantively within the scope of section 2255(a)—that is, any claim that collaterally attacks the validity of a federal conviction or sentence—should be filed as a section 2255 motion. *See Lloyd*, 398 F.3d at 979–80; *United States v. Holt*, 417 F.3d 1172, 1175 (11th Cir. 2005); *Okereke v. United States*, 307 F.3d 117, 120 (3d Cir. 2002) ("Motions pursuant to 28 U.S.C. § 2255 are the presumptive means by which federal prisoners can challenge their convictions or sentences"). If some other form of relief is sought, you must determine which other federal postconviction remedy is appropriate.

II. Habeas Corpus Petitions Under 28 U.S.C. § 2241

§ 3.04. Use section 2241 when the section 2255 remedy is "inadequate or ineffective."

Congress designed section 2255 to substitute for, but not entirely supersede, the traditional section 2241 habeas corpus remedy for federal prisoners. Section 2255 expressly states that a federal prisoner may resort to section 2241 when it "appears that the remedy by [section 2255] motion is inadequate or ineffective to test the legality of his detention." 28 U.S.C. § 2255(e).

§ 3.05. Resort to section 2241 is appropriate to attack the *execution* of a federal sentence.

Because of the breadth of the section 2255 remedy, the situations in which it has been found "inadequate or ineffective" are few. They are, however, important. Claims that attack the *execution* of a federal sentence by prison officials, or challenge a confinement that is not the result of a criminal court's judgment, are not cognizable in section 2255 proceedings. *United States v. Addonizio*, 442 U.S. 178, 185–86, 99 S. Ct. 2235, 2240–41, 60 L. Ed. 2d 805 (1979); *Bell v. United States*, 48 F.3d 1042, 1043 (8th Cir. 1995). Accordingly, section 2241, *not* section 2255, should be used to attack such things as:

(1) *the denial of sentence credits for items such as good time or pretrial detention. See Reno v. Koray*, 515 U.S. 50, 52–53, 115 S. Ct. 2021, 2023, 132 L. Ed. 2d 46 (1995) (credit for pretrial detention in treatment center); *Rogers v. United States*, 180 F.3d 349, 358 & n.16 (1st Cir. 1999) (credit for time served in state prison); *Graham v. Lanfong*, 25 F.3d 203, 204 (3d Cir. 1994) (good time credits); *Bell*, 48 F.3d at 1043 (credit for time served under "no bond" order); *McClain v. Bureau of Prisons*, 9 F.3d 503, 504–05 (6th Cir. 1993) (*per curiam*) (credit for time spent in federal prison while on state parole).

(2) *transfers or other changes in the type of detention. See Rogers*, 180 F.3d at 357 (1st Cir. 1999) (failure to designate state prison as place of confinement); *Dunne v. Keohane*, 14 F.3d 335, 336–37 (7th Cir. 1994) (transfers between state and federal facilities); *United States v. Harris*, 12 F.3d 735, 736 (7th Cir. 1994) (disciplinary segregation); *United States v. Barth*, 28 F.3d 253, 256 (2d Cir. 1994) (commitment to another facility for psychiatric examination to assist with determination of competence); *United States v. Fuller*, 86 F.3d 105, 106–07 (7th Cir. 1996) (same).

(3) *prison disciplinary procedures. See Kingsley v. United States Bureau of Prisons*, 937 F.2d 26, 30 n.5 (2d Cir. 1991) (denial of right to call witnesses at disciplinary hearing).

(4) *immigration orders, e.g., INS v. St. Cyr*, 533 U.S. 289, 121 S. Ct 2271, 150 L. Ed. 2d 347 (2001) (deportation/exclusion orders); *Zadvydas v. Davis*, 533 U.S. 678, 121 S. Ct. 2491, 150 L. Ed. 2d 653 (2001) (challenge to indefinite detention by immigration officials of person not likely to be deported). Note, however, that in May 2005, Congress passed the REAL ID Act, Pub. L. No. 109–13, Div. B, § 106, 119 Stat. 231, 310–11 (2005), which attempts to preclude the use of section 2241 as a means to obtain federal court review of immigration cases.

(5) *extradition to a foreign country. See In re Extradition of Drayer*, 190 F.3d 410, 412 n.2 (6th Cir. 1999); *Ludecke v. United States Marshal*, 15 F.3d 496, 497 (5th Cir. 1994); *Austin v. Healy*, 5 F.3d 598, 600–01 (2d Cir. 1993).

(6) *other detention orders issued by the executive branch. See Rasul v. Bush*, 542 U.S. 466, 124 S. Ct. 2686, 159 L. Ed. 2d 548 (2004) (challenges to legality of detention of foreign nationals captured by United States abroad and incarcerated at the Guantanamo Bay Naval Base, Cuba); *Hamdi v. Rumsfeld*, 542 U.S. 507, 124 S. Ct. 2633, 159 L. Ed. 2d 578 (2004) (habeas corpus available to review detention of an alleged "enemy combatant").

(7) *parole determinations. See Valona v. United States,* 138 F.3d 693, 694 (7th Cir. 1998); *Doganiere v. United States,* 914 F.2d 165, 169–70 (9th Cir. 1990).

§ 3.06. Bringing a claim under section 2255 or section 2241 has practical consequences.

Procedures differ depending on whether a federal prisoner's claims are brought under section 2255 or section 2241. For example, a section 2255 motion must be filed in the district where the prisoner was convicted and sentenced, whereas a section 2241 petition must be filed in the district of confinement. § 2255(e); Rules 3(b) & 4(a), Rules Governing Section 2255 Motions; *Rumsfeld v. Padilla*, 542 U.S. 426, 442–43, 124 S. Ct. 2711, 2722, 159 L. Ed. 2d 513 (2004). A petitioner seeking relief under section 2241 may have to exhaust administrative remedies before seeking federal court review. *See Skinner v. Wiley*, 355 F.3d 1293, 1295 (11th Cir. 2004). No such requirement pertains to section 2255 motions.

But most importantly, many of the changes to section 2255 practice worked by the AEDPA do not apply to section 2241 proceedings initiated by federal prisoners. A federal prisoner seeking habeas corpus relief via section 2241 need not file an application within the one-year limitations period applicable to section 2255 motions, nor obtain a certificate of appealability to appeal the denial of relief by the district court.[3] *See* § 2255(f); 28 U.S.C. § 2253(c)(1); *Harrison v. Ollison*, 519 F.3d 952, 958–59 (9th Cir. 2008); *Binford v. United States*, 436 F.3d 1252, 1253 n.2 (10th Cir. 2006); *Murphy v. United States*, 199 F.3d 599, 601 n.2 (2d Cir. 1999). And although the AEDPA greatly restricts the ability to obtain relief on a second or successive section 2255 motion, a section 2255 motion is not considered "second or successive" where the prior application sought relief under section 2241; and, conversely, a section 2241 petition filed after the denial of a prior application under section 2255 is not considered "second or successive." *See, e.g., Stantini v. United States*, 140 F.3d 424, 426–27 (2d Cir. 1998); *Romandine v. United States*, 206 F.3d 731, 736 (7th Cir. 2000).[4]

§ 3.07. Do section 2255's statute of limitations or restrictions on second or successive motions make it inadequate or ineffective?

In general, the section 2255 remedy is not "inadequate" or "ineffective," and a prisoner cannot invoke section 2241 simply because of his or her inability to comply with section 2255's statute of limitations or its requirements for second or successive motions. *See Okereke*, 307 F.3d at 120; *Tolliver v. Dobre*, 211 F.3d 876, 878 (5th Cir. 2000) (collecting cases).

The courts of appeal, however, have carved out a narrow exception to this general rule. They have found the statute of limitations and restrictions on second or successive motions render the section 2255 remedy inadequate or ineffective in certain rare circumstances, although they disagree slightly about what those circumstances are. *See Harrison*, 519 F.3d at 959 (section 2241 remedy available when a petitioner (1) makes a claim of actual innocence and (2) has not had an unobstructed procedural shot at presenting that claim); *In re Jones*, 226 F.3d 328, 333–34 (4th Cir. 2000) (holding section 2255 is inadequate and ineffective "when: (1) at the time of conviction, settled law of this circuit or the Supreme Court established

3. The statute of limitations for section 2255 motions is discussed in Chapter 5; certificates of appealability are discussed in Chapter 18.

4. Note, however, that the pre-AEDPA rule that claims raised and litigated in a prior section 2241 proceeding cannot be relitigated in a subsequent section 2241 petition survived the AEDPA. *See* 28 U.S.C. § 2244(a); Queen v. Miner, 530 F.3d 253, 255 (3d Cir. 2008).

the legality of the conviction; (2) subsequent to the prisoner's direct appeal and first § 2255 motion, the substantive law changed such that the conduct of which the prisoner was convicted is deemed not to be criminal; and (3) the prisoner cannot satisfy the gatekeeping provisions of § 2255 because the new rule is not one of constitutional law"); *Wofford v. Scott*, 177 F.3d 1236, 1244 (11th Cir. 1999) (section 2241 remedy available where claim is based on a retroactively applicable Supreme Court decision, where that decision establishes prisoner was convicted for a nonexistent offense, and where circuit law squarely foreclosed such a claim at the time it otherwise should have been raised); *In re Davenport*, 147 F.3d 605, 610–12 (7th Cir. 1998) (section 2241 remedy available where federal prisoner had no reasonable opportunity to obtain an earlier judicial correction of a fundamental defect in his conviction or sentence); *Triestman v. United States*, 124 F.3d 361, 377 (2d Cir. 1997) (section 2241 remedy available where the failure to provide relief would raise a serious question as to section 2255's constitutionality); *In re Dorsainvil*, 119 F.3d 245, 250–51 (3d Cir. 1997) (section 2255 inadequate if prisoner "had no earlier opportunity to challenge his conviction for a crime that an intervening change in the substantive law may negate").

III. *Coram Nobis*[5]

§ 3.08. *Coram nobis* is available only when all other statutory remedies are not.

The common-law writ of *coram nobis* is considered an "extraordinary remedy" available only to correct errors "of the most fundamental character." *Morgan*, 346 U.S. at 511–12, 74 S. Ct. at 252–53 (internal quotation marks omitted). In light of its "extraordinary" nature, *coram nobis* relief is limited to those circumstances in which no statutory remedy is adequate or available. *See United States v. Brown*, 117 F.3d 471, 474–75 (11th Cir. 1997); *Matus-Leva*, 287 F.3d at 761.

As a result, individuals who are "in custody"[6] pursuant to a federal conviction and sentence are barred from seeking a writ of error *coram*

5. The writ of *audita querela* is similar, but not identical to, the writ of *coram nobis*. United States v. Torres, 282 F.3d 1241, 1245 n.6 (10th Cir. 2002). A writ of *coram nobis* is used to attack a judgment that was infirm at the time of judgment for reasons that later came to light, whereas a writ of *audita querela* is used to attack a judgment that was correct at the time of judgment but became infirm by matters that later arose. *Id.* At least five federal courts of appeal have assumed, without deciding, that *audita querela* may be used to vacate an otherwise final conviction. *See id.* Nonetheless, every court of appeal to consider the question has held that a writ of *audita querela* may not be granted when relief is cognizable under section 2255 or *coram nobis*. *See United States v. Holt*, 417 F.3d 1172, 1175 (11th Cir. 2005) (collecting cases). It will not be discussed further here.

6. *See* Chapter 6 for a discussion of the custody requirement for section 2255 motions.

nobis, because relief is available via section 2255 or section 2241. *See Brown*, 117 F.3d at 475; *Matus-Leva*, 287 F.3d at 761; *United States v. Torres*, 282 F.3d 1241, 1245 (10th Cir. 2002). Importantly, the section 2255 remedy is considered "available" if the claims presented in the *coram nobis* petition could have been raised earlier in a section 2255 motion, but were not. *United States v. Baptiste*, 223 F.3d 188, 189–90 (3d Cir. 2002). Moreover, the fact that the individual simply failed to comply with section 2255's statute of limitations or its provisions governing second or successive motions does not make the section 2255 remedy unavailable: "A petitioner may not resort to *coram nobis* merely because he has failed to meet the AEDPA's gatekeeping requirements. To hold otherwise would circumvent the AEDPA's overall purpose of expediting the presentation of claims in federal court and enable prisoners to bypass the limitations and successive petitions provisions." *Matus-Leva*, 287 F.3d at 761. *See Baptiste*, 223 F.3d at 189–90; *Godoski v. United States*, 304 F.3d 761, 763 (7th Cir. 2002) ("*coram nobis* is a common-law writ, and it is entirely inappropriate for the judiciary to invoke the common law to override limitations enacted by Congress, such as the period of limitations in § 2255").

Given that it is available only when all other statutory remedies are not, the situations in which *coram nobis* relief has been found to be appropriate are few. Most courts have found it available only to attack a fundamentally unfair conviction where the prisoner has already served the entire sentence and is therefore no longer in custody. *See United States v. Kwan*, 407 F.3d 1005, 1009 (9th Cir. 2005); *Baptiste*, 223 F.3d at 189; *United States v. Peter*, 310 F.3d 709, 712 (11th Cir. 2002).

§ 3.09. *Coram nobis* is available only to correct "fundamental" errors.

The Supreme Court has held that the writ of error *coram nobis* is available only when the challenged conviction is one that has been obtained as a result of errors "of the most fundamental character" that have "rendered the proceeding itself irregular and invalid." *Morgan*, 346 U.S. at 509 n.15, 74 S. Ct. at 251 n.15 (internal quotation marks omitted); *Kwan*, 407 F.3d at 1009-1010 (*coram nobis* "provides a remedy for those suffering from the lingering collateral consequences of an unconstitutional or unlawful conviction based on errors of fact and egregious legal errors") (internal quotation marks omitted).

"Fundamentally unfair" errors cognizable in *coram nobis* include:

(1) *the failure of the indictment to charge an offense. See Peter*, 310 F.3d at 712–13 (granting *coram nobis* relief after concluding district court had no jurisdiction to accept defendant's plea to an indictment that alleged only a non-offense);

(2) *ineffective assistance of counsel. See Kwan*, 407 F.3d at 1017–18 (concluding that counsel was ineffective for misadvising petitioner that his guilty plea would have no adverse immigration consequences, and granting *coram nobis* relief);

(3) *denial of the right to counsel. See Morgan*, 346 U.S. at 511–12, 74 S. Ct. at 252–53 (granting *coram nobis* relief and vacating federal conviction on grounds that defendant was not provided legal representation at taking of plea).

§ 3.10. Procedural considerations for writs of error *coram nobis*.

Like section 2255 motions, writs of error *coram nobis* must be filed in the sentencing court. *United States v. Monreal*, 301 F.3d 1127, 1131 (9th Cir. 2002). Unlike section 2255 motions, however, no statute of limitations applies.[7] *See Kwan*, 407 F.3d at 1012; *Morgan*, 346 U.S. at 507, 74 S. Ct. at 250 (explaining that *coram nobis* petitions are allowed "without limitation of time"). In lieu of a specific limitations period, courts have required a *coram nobis* petitioner to provide sound reasons explaining why the conviction or sentence was not attacked earlier. *See Morgan*, 346 U.S. at 512, 74 S. Ct. at 253; *Kwan*, 407 F.3d at 1012.

An appeal in a *coram nobis* proceeding is considered "civil" in nature, Fed. R. App. P. 4(a)(1)(C), and therefore must be filed within 60 days after entry of the order granting or denying the writ, Fed. R. App. P. 4(a)(1)(B).

IV. Motions Under Federal Rule of Criminal Procedure 33

§ 3.11. Rule 33 allows for granting a new trial in the interests of justice or based on newly discovered evidence.

Federal Rule of Criminal Procedure 33 authorizes the grant of a new trial on motion of a defendant in two circumstances. First, newly discovered evidence may form the basis for a new trial motion if the motion is filed within three years after the verdict or finding of guilty. Fed. R. Crim. P. 33(b)(1). Second, a new trial may be granted "on any reason other than newly discovered evidence" if the motion is filed within seven days after the verdict or finding of guilty. Fed. R. Crim. P. 33(b)(2). Thus, the remedies provided by Rule 33 and section 2255 overlap in some respects.

7. The statute of limitations applicable to section 2255 motions is discussed in detail in Chapter 5.

§ 3.12. Beware the traps created by the overlap between Rule 33(b)(1) and section 2255.

The overlap between a motion for new trial based on Rule 33(b)(1) and a section 2255 motion can create at least two potential traps for the unwary. The first involves timing: a pending Rule 33(b)(1) motion does *not* toll the one-year limitation period for a section 2255 motion, unless it is filed within ten days of the entry of the underlying criminal judgment and therefore tolls the time for filing a direct appeal under Federal Rule of Appellate Procedure 4(b). *See, e.g., Barnes v. United States*, 437 F.3d 1074, 1078–79 (11th Cir. 2006); *Johnson v. United States*, 246 F.3d 655, 658–59 (6th Cir. 2001).

The second potential trap for the unwary can arise from an overlap between the claims presented in a Rule 33(b)(1) motion and those presented in a section 2255 motion. If the claim or claims presented in a Rule 33(b)(1) motion do not involve newly discovered evidence, but appear to more closely resemble the claims typically brought in a section 2255 proceeding—*e.g.*, ineffective assistance of counsel—the court may recharacterize the Rule 33(b)(1) motion as a section 2255 motion. *See United States v. Evans*, 224 F.3d 670, 674–75 (7th Cir. 2000). Why is this a trap? First, a recharacterized motion filed within Rule 33(b)(1)'s three-year period may be instantly untimely if it was filed outside the one-year limitation period applicable to section 2255 motions. Second, a certificate of appealability (COA) will be required to appeal the denial of a recharacterized motion, whereas a COA is *not* required to appeal the denial of a Rule 33 motion. *See United States v. Campbell*, 463 F.3d 1, 2 (D.C. Cir. 2006), *cert. denied*, ___ U.S. ___, 127 S. Ct. 2993, 168 L. Ed. 2d 718 (2007). And finally, any section 2255 motion filed after the recharacterized motion will likely be subject to section 2255's strict limitations on second or successive motions. *See Evans*, 224 F.3d at 673–74.

Recharacterization is discussed later; the interplay between Rule 33 and section 2255's statute of limitations provision is discussed in detail in Chapter 5, certificates of appealability are discussed in Chapter 18, and second and successive section 2255 motions are discussed in Chapter 19.

V. Motions to Modify Sentence Under 18 U.S.C. § 3582(c)

Under 18 U.S.C. § 3582(c), a district court may modify a term of imprisonment in one of three limited circumstances.

§ 3.13. Section 3582(c)(1)(A) allows the Bureau of Prisons to seek "compassionate release."

First, under § 3582(c)(1)(A), upon motion of the Bureau of Prisons (BOP), the district court may grant a sentence reduction "in any case" if, after considering the sentencing factors in 18 U.S.C. § 3553(a), it finds either: (1) that the defendant is at least 70 years old, has served at least 30 years, and the BOP has determined that he is not a danger to "any other person or the community," § 3582(c)(1)(A)(ii), or (2) "extraordinary and compelling reasons warrant such a reduction," § 3582(c)(1)(A)(i).[8] In a policy statement, the U.S. Sentencing Commission instructs judges that "extraordinary and compelling reasons" warrant a sentence reduction under § 3582(c)(1)(A)(i) when: "[t]he defendant is suffering from a terminal illness;" or "[t]he defendant is suffering from a permanent physical or medical condition, or is experiencing deteriorating physical or mental health because of the aging process, that substantially diminishes the ability of the defendant to provide self-care within the environment of a correctional facility and for which conventional treatment promises no substantial improvement;" or "[t]he death or incapacitation of the defendant's only family member capable of caring for the defendant's minor child or minor children" has occurred. U.S.S.G. § 1B1.13 (2007). Compassionate release is also appropriate when the BOP decides that some other compelling reason exists that warrants a reduction. *Id.* However, the "rehabilitation of the defendant is not, by itself," a basis for a reduction under § 3582(c)(1)(A). *Id.* Although it is *only* the BOP that may move for a compassionate release, it is the prisoner who starts the process through an internal BOP inmate procedure. *See* BOP Program Statement 5050.46.

§ 3.14. Section 3582(c)(1)(B) permits sentence modification as allowed by Rule 35 or statute.

Second, under § 3582(c)(1)(B), the court may, "in any case," modify a term of imprisonment "to the extent otherwise expressly permitted by statute or by Rule 35 of the Federal Rules of Criminal Procedure." § 3582(c)(1)(B). Rule 35 allows a court to correct a prisoner's sentence (1) for an "arithmetical, technical, or other clear error" within seven days of sentencing,

8. For inmates whose offense was committed prior to November 1, 1987, the BOP may file a motion with the sentencing court seeking to reduce the term of imprisonment to the time the inmate has served, thereby making him or her eligible for parole consideration. *See* 18 U.S.C. § 4205(g).

or (2) if the government files a substantial assistance motion. See Fed. R. Crim. P. 35(a), (b). Other than the circumstances allowed by Rule 35, the district court has no power to modify a sentence under § 3582(c)(1)(B) except as "otherwise expressly permitted by statute"—that is, as is allowed following (1) a remand from the court of appeals or Supreme Court under 28 U.S.C. § 2106, (2) a grant of relief under section 2255, or (3) a grant of habeas corpus relief under 28 U.S.C. § 2241. *See United States v. Ross*, 245 F.3d 577, 586 (6th Cir. 2001); *United States v. Harrison*, 113 F.3d 135, 137 (8th Cir. 1997); *United States v. Triestman*, 178 F.3d 624, 629 (2d Cir. 1999).

§ 3.15. Section 3582(c)(2) permits sentence modification when an amendment to the Sentencing Guidelines applies retroactively.

Third, a sentence can be modified under § 3582(c)(2) when the U.S. Sentencing Commission amends the Sentencing Guidelines and makes that amendment apply retroactively. § 3582(c)(2). This provision applies only when an action "by the Sentencing Commission" itself has reduced the defendant's sentencing range. Reductions based on court decisions are not allowed. *See United States v. Carter*, 500 F.3d 486, 490 (6th Cir. 2007) (§ 3582 does not allow for reductions based on *United States v. Booker*, 543 U.S. 220, 125 S. Ct. 738, 160 L. Ed. 2d 621 (2005)). Moreover, a defendant is not entitled to a reduction based on an amendment to the Guidelines unless the Sentencing Commission has made the amendment retroactive. *See United States v. Stoneking*, 60 F.3d 399, 403 (8th Cir. 1999). Finally, any retroactive amendment of the Guidelines must actually reduce the defendant's sentencing range. If the defendant is subject to a mandatory minimum sentence, or the Commission's actions otherwise have no effect on the defendant's ultimate sentencing range, relief under § 3582(c)(2) is unavailable. *See United States v. Smartt*, 129 F.3d 539, 542 (10th Cir. 1997).

§ 3.16. Procedural considerations for section 3582 motions.

A defendant has no right to counsel for a proceeding under § 3582, *see United States v. Whitebird*, 55 F.3d 1007, 1010–11 (5th Cir. 1995), and has no right to be present for any resentencing pursuant to § 3582, Fed. R. Crim. P. 43(b)(4). Finally, the ten-day period for appeals in criminal cases applies to appeals from the denial of a motion under § 3582(c). *See United States v. Espinosa-Talamantes*, 319 F.3d 1245, 1246 (10th Cir. 2003) (collecting cases).

VI. Recharacterization of a Pleading as a Section 2255 Motion

§ 3.17. Courts will characterize mislabeled filings consistent with the relief requested.

Despite the variety of federal postconviction remedies available, the label placed on a filing will not control its treatment by the court. Rather, the court will determine whether a filing is indeed a section 2255 motion, although not labeled as such. *See, e.g., Lloyd*, 398 F.3d at 979–80; *Evans*, 224 F.3d at 672 ("we hold that any post-judgment motion in a criminal proceeding that fits the description of [§ 2255(a)] is a motion under § 2255"); *United States v. Rich*, 141 F.3d 550, 551 (5th Cir. 1998) ("there is a trend among circuit courts to look beyond the formal title affixed to a motion if the motion is the functional equivalent of a motion under section 2255"). Courts may therefore recharacterize as a section 2255 motion a filing mislabeled as a section 2241 habeas corpus petition, *see Tolliver*, 211 F.3d at 877–78, or a writ of error *coram nobis*, *see Torres*, 282 F.3d at 1246, or a motion under Federal Rule of Criminal Procedure 33, *see Evans*, 224 F.3d at 672. As a result of this recharacterization, a movant may run up against section 2255's statute of limitations. Moreover, litigants who mistakenly file an improperly characterized motion may seriously harm their ability to obtain relief on any section 2255 motion filed thereafter, as it will likely be treated as a second or successive motion.[9]

§ 3.18. A court must mitigate the effect of recharacterization on *pro se* litigants.

In *Castro v. United States*, 540 U.S. 375, 124 S. Ct. 786, 157 L. Ed. 2d 778 (2003), the Supreme Court held that district courts must take steps to mitigate the effect that recharacterization may have on a *pro se* movant's right to bring a future initial application for section 2255 relief. The Court held that

> when a court recharacterizes a *pro se* litigant's motion as a first § 2255 motion . . . the district court must notify the *pro se* litigant that it intends to recharacterize the pleading, warn the litigant that this recharacterization means that any subsequent § 2255 motion will be subject to the restrictions on "second or successive"

9. Section 2255's statute of limitations is discussed in Chapter 5; the restrictions on the ability to obtain relief on a second or successive section 2255 motion are discussed in Chapter 19.

> motions, and provide the litigant an opportunity to withdraw the motion or to amend it so that it contains all the § 2255 claims he believes he has.

Id., 540 U.S. at 383, 124 S. Ct at 792. If the district court fails to give the required notice, "the motion cannot be considered to have become a § 2255 motion for purposes of applying to later motions the law's 'second or successive' restrictions." *Id.*, 540 U.S. at 383, 124 S. Ct at 792.

Castro's "notice before recharacterization" requirement, however, applies only when a court recharacterizes a pleading as a *first* section 2255 motion. *Castro* is rooted in the concern that a prisoner may be unaware that such a recharacterization may cause any later section 2255 motion to be barred as second or successive. This concern, however, does not arise when a federal prisoner has already had a previous section 2255 motion dismissed on the merits. *See Evans*, 224 F.3d at 674–75; *Torres*, 282 F.3d at 1246. As such, when the court recharacterizes a section 2241 motion or *coram nobis* petition or other pleading filed by a federal prisoner as a *second or successive* section 2255 motion, no prior notice nor opportunity to withdraw the motion is required. In addition, *Castro*'s notice requirement applies only when the pleading at issue was filed by a *pro se* litigant. No such notice is required when the mislabeled pleading is filed by counsel.

Finally, the Second Circuit has extended *Castro*'s prescription to cases where a first pleading is converted into a habeas corpus petition under 28 U.S.C. § 2241. *See Simon v. United States*, 359 F.3d 139, 140 (2d Cir. 2004).

VII. Appendix

A. 28 U.S.C. § 2241 (2008)

§ 2241. Power to grant writ.

(a) Writs of habeas corpus may be granted by the Supreme Court, any justice thereof, the district courts, and any circuit judge within their respective jurisdictions. The order of a circuit judge shall be entered in the records of the district court of the district wherein the restraint complained of is had.

(b) The Supreme Court, any justice thereof, and any circuit judge may decline to entertain an application for a writ of habeas corpus and may transfer the application for hearing and determination to the district court having jurisdiction to entertain it.

(c) The writ of habeas corpus shall not extend to a prisoner unless—

(1) He is in custody under or by color of the authority of the United States or is committed for trial before some court thereof; or

(2) He is in custody for an act done or omitted in pursuance of an Act of Congress, or an order, process, judgment or decree of a court or judge of the United States; or

(3) He is in custody in violation of the Constitution or laws or treaties of the United States; or

(4) He, being a citizen of a foreign state and domiciled therein is in custody for an act done or omitted under any alleged right, title, authority, privilege, protection, or exemption claimed under the commission, order or sanction of any foreign state, or under color thereof, the validity and effect of which depend upon the law of nations; or

(5) It is necessary to bring him into court to testify or for trial.

(d) Where an application for a writ of habeas corpus is made by a person in custody under the judgment and sentence of a State court of a State which contains two or more Federal judicial districts, the application may be filed in the district court for the district wherein such person is in custody or in the district court for the district within which the State court was held which convicted and sentenced him and each of such district courts shall have concurrent jurisdiction to entertain the application. The district court for the district wherein such an application is filed in the exercise of its discretion and in furtherance of justice may transfer the application to the other district court for hearing and determination.

(e) **(1)** No court, justice, or judge shall have jurisdiction to hear or consider an application for a writ of habeas corpus filed by or on behalf of an alien detained by the United States who has been determined by the United States to have been properly detained as an enemy combatant or is awaiting such determination.

(2) Except as provided in paragraphs (2) and (3) of section 1005(e) of the Detainee Treatment Act of 2005 (10 U.S.C. 801 note), no court, justice, or judge shall have jurisdiction to hear or consider any other action against the United States or its agents relating to any aspect of the detention, transfer, treatment, trial, or conditions of confinement of an alien who is or was detained by the United States and has been determined by the United States to have been properly detained as an enemy combatant or is awaiting such determination.

B. Federal Rule of Criminal Procedure 33 (2008)

Rule 33. New trial.

(a) Defendant's Motion. Upon the defendant's motion, the court may vacate any judgment and grant a new trial if the interest of justice so requires. If the case was tried without a jury, the court may take additional testimony and enter a new judgment.

(b) Time to File.

(1) ***Newly Discovered Evidence.*** Any motion for a new trial grounded on newly discovered evidence must be filed within 3 years after the verdict or finding of guilty. If an appeal is pending, the court may not grant a motion for a new trial until the appellate court remands the case.

(2) ***Other Grounds.*** Any motion for a new trial grounded on any reason other than newly discovered evidence must be filed within 7 days after the verdict or finding of guilty.

C. 18 U.S.C. § 3582 (2008)

§ 3582. Imposition of a sentence of imprisonment.

(a) Factors to be considered in imposing a term of imprisonment.— The court, in determining whether to impose a term of imprisonment, and, if a term of imprisonment is to be imposed, in determining the length of the term, shall consider the factors set forth in section 3553(a) to the extent that they are applicable, recognizing that imprisonment is not an appropriate means of promoting correction and rehabilitation. In determining whether to make a recommendation concerning the type of prison facility appropriate for the defendant, the court shall consider any pertinent policy statements issued by the Sentencing Commission pursuant to 28 U.S.C. 994(a)(2).

(b) Effect of finality of judgment.—Notwithstanding the fact that a sentence to imprisonment can subsequently be—

(1) modified pursuant to the provisions of subsection (c);

(2) corrected pursuant to the provisions of rule 35 of the Federal Rules of Criminal Procedure and section 3742; or

(3) appealed and modified, if outside the guideline range, pursuant to the provisions of section 3742;

a judgment of conviction that includes such a sentence constitutes a final judgment for all other purposes.

(c) Modification of an imposed term of imprisonment.—The court may not modify a term of imprisonment once it has been imposed except that—

(1) in any case—

(A) the court, upon motion of the Director of the Bureau of Prisons, may reduce the term of imprisonment (and may impose a term of probation or supervised release with or without conditions that does not exceed the unserved portion of the original term of imprisonment), after considering the factors set forth in section 3553(a) to the extent that they are applicable, if it finds that—

(i) extraordinary and compelling reasons warrant such a reduction; or

(ii) the defendant is at least 70 years of age, has served at least 30 years in prison, pursuant to a sentence imposed under section 3559(c), for the offense or offenses for which the defendant is currently imprisoned, and a determination has been made by the Director of the Bureau of Prisons that the defendant is not a danger to the safety of any other person or the community, as provided under section 3142(g);

and that such a reduction is consistent with applicable policy statements issued by the Sentencing Commission; and

(B) the court may modify an imposed term of imprisonment to the extent otherwise expressly permitted by statute or by Rule 35 of the Federal Rules of Criminal Procedure; and

(2) in the case of a defendant who has been sentenced to a term of imprisonment based on a sentencing range that has subsequently been lowered by the Sentencing Commission pursuant to 28 U.S.C. 994(o), upon motion of the defendant or the Director of the Bureau of Prisons, or on its own motion, the court may reduce the term of imprisonment, after considering the factors set forth in section 3553(a) to the extent that they are applicable, if such a reduction is consistent with applicable policy statements issued by the Sentencing Commission.

(d) Inclusion of an order to limit criminal association of organized crime and drug offenders.—The court, in imposing a sentence to a term of imprisonment upon a defendant convicted of a felony set forth in chapter 95 (racketeering) or 96 (racketeer influenced and corrupt organizations) of this title or in the Comprehensive Drug Abuse Prevention and Control Act of 1970 (21 U.S.C. 801 et seq.), or at any time thereafter upon motion by the Director of the Bureau of Prisons or a United States attorney, may include as a part of the sentence an order that requires that the defendant not associate or communicate with a specified person, other than his attorney, upon a showing of probable cause to believe that association or communication with such person is for the purpose of enabling the defendant to control, manage, direct, finance, or otherwise participate in an illegal enterprise.

Part II:

Timing Considerations

CHAPTER 4

The Timing of a Section 2255 Motion

Contents

Introduction

§4.01. Don't file either too early or too late.

A section 2255 motion may be filed either too early or too late. Generally, a motion is considered too early if filed while direct appeal proceedings are still pending and too late if filed outside the applicable one-year limitations period.

I. Exhaust Appellate Remedies Before Filing a Section 2255 Motion

§4.02. Don't file until after you have exhausted appellate remedies.

In general, don't file a section 2255 motion until after you have exhausted appellate remedies. That is, you should not file a motion until the following have been completed: (1) the trial or guilty plea; (2) the sentencing hearing; (3) direct appeal to the United States Court of Appeals, including any petition for rehearing and/or rehearing *en banc;* and, (4) in many cases, *certiorari* proceedings to the United States Supreme Court.

§4.03. Most courts will not entertain a section 2255 motion while an appeal is pending.

The first reason to exhaust appellate remedies is that most courts generally will not allow both a section 2255 motion and a direct appeal brought by the same prisoner to be pending at the same time. Although "there is no jurisdictional barrier to a district court entertaining a § 2255 motion while a direct appeal is pending," this general rule has been adopted for reasons of judicial economy. *United States v. Prows*, 448 F.3d 1223, 1228 (10th Cir. 2006) (collecting cases). *See* Advisory Committee Note to Rule 5, Rules Governing § 2255 Proceedings. Disposition of the direct appeal could render the section 2255 motion moot. *See Capaldi v. Pontesso*, 135 F.3d 1122, 1124 (6th Cir. 1998). District courts, therefore, will dismiss without prejudice any section 2255 motion filed while a defendant's direct appeal proceedings are ongoing, unless there are extraordinary circumstances. *See, e.g., id.* (collecting cases); *United States v. Cook*, 997 F.2d 1312, 1319 (10th Cir. 1993).

Such "extraordinary circumstances" exist, however, where a federal prisoner files a section 2255 motion while the *government's* direct appeal is pending, and the government's appeal raises issues that are completely different from those raised in the section 2255 motion. *See Prows*, 448 F.3d at 1229. Otherwise, "the government could effectively keep [the movant] in custody for years while it exercises its appellate rights." *Id.* Proceeding with the section 2255 motion while a direct appeal is pending is also proper "when the motion raises a substantial question about the integrity of the government's prosecution, [because t]hat integrity is a concern of the highest order, and questions regarding it can take precedence over matters pending on appeal." *United States v. Rangel*, 519 F.3d 1258, 1266 (10th Cir. 2008) (abating direct appeal to allow proceedings on section 2255 motion raising claim that the government knowingly presented perjured testimony at movant's trial).

§ 4.04. Courts will default most record-based claims not raised on appeal.

The second reason to exhaust appellate remedies before seeking section 2255 relief arises out of the long-standing rule that a section 2255 motion "will not be allowed to do service for an appeal." *Bousley v. United States*, 523 U.S. 614, 621, 118 S. Ct. 1604, 1610, 140 L. Ed. 2d 828 (1998) (internal quotation marks omitted). Indeed, to ensure that prisoners do not use section 2255 proceedings as a substitute for direct appeal, the courts have created a "procedural default" doctrine. Under that doctrine, except for claims of ineffective assistance of counsel, section 2255 relief is generally barred for any claim that could have been raised on direct appeal, but was not.

Procedural default is discussed in detail in Chapter 9, but briefly, the best way to avoid its application is to exhaust appellate remedies before filing a section 2255 motion. That is, except for claims of ineffective assistance of counsel, you must raise *on direct appeal* any and all claims that arise on the face of the record of the proceedings that resulted in the conviction and sentence. If you fail to raise a record-based issue on appeal, you are, in most cases, precluded from obtaining section 2255 relief on that claim.

By definition, however, the procedural default doctrine applies only to claims that *could* have been raised on direct appeal. It does not apply to claims that require development of facts outside the trial record. *See Bousley*, 523 U.S. at 621–22, 118 S. Ct. at 1610–11. Accordingly, no procedural default will arise from the failure to raise an extra-record claim on direct appeal.

§ 4.05. Ineffective assistance of counsel claims *cannot* be procedurally defaulted.

Importantly, the procedural default doctrine *never* bars section 2255 relief on an ineffective assistance of counsel claim, even if that claim could have been, but was not, raised on direct appeal. Ineffective assistance of counsel claims may *always* be litigated in the first instance by way of section 2255. *Massaro v. United States*, 538 U.S. 500, 509, 123 S. Ct. 1690, 1696, 155 L. Ed. 2d 714 (2003).

Not all ineffective assistance of counsel claims must await collateral proceedings, however. There are instances where such claims are "so apparent from the record that appellate counsel will consider it advisable to raise the issue on direct appeal." *Id.*, 538 U.S. at 508, 123 S. Ct. at 1696. In addition, the District of Columbia Circuit allows federal prisoners to raise ineffective assistance of trial counsel claims on direct appeal—even if those claims are based on matters outside the trial record. *United States v. Rashad*, 331 F.3d 908, 909–10 (D.C. Cir. 2003).[1]

§ 4.06. Think carefully before you skip *certiorari* prior to filing a section 2255 motion.

Finally, when exhausting your appellate remedies prior to filing a section 2255 motion, you should carefully consider seeking *certiorari* review to the United States Supreme Court following the conclusion of proceedings before the court of appeals. There are risks from failing to do so.

1. If the ineffective assistance of counsel claim involves matters outside the record, the District of Columbia Circuit's "general practice is to remand the claim for an evidentiary hearing unless the trial record alone conclusively shows that defendant either is or is not entitled to relief." *United States v. Rashad*, 331 F.3d 908, 909–10 (D.C. Cir 2003) (internal quotation marks omitted). Note, however, that the District of Columbia Circuit requires that claims of ineffective assistance of *appellate* counsel be raised in a section 2255 motion. *See* United States v. Henry, 472 F.3d 910, 915 (D.C. Cir. 2007).

For example, a petition for writ of *certiorari* should be filed if you feel that the court of appeals erred in resolving any of the claims raised on direct appeal. As discussed in greater detail in Chapter 8, a section 2255 motion may not be used to relitigate questions that have already been raised and rejected on direct appeal, except in rare circumstances. In most cases, *certiorari* proceedings will be a federal prisoner's last chance to obtain relief on record-based claims.

In particular, you should not skip *certiorari* proceedings if, in your direct appeal, you raised a claim that sought the development of new law. *Teague v. Lane*, 489 U.S. 288, 109 S. Ct. 1060, 103 L. Ed. 2d 334 (1989), generally bars section 2255 relief on any claim based on a new rule of criminal procedure promulgated since the case became final on direct review.[2] Consequently, the last opportunity a federal prisoner may have to argue that he or she is entitled to the benefit of a new legal development is in a *certiorari* petition to the United States Supreme Court following direct appeal.

For these reasons, federal prisoners are well advised to file *certiorari* petitions following direct appeal, and, where applicable, to focus any such petitions on new rules of criminal procedure. There is little chance of obtaining section 2255 relief on such claims.

II. Statute of Limitations Considerations

§ 4.07. File a section 2255 motion before the statute of limitations has run.

In addition to being filed too early, a section 2255 motion can be too late if filed beyond the applicable one-year limitation period. The statute of limitations for section 2255 motions, 28 U.S.C. § 2255(f), is discussed in Chapter 5.

2. The *Teague* nonretroactivity doctrine is discussed in detail in Chapter 10.

The Statute of Limitations

Contents

Introduction

§ 5.01. The AEDPA created a new statute of limitations for section 2255 motions.

One of the most dramatic changes to section 2255 practice caused by the Antiterrorism and Effective Death Penalty Act of 1996 (AEDPA) is the creation of a one-year limitation period within which federal prisoners must file a section 2255 motion.[1] Prior to the AEDPA, section 2255 provided that a motion could be made "at any time," 28 U.S.C. § 2255 (1994). The one-year statute of limitations applies to all section 2255 motions filed *after* the AEDPA was enacted on April 24, 1996. *See Lindh v. Murphy*, 521 U.S. 320, 336, 117 S. Ct. 2059, 2068, 138 L. Ed. 2d 481 (1997).

1. The AEDPA is discussed in Chapter 2.

§ 5.02. File a timely and complete motion.

If you are considering filing a section 2255 motion, one of the first things you must do is determine the date by which it must be filed in order for it to be timely. This can be accomplished only with a full understanding of section 2255's statute of limitations. Moreover, simply filing a *timely* section 2255 motion is not enough. You must also be sure to file a *complete* motion containing all colorable claims. As discussed later, once the limitation period has run, an attempt to amend a timely filed motion to include *new* claims will likely result in the new claims being dismissed as untimely. You must therefore allot sufficient time prior to the date of filing to allow for the investigation and development of *all* potential claims so that they may be included in the initial, timely filed motion.

§ 5.03. The statute of limitations is an affirmative defense.

The one-year time limit for filing a section 2255 motion is not jurisdictional, but an affirmative defense. *See Day v. McDonough*, 547 U.S. 198, 205, 126 S. Ct. 1675, 1681, 164 L. Ed. 2d 376 (2006). It can be therefore be "waived" by the government explicitly. *See United States v. Green*, 260 F.3d 78, 85 (2d Cir. 2001).

That said, even if the government waives the limitations defense, the district court has the discretion to dismiss a motion as untimely *sua sponte,* so long as it provides notice that the motion may be time-barred, gives the movant the opportunity to argue the motion is timely, and the movant "is not significantly prejudiced by the delayed focus on the limitation issue." *See Day*, 547 U.S. at 210, 126 S. Ct. at 1684. Indeed, the local rules of many district courts require section 2255 motions to be filed on the "Model Form" appended to the Rules Governing § 2255 Proceedings, and the Model Form requires movants to affirmatively establish the timeliness of their motion. *See* Rules Governing § 2255 Proceedings (Appendix, Motion Under 28 U.S.C. § 2255 at ¶18), 28 U.S.C. foll. § 2255.[2] Accordingly, if a motion is untimely, that fact will likely be noticed by either the government or the court.

§ 5.04. Err on the side of caution.

Although creativity and zealous advocacy are the hallmarks of criminal defense practice, do not push the legal envelope when it comes to section 2255's statute of limitations. If a section 2255 motion is not timely filed, the results are harsh and complete; the motion will be dismissed with prejudice, and any motion filed thereafter will be considered "second or successive." *See, e.g., Villaneueva v. United States*, 346 F.3d 55, 61 (2d Cir. 2003)

2. The Model Form is discussed in Chapter 12. A copy of it can be found in the Appendix.

("the dismissal of a § 2255 petition as untimely . . . presents a 'permanent and incurable' bar to federal review of the merits" of the claims presented in the motion). Caution is the watchword for statute of limitations issues.

I. You Have One Year to File a Motion

§ 5.05. Section 2255's statute of limitations is found in subsection (f).

Subsection (f) of section 2255 establishes a one-year limitation period for federal prisoners seeking section 2255 relief. Because a complete understanding of its text is critical, subsection (f) is reproduced here in full. It states:

> **(f)** A 1-year period of limitation shall apply to a motion under this section. The limitation period shall run from the latest of—
> **(1)** the date on which the judgment of conviction becomes final;
> **(2)** the date on which the impediment to making a motion created by governmental action in violation of the Constitution or laws of the United States is removed, if the movant was prevented from making a motion by such governmental action;
> **(3)** the date on which the right asserted was initially recognized by the Supreme Court, if that right has been newly recognized by the Supreme Court and made retroactively applicable to cases on collateral review; or
> **(4)** the date on which the facts supporting the claim or claims presented could have been discovered through the exercise of due diligence.

28 U.S.C. § 2255(f)(1)–(4). For a section 2255 motion to be timely, it must be filed within one year of one of the four triggering dates listed in subsections (f)(1) to (f)(4).

§ 5.06. The "mailbox rule" determines when a motion is "filed" for *pro se* prisoners.

For prisoners appearing *in propria persona,* the "mailbox rule"[3] applies such that a section 2255 motion is "filed," for purposes of the one-year

3. The Supreme Court established the "mailbox rule" in Houston v. Lack, 487 U.S. 266, 108 S. Ct. 2379, 101 L. Ed. 2d 245 (1988). There, the Court decided that a notice of appeal filed by a *pro se* prisoner would be considered "filed" at the time of delivery to prison authorities, rather than at the later point in time when the notice arrived at the court. The "mailbox rule" has since been extended to cover numerous other court filings by *pro se* prisoners.

statute of limitations, on the date the prisoner delivers it to prison authorities for mailing. *See, e.g., Morales-Rivera v. United States*, 184 F.3d 109, 110 (1st Cir. 1999) *(per curiam); United States v. Patterson*, 211 F.3d 927, 930 (5th Cir. 2000). As such, a motion "filed by an inmate confined in an institution is timely if deposited in the institution's internal mailing system on or before the last day for filing." Rule 3(d), Rules Governing § 2255 Proceedings. Note, however, that "[i]f an institution has a system designed for legal mail, the inmate must use that system to receive the benefit of" the mailbox rule. *Id.*

§ 5.07. How is the one year to be counted?

Federal Rule of Civil Procedure 6(a) is used to calculate the end of the limitation period for section 2255 motions. *See Wilson v. Beard*, 426 F.3d 653, 662 n.6 (3d Cir. 2005) (collecting cases). Under Rule 6(a), when computing any period of time specified in a statute, "[e]xclude the day of the act, event, or default that begins the period." Fed. R. Civ. P. 6(a)(1).[4] For example, if the statute of limitations began to run on April 1, 2007, then the section 2255 motion must be filed by April 1, 2008.

Nonetheless, the better practice is *not* to wait until the last day of the one-year limitation period to file a motion. Section 2255 motions have been dismissed as untimely because they were filed one day late. *See United States v. Marcello*, 212 F.3d 1005, 1010 (7th Cir. 2000). "Foreclosing litigants from bringing their claim because they missed the filing deadline by one day may seem harsh, but courts have to draw lines somewhere." *Id.* To be cautious, file your motion with some time to spare on the limitations clock.

II. When Does the Limitation Period Begin to Run?

§ 5.08. The one year runs from the "latest" of four triggering dates.

Under subsection (f) of section 2255, the one-year limitation period runs from the "latest" of the four possible triggering dates delineated in subsections (f)(1) to (f)(4). The main triggering date is that found in § 2255(f)(1)—"the date on which the judgment of conviction becomes final." § 2255(f)(1). In addition, there are three other possible triggering dates, each of which may refer to a point in time arising *after* the finality of conviction: the date on which an unlawful or unconstitutional governmental action

4. The complete text of Federal Rule of Civil Procedure 6 can be found in the Appendix to this chapter.

impeding the filing of the motion was removed, § 2255(f)(2); the date on which a new and retroactively applicable right was initially recognized by the Supreme Court, § 2255(f)(3); or the date on which the facts supporting the claim or claims presented "could have been discovered through the exercise of due diligence," § 2255(f)(4).

These latter three triggering dates are not "tolling provision[s] that extend[] the length of the available filing time by excluding certain periods that post-date the start of the limitations clock from the calculation of how much time has run. Rather, [they reset] the limitations period's beginning date, moving it from the time when the conviction became final . . . to the later date on which the particular claim accrued." *Wims v. United States*, 225 F.3d 186, 190 (2d Cir. 2000) (internal citation omitted).

§ 5.09. File within one year of the date on which the judgment of conviction became final.

It is not yet clear when the limitation period begins to run if a motion contains multiple claims with different triggering dates. The Eleventh Circuit has held that the existence of *one* claim in the motion that has been filed within one year of *any* of the triggering dates is enough to render the *entire motion* timely. *See Walker v. Crosby*, 341 F.3d 1240, 1245 (11th Cir. 2003). In contrast, the Third and Sixth Circuits have held that if the motion is filed more than a year after the judgment of conviction becomes final under § 2255(f)(1), they will review the motion claim-by-claim and will deem timely *only* those claims impeded by state action under § 2255(f)(2), or based on a newly recognized right under § 2255(f)(3), or newly discovered evidence under § 2255(f)(4). *See Fielder v. Varner*, 379 F.3d 113, 117–18 (3d Cir. 2004) (expressly disagreeing with *Walker*), *cert. denied*, 543 U.S. 1067, 125 S. Ct. 904, 160 L. Ed. 2d 801 (2005); *Bachman v. Bagley*, 487 F.3d 979, 983–84 (6th Cir. 2007) (same). Until this split is resolved, the safest course is to file all potential claims in a single application within one year of the main triggering date found in § 2255(f)(1)—"the date on which the judgment of conviction becomes final." The other three triggering dates should be relied upon only when it is clear that more than one year has passed from the date of finality.

III. Section 2255(f)(1): Finality of Conviction

§ 5.10. When does the conviction become "final" under § 2255(f)(1)?

For the vast majority of section 2255 motions, the limitation period begins to run on "the date on which the judgment of conviction becomes final."

§ 2255 (f)(1). So when is that? It depends on whether a petition for writ of *certiorari* was filed following the movant's direct appeal, whether an appeal was filed at all, and whether the court of appeals reversed all or part of the judgment and remanded to the district court for further proceedings.

§ 5.11. If *certiorari* is sought following affirmance on direct appeal.

For a federal prisoner who files a petition for writ of *certiorari* following affirmance on direct appeal, the judgment becomes final on the day that the United States Supreme Court either denies *certiorari* or affirms on the merits. *See Clay v. United States*, 537 U.S. 522, 527, 123 S. Ct. 1072, 1076, 155 L. Ed. 2d 88 (2003). For those cases in which the Supreme Court denies *certiorari,* it is the date of that denial that triggers the one-year limitation period under § 2255(f)(1). *Id.* It is *not* the date on which the denial of *certiorari* is filed and docketed with the court of appeals. *See Marcello*, 212 F.3d at 1008; *United States v. McIntosh*, 332 F.3d 550, 550 (8th Cir. 2003). Importantly, even if a petition for rehearing from the denial of *certiorari* has been filed in the Supreme Court, the one-year period nonetheless begins to run on the date on which *certiorari* was denied, unless the Court or a justice suspends the order denying *certiorari* in response to the rehearing petition. *See Drury v. United States*, 507 F.3d 1295, 1296 (11th Cir. 2007) (collecting cases).

§ 5.12. If *certiorari* is *not* sought following affirmance on direct appeal.

If *certiorari* is not sought following affirmance on direct appeal, the judgment becomes "final" for purposes of § 2255(f)(1) when the 90-day period for filing a *certiorari* petition expires. *Clay*, 537 U.S. at 527, 123 S. Ct. at 1076. Even if a prisoner voluntarily dismisses her direct appeal, that appeal does not become final, and the limitations period under § 2255(f)(1) does not begin to run, until the 90 days to seek *certiorari* have run. *See Latham v. United States*, 527 F.3d 651, 653 (7th Cir. 2008).

Supreme Court Rule 13[5] determines the expiration date for the 90-day period for filing a *certiorari* petition. *See, e.g., United States v. Wall*, 456 F.3d 316, 318–20 (3d Cir. 2006).

5. The text of Supreme Court Rule 13 can be found in the Appendix to this chapter.

§ 5.13. If the conviction or sentence is reversed on direct appeal.

"'Final judgment in a criminal case means sentence. The sentence is the judgment.'" *Burton v. Stewart*, 549 U.S. 147, ___, 127 S. Ct. 793, 798–99, 166 L. Ed. 2d 628 (2007) (quoting *Berman v. United States*, 302 U.S. 211, 212, 58 S. Ct. 164, 166, 82 L. Ed 204 (1937)). For this reason, where the appellate court wholly or partially reverses a defendant's conviction or sentence, the "limitations period [does] not begin until both his conviction *and* sentence 'became final.'" *Id.*, 549 U.S. at ___, 127 S. Ct. at 799 (emphasis in original); *accord United States v. LaFromboise*, 427 F.3d 680, 684 (9th Cir. 2005).

This rule holds even if a defendant is convicted on multiple counts. In such circumstances, the judgment of conviction cannot be disaggregated so that individual counts become final at different times. *See United States v. Dodson*, 291 F.3d 268, 274 (4th Cir. 2002). This is because "only a single 'judgment of conviction' arises from a case . . . in which a defendant is convicted at one trial on multiple counts of an indictment." *Id.* at 272. Accordingly, in cases where a defendant is convicted on multiple counts, and the court of appeals affirms as to some counts but remands as to others, the "judgment of conviction" is not final until both the conviction and sentence are final for *all* counts. *Id.*

The Ninth Circuit has applied this rule broadly, concluding that any remand from the appellate court for further proceedings in the district court delays finality, even in circumstances where the mandate of the court of appeals does not appear to leave any matters open for the district court's consideration. *See United States v. Colvin*, 204 F.3d 1221, 1225 (9th Cir. 2000). The Second and Fourth Circuits, however, have held to the contrary, concluding that finality is *not* delayed in those circumstances where "an appellate court disposes of all counts in a judgment of conviction but remands for a ministerial purpose that could not result in a valid second appeal." *Dodson*, 291 F.3d at 275. *Accord Burrell v. United States*, 467 F.3d 160, 166 (2d Cir. 2006) (appellate court's remand ordering district court to vacate conviction was "strictly ministerial" and did not delay finality for purposes of section 2255, where "reversal of a conviction did not affect the 'knot of calculations' under the Guidelines and where remand for resentencing was unnecessary"), *cert. denied*, ___ U.S. ___, 127 S. Ct. 2031, 167 L. Ed. 2d 773 (2007). The upshot of this circuit split? Until it is resolved, you must closely review the language of the court of appeals' mandate to determine whether it allows the district court to exercise any discretion or is merely for a ministerial purpose. If the latter, or if the language used by the court of appeals is unclear, you must err on the side of caution and assume that, for purposes of § 2255(f)

(1), the "judgment of conviction" becomes final when the court of appeals' remand order does.

§ 5.14. If no appeal is filed.

There is a split in the circuits as to when a judgment of conviction becomes final for purposes of § 2255(f)(1) if no appeal is filed. The Second, Third, Sixth, Tenth, and Eleventh Circuits have held that "the judgment becomes final upon the expiration of the period in which the defendant could have appealed to the court of appeals." *Sanchez-Castellano v. United States*, 358 F.3d 424, 427 (6th Cir. 2004). *Accord United States v. Prows*, 448 F.3d 1223, 1227–28 (10th Cir. 2006); *Moshier v. United States*, 402 F.3d 116, 118 (2d Cir. 2005); *Mederos v. United States*, 218 F.3d 1252, 1253 (11th Cir. 2000); *Kapral v. United States*, 166 F.3d 565, 577 (3d Cir. 1999). In most cases, that is ten days after the entry of judgment, when the time to file a notice of appeal has expired under Federal Rule of Appellate Procedure 4(b)(1).[6] *See, e.g., Sanchez-Castellano*, 358 F.3d at 427. In contrast, the Fourth Circuit has held that if no appeal is filed, the judgment of conviction becomes final on the date that the district court entered judgment. *See United States v. Sanders*, 247 F.3d 139, 142 (4th Cir. 2001). To be safe, until this circuit split is resolved, in cases where no direct appeal of the conviction or sentence was filed, a section 2255 motion should be filed within one year of the date on which the district court entered judgment.

§ 5.15. Effect of motions under Federal Rules of Criminal Procedure 33 and 35.

A pending Rule 33 motion does *not* toll the one-year limitation period for a section 2255 motion, unless the Rule 33 motion was filed within 10 days of the entry of the underlying criminal judgment and therefore tolled the time for filing a direct appeal under Federal Rule of Appellate Procedure 4(b)(3)(A). *See Barnes v. United States*, 437 F.3d 1074, 1078–79 (11th Cir. 2006) (collecting cases).

Similarly, a modification of sentence under Federal Rule of Criminal Procedure 35(b) does *not* affect the date on which a federal prisoner's judgment of conviction becomes final under § 2255(f)(1) and therefore does not delay the running of the limitation period. *See Sanders*, 247 F.3d at 142–43; *United States v. Schwartz*, 274 F.3d 1220, 1223–24 (9th Cir. 2001).

6. The text of Federal Rule of Appellate Procedure 4(b) is contained in the Appendix to this chapter.

§ 5.16. Cases where the judgment of conviction became final before April 24, 1996.

For prisoners whose conviction became final before the AEDPA was enacted on April 24, 1996, the limitation period under § 2255(f)(1) began to run on that date, providing a one-year "grace period," to April 24, 1997, for filing a section 2255 motion. *See, e.g., Solomon v. United States*, 467 F.3d 928, 931 n.2 (6th Cir. 2006); *Rogers v. United States*, 180 F.3d 349, 355 (1st Cir. 1999).

IV. Section 2255(f)(2): Unconstitutional or Unlawful Impediment to Filing

Under section 2255(f)(2), a motion is timely if filed within one year of "the date on which the impediment to making a motion created by governmental action in violation of the Constitution or laws of the United States is removed, if the movant was prevented from making a motion by such governmental action." 28 U.S.C. § 2255(f)(2). This is an extraordinarily difficult standard to meet, and, as a result, the situations in which § 2255(f)(2) can trigger a new one-year limitation period are few.

§ 5.17. An "impediment" to filing is required.

The word "impediment" implies that an obstacle, obstruction, or hindrance caused by the government's actions is required before § 2255(f)(2) applies. *See Minter v. Beck*, 230 F.3d 663, 666 (4th Cir. 2000). It is not enough that the government's actions simply rendered filing a motion "futile." *See id.* Consequently, § 2255(f)(2) is unavailable to a section 2255 movant where the government's actions did not prevent the filing of a motion. *See United States v. Cottage*, 307 F.3d 494, 500 (6th Cir. 2002) (movant has not shown an "impediment created by governmental action" where it is clear from movant's allocution at sentencing that he was aware of the government's failure to disclose exculpatory evidence).

§ 5.18. The governmental action must also be "unlawful" or "unconstitutional."

In addition to constituting an "impediment" to filing, the government's actions must also be either unconstitutional or unlawful in order to trigger a new limitation period under § 2255(f)(2). *See Akins v. United States*, 204 F.3d 1086, 1090 (11th Cir. 2000) (movant's failure to prove that his constitutional right of access to the courts was violated is "fatal to his claim of an unconstitutional impediment" under § 2255(f)(2)); *United States v.*

Cicero, 214 F.3d 199, 204 (D.C. Cir. 2000) (movant concedes that "his transfer and incidental separation from his papers were not unlawful, and therefore do not implicate § 2255(f)(2)").

Such an unconstitutional or unlawful impediment may be found if the movant can demonstrate that the government withheld exculpatory material that formed the basis for the claim in violation of *Brady v. Maryland*, 373 U.S. 83, 83 S. Ct. 1194, 10 L. Ed. 2d 215 (1963). *See Cottage*, 307 F.3d at 499–500 (analyzing *Brady* claim under § 2255(f)(2)). In addition, a *pro se* prisoner who can demonstrate a constitutional violation of the right of access to the courts under *Lewis v. Casey*, 518 U.S. 343, 116 S. Ct. 2174, 135 L. Ed. 2d 606 (1996)—that is, that he diligently pursued his federal claims but was prevented from doing so as a result of deficiencies in the prison law library—may be able to rely on § 2255(f)(2) to trigger the one-year limitations period. *See Akins*, 204 F.3d at 1090.

V. Section 2255(f)(3): Newly Recognized and Collaterally Applicable Right

Under section 2255(f)(3), a motion is timely if it asserts a right "newly recognized by the Supreme Court" and is filed within a year of "the date on which the right asserted was initially recognized by the Supreme Court, if that right has been newly recognized by the Supreme Court and made retroactively applicable to cases on collateral review." 28 U.S.C. § 2255(f)(3). Either a statutory right or a constitutional right that has been newly recognized can trigger a renewed limitation period under § 2255(f)(3). *See United States v. Lopez*, 248 F.3d 427, 430 (5th Cir. 2001) (collecting statutory right cases); *Ashley v. United States*, 266 F.3d 671, 672 (7th Cir. 2001) (constitutional right). But the right asserted must have been recognized *by the Supreme Court*—lower court decisions do not suffice. *See Nichols v. United States*, 285 F.3d 445, 447 (6th Cir. 2002).

§ 5.19. Under § 2255(f)(3), file within a year of when the Supreme Court initially recognized the right asserted.

In *Dodd v. United States*, 545 U.S. 353, 357, 125 S. Ct. 2478, 2482, 162 L. Ed. 2d 343 (2005), the Supreme Court considered § 2255(f)(3)'s confusing language, and held that the one-year limitation period runs from the date on which it initially recognized the right asserted, *not* from the date on which the right asserted was made retroactively applicable to cases on collateral review.[7] Accordingly, when the Supreme Court issues a decision recognizing a new right, a section 2255 motion seeking the benefit of that right must be filed within one year of that decision.

§ 5.20. For initial motions, don't wait for the right to be applied retroactively before filing.

For initial section 2255 motions, there is no need to wait for a court decision holding that the new right is retroactively applicable to collateral cases before filing under § 2255(f)(3). The district court in which the section 2255 motion is filed can *itself* determine whether the right newly recognized by the Supreme Court applies retroactively. *See Ashley*, 266 F.3d at 674. If the new right *does* apply retroactively, the district court will then consider the motion on its merits. But if the court determines that the newly recognized right is *not* retroactively applicable, it will deny the motion as untimely. *Id.*

§ 5.21. When is a right "newly recognized?"

So when does a Supreme Court decision constitute an initial recognition of a "newly recognized" right, thereby triggering a new limitation period under § 2255(f)(3)? In some ways, it is easier to describe when a right is *not* "newly" or "initially" recognized. "[A] new right cannot be 'initially recognized' when the Court has merely applied its precedent to a particular factual setting." *United States v. Hopkins*, 268 F.3d 222, 225 (4th Cir. 2001) (concluding that the Supreme Court's decision *Florida v. J.L.*, 529 U.S. 266, 120 S. Ct. 1375, 146 L. Ed. 2d 254 (2000), did not create a "newly recognized" right because it "resulted from the logical application of [the Court's] stop and frisk jurisprudence"). In contrast, a Supreme Court decision may initially recognize a "new" right if that decision overrules numerous lower court decisions. *See Ashley*, 266 F.3d at 672. For example, when the Supreme Court issued its decision in *Apprendi v. New Jersey*, 530 U.S. 466, 120 S. Ct. 2348, 147 L. Ed. 2d 435 (2000), "No one could doubt that *Apprendi* 'newly' or 'initially' recognize[d] a constitutional right." *Ashley*, 266 F.3d at 672.

When a statutory right is at issue, that right is "newly recognized" when "the Supreme Court officially acknowledges the appropriate statutory meaning." *Lopez*, 248 F.3d at 431. For example, when the Supreme

7. The retroactivity criteria established by the Supreme Court in Teague v. Lane, 489 U.S. 288, 109 S. Ct. 1060, 103 L. Ed. 2d 334 (1989), govern whether a new right is retroactively applicable to cases on collateral review. *Teague* is discussed in Chapter 10.

Court recognized for the first time, in *Bailey v. United States*, 516 U.S. 137, 116 S. Ct. 501, 133 L. Ed. 2d 472 (1995), a defendant's right to be free of criminal liability under 18 U.S.C. § 924(c)(1) for conduct that had previously supported a conviction in virtually every circuit, that right was "newly recognized" and triggered a new limitation period under § 2255(f)(3). *See Haugh v. Booker*, 210 F.3d 1147, 1149 (10th Cir. 2000); *United States v. Lloyd*, 188 F.3d 184, 187 (3d Cir. 1999). *Richardson v. United States*, 526 U.S. 813, 119 S. Ct. 1707, 143 L. Ed. 2d 985 (1999), is another decision in which the Supreme Court newly recognized a statutory right, thereby triggering § 2255(f)(3). *See Lopez*, 248 F.3d at 430–31.

§ 5.22. Section 2255(f)(3) complicates obtaining relief on second or successive motions.

A section 2255 movant may obtain relief on a claim brought in a second or successive motion only if that claim "relies on a new rule of constitutional law, made retroactive to cases on collateral review by the Supreme Court, that was previously unavailable." § 2255(h)(2).[8] Given its similarity to the language used in subsection (h)(2), the statute of limitations provision in subsection (f)(3) may also establish a time limit for filing a second or successive section 2255 motion based on a newly recognized right. *See In re Vial*, 115 F.3d 1192, 1197 n.9 (4th Cir. 1997); *Libby v. Magnusson*, 177 F.3d 43, 47–48 (1st Cir. 1999). Note, however, that because § 2255(h)(2) requires that the new rule of law has *already been made* retroactively applicable *by the Supreme Court* before a second or successive application can be filed, the statute of limitations provision in § 2255(f)(3) makes it difficult for applicants filing such motions to obtain any relief, because the Supreme Court rarely both announces a new rule of law *and* makes it retroactive within a year. *See Dodd*, 543 U.S. at 359, 125 S. Ct. at 2481–83.

VI. Section 2255(f)(4): Newly Discovered Evidence

The one-year period for section 2255 motions may also begin to run from "the date upon which the facts supporting the claim or claims presented could have been discovered through the exercise of due diligence." 28 U.S.C. § 2255(f)(4). In cases of newly discovered evidence, § 2255(f)(4) ensures that section 2255 relief may be sought even though the movant's conviction has been final for more than one year. *See Wims*, 225 F.3d at 190. Subsection (f)(4) may also apply to second or successive motions

8. Second or successive motions are discussed in Chapter 19.

based on a claim of newly discovered evidence under § 2255(h)(1). *See Libby*, 177 F.3d at 47–48.[9]

§ 5.23. "Due" diligence requirement.

Section 2255(f)(4) "does not require the maximum feasible diligence, but only 'due' or reasonable, diligence." *Aron v. United States*, 291 F.3d 708, 712 (11th Cir. 2002) (citing *Wims*, 225 F.3d at 190 n.4). "Due diligence therefore does not require a prisoner to undertake repeated exercises in futility or to exhaust every imaginable option, but rather to make reasonable efforts." *Id.* Nonetheless, § 2255(f)(4) "does not convey a statutory right to an extended delay . . . while a [movant] gathers every possible scrap of evidence that might, by negative implication, support his claim." *Flanagan v. Johnson*, 154 F.3d 196, 199 (5th Cir. 1998).

§ 5.24. If the movant did not exercise "due" diligence, the court must determine when the facts could have been discovered had the movant done so.

Under § 2255(f)(4), the one-year limitation period "begins to run when the facts *could have been* discovered through the exercise of due diligence, not when they were *actually* discovered." *Aron*, 291 F.3d at 711 (emphasis in original). *Accord Wims*, 225 F.3d at 190. Thus, "the beginning of the one-year period is triggered by a date that is not necessarily related to a petitioner's actual efforts or actual discovery of the relevant facts." *Aron*, 291 F.3d at 711. "Of course, if a court finds that a petitioner exercised due diligence, then the one-year limitation period would begin to run on the date the petitioner actually discovered the relevant facts, because the dates of actual and possible discovery would be identical." *Id.*

However, a finding of due diligence is not required before a motion may be deemed timely under § 2255(f)(4). Even "if the court finds that the petitioner did *not* exercise due diligence, the statute does not preclude the possibility that the petitioner's motion could still be timely under § 2255(f)(4)." *Id.* at 711 (emphasis in original).

> For example, if the court concludes that, with the exercise of due diligence, the relevant facts could have been discovered two months earlier than the petitioner (who it finds did not exercise due diligence) actually discovered them, then the motion would still be timely if filed within ten months of the date of actual discovery.

9. Second or successive motions are discussed in detail in Chapter 19.

Id. See also Wims, 225 F.3d at 190. Accordingly, application of § 2255(f)(4) requires a two-step process: (1) the court must consider whether the movant exercised due diligence, and (2) if it finds the movant did *not* exercise due diligence, it must determine when the relevant facts *could have been* discovered had the movant done so.

For this reason, a movant relying on § 2255(f)(4) must prove her claim through facts that she could have discovered only in the year before she filed her § 2255 motion. *See Wims*, 225 F.3d at 189–90. Generally speaking, where the facts supporting the claims presented were known to the applicant at the time of trial, § 2255(f)(4) does not apply. *See United States v. Battles*, 362 F.3d 1195, 1198 (9th Cir. 2004) ("Surely due diligence requires that Battles at least consult his own memory of the trial proceedings.").

§ 5.25. Under § 2255(f)(4), "facts" include court rulings or the legal consequences of known facts.

In *Johnson v. United States*, 544 U.S. 295, 308, 125 S. Ct. 1571, 1580, 161 L. Ed. 2d 542 (2005), the Supreme Court held that, for purposes of § 2255(f)(4), the "facts" supporting a claim may include court rulings or the legal consequences of known facts, including the vacatur of prior convictions used to enhance a later sentence. In such circumstances, the one year is triggered by the notice of the order vacating the prior convictions, so long as the prisoner has shown "due diligence" in seeking that order. *Id.*, 544 U.S. at 308, 125 S. Ct. at 1580. In this context, the "due diligence" standard requires a movant to begin seeking vacatur of any prior convictions used to enhance his federal sentence *immediately after sentencing* in the federal case; if the movant waits until after any appeal of the enhanced sentence is completed, the due diligence standard will likely not be met. *Id.*, 544 U.S. at 308–09, 125 S. Ct. at 1580–81.

Applying this analysis, the Supreme Court found that a movant had not demonstrated "due diligence," because he waited more than three years to begin the process that uncovered the facts to support his claim. *See Johnson*, 544 U.S. at 311, 125 S. Ct. at 1582. In contrast, a movant who waited only five months to begin the process of uncovering the facts to support his claim acted with "due diligence" under § 2255(f)(4). *See Wims*, 225 F.3d at 190–91.

§ 5.26. Fact-specific inquiry.

Under § 2255(f)(4), "[t]he date on which the limitations clock [begins] to tick is a fact-specific issue." *Wims*, 225 F.3d at 190. For this reason, an evidentiary hearing may be required to determine the facts supporting the due diligence exception. *See id.* at 190–91; *Aron*, 291 F.3d at 714–15 (remanding for evidentiary hearing on whether petitioner exercised due diligence).

§ 5.27. Subsection (f)(4) and incarcerated *pro se* movants.

Under § 2255(f)(4), "the due diligence inquiry is an individualized one that must take into account the conditions of confinement and the reality of the prison system." *Aron*, 291 F.3d at 712 (internal quotation marks omitted). *See Wims*, 225 F.3d at 191. "Unlike the general population which has greater access to court opinions, prisoners must rely exclusively upon the prison law library to discover information contained in new cases." *Easterwood v. Champion*, 213 F.3d 1321, 1323 (10th Cir. 2000). Thus, where the factual predicate of the claim can be found in a court decision, the claim is not discoverable by an incarcerated prisoner exercising "due diligence" until the date the opinion became accessible in the prison law library, rather than the date the opinion was issued. *Id.*

VII. Actual Innocence and the Statute of Limitations

§ 5.28. A showing of actual innocence can render a section 2255 motion timely.

The Eleventh Circuit has held that a showing of actual innocence "serves . . . to lift the procedural bar caused by [the movant's] failure timely to file his § 2255 motion." *United States v. Montano*, 398 F.3d 1276, 1284 (11th Cir. 2005). And, as discussed next, some courts have held that actual innocence can provide a basis for equitable tolling of the limitation period.

Courts considering whether "actual innocence" excuses the untimely filing of a section 2255 motion have required the same showing of "actual innocence" as that required to excuse a procedural default. *See id.* at 1285 n.8 (collecting cases). What constitutes "actual innocence" sufficient to excuse a procedural default is discussed in Chapter 9.

§ 5.29. Actual innocence and the Suspension Clause.

The Suspension Clause provides that "[t]he Privilege of the Writ of Habeas Corpus shall not be suspended, unless when in Cases of Rebellion or Invasion the public Safety may require it." U.S. Const., Art. I, § 9, cl. 2. Although it does not violate the Suspension Clause *per se* to apply the statute of limitations to bar consideration of an initial section 2255 motion filed outside the limitation period, if the applicant makes a colorable showing of actual innocence, the foreclosure of collateral review in such circumstances may suspend the writ. *See Wyzykowski v. Dept. of Corrections*, 226 F.3d 1213, 1218 (11th Cir. 2000) (collecting cases).

VIII. Equitable Tolling

§ 5.30. Section 2255's statute of limitations is subject to equitable tolling.

The Supreme Court has not yet decided whether section 2255's statute of limitations is subject to equitable tolling. *See Pace v. DiGuglielmo*, 544 U.S. 408, 418 n.8, 125 S. Ct. 1807, 1814 n.8, 161 L. Ed. 2d 669 (2005). Nonetheless, every circuit to decide the question has held that it is. *See United States v. Pollard*, 416 F.3d 48, 56 n.1 (D.C. Cir. 2005), *cert. denied*, 547 U.S. 1021, 126 S. Ct. 1590, 164 L. Ed. 2d 303 (2006) (collecting cases). The District of Columbia Circuit has expressly reserved the question. *Id.* Where applicable, equitable tolling can extend section 2255's limitation period beyond one year.

§ 5.31. Showing required for equitable tolling.

"Generally, a litigant seeking equitable tolling bears the burden of establishing two elements: (1) that he has been pursuing his rights diligently, and (2) that some extraordinary circumstance stood in his way." *Pace*, 544 U.S. at 418, 125 S. Ct. at 1814 (citing *Irwin v. Department of Veterans Affairs*, 498 U.S. 89, 96, 111 S. Ct. 453, 112 L. Ed. 2d 435 (1990)).[10] In *Pace*, the petitioner failed to establish the requisite diligence because he "waited years, without any valid justification," to assert his claims. *Id.*, 544 U.S. at 419, 125 S. Ct. at 1815.

Because equitable tolling is a fact-based inquiry, the court may be required to hold a hearing in order to determine whether tolling is warranted. *See Battles*, 362 F.3d at 1198.

§ 5.32. Do not rely on equitable tolling.

Given that equitable tolling is available only in "extraordinary" circumstances, a court may not allow equitable tolling, whatever the equities

10. The Sixth Circuit has adopted a slightly different test. There, the decision to grant equitable tolling is governed by the following criteria: "(1) the petitioner's lack of notice of the filing requirement; (2) the petitioner's lack of constructive knowledge of the filing requirement; (3) diligence in pursuing one's rights; (4) absence of prejudice to the respondent; and (5) the petitioner's reasonableness in remaining ignorant of the legal requirement for filing his claim." Dunlap v. United States, 250 F.3d 1001, 1008–09 (6th Cir. 2001).

may be. *See Poe v. United States*, 468 F.3d 473, 476 (7th Cir. 2006) (noting that the Seventh Circuit has "yet to identify a circumstance that justifies equitable tolling in the collateral relief context") (internal quotation marks omitted); *Marcello*, 212 F.3d at 1010 (rejecting argument that statute of limitations should be tolled for *one day*). To be safe, do not rely on equitable tolling as a means to extend the limitation period. Instead, make every possible effort to timely file your motion under § 2255(f)(1)—that is, within one year of the date on which the judgment of conviction becomes final. Equitable tolling should be relied upon only when it is clear that more than one year has passed from the date of finality, and none of the other three triggering dates in §§ 2255(f)(2), (f)(3), or (f)(4) apply.

§ 5.33. Situations where equitable tolling is generally *not* available.

So, what are the rare "extraordinary circumstances" where equitable tolling is available? This is a difficult question, because the availability of equitable tolling is necessarily a case-specific inquiry. *See Warren v. Garvin*, 219 F.3d 111, 113 (2d Cir. 2000). However, some generalizations can be made. Generally, the following are *not* sufficient to warrant equitable tolling:

(1) *mere error, excusable neglect, or mistake, whether by counsel or by movant. See Baldayaque v. United States*, 338 F.3d 145, 151–52 (2d. Cir. 2003) (mistakes of counsel as to the calculation of time remaining in limitation period or when the limitation period begins to run does not justify equitable tolling); *McIntosh*, 332 F.3d at 551 ("equitable tolling based on [movant's] mistake about the deadline is not warranted"); *United States v. Riggs*, 314 F.3d 796, 799 (5th Cir. 2002) ("'[M]ere attorney error or neglect is not an extraordinary circumstance such that equitable tolling is justified.' . . . Likewise, a petitioner's *own* ignorance or mistake does not warrant equitable tolling.") (emphasis in original) (internal quotation marks omitted); *Marcello*, 212 F.3d at 1010 (no equitable tolling where counsel's miscalculation resulted in motion being filed *one day* late: "The deadline was simply missed. That is not grounds for equitable tolling.").

(2) *ignorance of the law, lack of legal training, or lack of legal representation. See United States v. Sosa*, 364 F.3d 507, 512 (4th Cir. 2004) ("even in the case of an unrepresented prisoner, ignorance of the law is not a basis for equitable tolling"); *Riggs*, 314 F.3d at 799 ("[A] petitioner's *own* ignorance or mistake does not warrant equitable tolling.") (emphasis in original); *United States v. Wynn*,

292 F.3d 226, 230 (5th Cir. 2002) (prisoner's *pro se* status does not warrant equitable tolling).

(3) *reliance on an inmate law clerk. Marsh v. Soares*, 223 F.3d 1217, 1220 (10th Cir. 2000).

(4) *the fact of incarceration, including an inadequate law library. See Wynn*, 292 F.3d at 230.

(5) *a pending motion under Federal Rule of Criminal Procedure 33. See Trenkler v. United States*, 268 F.3d 16, 22 (1st Cir. 2001); *United States v. Prescott*, 221 F.3d 686, 688 (4th Cir. 2000).

§ 5.34. Situations where equitable tolling may be available.

A nonexclusive list of situations where equitable tolling may be available includes:[11]

(1) *judicial interference with timely filing. See, e.g., Pliler v. Ford*, 542 U.S. 225, 235, 124 S. Ct. 2441, 2448, 159 F.3d 338 (2004) (O'Connor, J., concurring) ("if the petitioner is affirmatively misled . . . by the court . . . , equitable tolling might well be appropriate"); *Riddle v. Kemna*, 523 F.3d 850, 857 (8th Cir. 2008) *(en banc)* ("abrogation of *en banc* precedent is an extraordinary circumstance, external to [petitioner] and not attributable to him," and therefore equitable tolling is warranted); *Patterson*, 211 F.3d at 931–32 (concluding equitable tolling warranted where petitioner "relied to his detriment on the district court's granting of his request to dismiss the initial, timely filed § 2255 motion in order to refile it at a later date"); *United States v. Miller*, 197 F.3d 644, 652–53 (3d Cir. 1999) (allowing equitable tolling where district court failed to provide *pro se* litigant required warnings about the AEDPA before ruling on the merits); *Calderon v. United States District Court (Kelly)*, 163 F.3d 530, 541 (9th Cir. 1998) (holding equitable tolling was appropriate where the district court stayed "all other aspects" of the case pending a determination of petitioner's competency, thus precluding petitioner from timely filing), *overruled in part on other grounds by Woodford v. Garceau*, 538 U.S. 202, 123 S. Ct. 1398, 155 L. Ed. 2d 363 (2003); *Davis v. Johnson*, 158 F.3d 806, 811–12 (5th Cir. 1998) (equitable tolling may be warranted where district court granted petitioner extension of time to file federal petition and petitioner filed within time period allowed by court's order).

11. Note that this list is nonexclusive and that courts may look to non-habeas cases "for further elucidation of when to toll." *Fisher v. Johnson*, 174 F.3d 710, 713 n.11 (5th Cir. 1999).

(2) *government interference with timely filing. See Irwin*, 498 U.S. at 96, 111 S. Ct. at 458 (equitable tolling traditionally allowed where "the complainant has been induced or tricked by his adversary's misconduct into allowing the filing deadline to pass"); *Pliler*, 542 U.S. at 235, 124 S. Ct. at 2448 (O'Connor, J., concurring) ("if the petitioner is affirmatively misled . . . by the State, equitable tolling might well be appropriate"); *United States v. Gabaldon*, 522 F.3d 1121–26 (10th Cir. 2008) (remanding for an evidentiary hearing on equitable tolling where prison officials confiscated all of movant's legal documents, including his section 2255 motion and brief, and refused to return them despite his numerous requests before the deadline that they do so, and movant ultimately filed motion 22 days after his legal materials were returned to him); *Solomon v. United States*, 467 F.3d 928, 934 (6th Cir. 2006) (granting equitable tolling where movant "was impeded from completing his petition more than one month before it was due and one month thereafter because of his transfer to other facilities [without his legal materials] to secure his testimony in a trial."); *Stillman v. LeMarque*, 319 F.3d 1199, 1202 (9th Cir. 2003) (granting equitable tolling because the "prison litigation coordinator promised Stillman's lawyer to obtain Stillman's signature in time for filing, but then broke his promise, causing the filing to be late"); *Valverde v. Stinson*, 224 F.3d 129, 133 (2d Cir. 2000) ("confiscation of a prisoner's legal papers by a corrections officer shortly before the filing deadline may justify equitable tolling and permit the filing of a petition after the statute of limitations ordinarily would have run.").

(3) *counsel's serious errors or misconduct.* Although mere negligence by counsel, such as miscalculation of a filing deadline, is not a sufficient basis for finding the statute of limitations equitably tolled, the vast majority of circuits have held that there are circumstances where the limitation period may be tolled by a *serious* error or misconduct by counsel, if those actions permitted the statute of limitations to run. *See Downs v. McNeil*, 520 F.3d 1311, 1321 (11th Cir. 2008) (collecting cases). *But see Powell v. Davis*, 415 F.3d 722, 727 (7th Cir. 2005) (holding severity of counsel misconduct is irrelevant for purposes of equitable tolling).

(4) *mental incompetence. See Laws v. Lamarque*, 351 F.3d 919, 923 (9th Cir. 2003) ("Where a habeas petitioner's mental incompetence in fact caused him to fail to meet the AEDPA filing deadline, his delay was caused by an 'extraordinary circumstance beyond [his] control,' and the deadline should be equitably tolled."); *Nara v. Frank*, 264 F.3d 310, 320 (3d Cir. 2001), *overruled in part on*

other grounds by Carey v. Saffold, 536 U.S. 214, 122 S. Ct. 2134, 153 L. Ed. 2d 260 (2002).

(5) *the applicant filed a defective pleading during the statutory period. See Irwin*, 498 U.S. at 96, 111 S. Ct. at 457–58 ("We have allowed equitable tolling in situations where the claimant has actively pursued his judicial remedies by filing a defective pleading during the statutory period."); *De Aza-Paez v. United States*, 343 F.3d 552, 553 (1st Cir. 2003) (lack of signature on original, timely filed motion was cured by signed copy of same motion filed soon thereafter).

(6) *actual innocence.* Although simply alleging a *claim* of actual innocence may not warrant equitable tolling, *see Felder v. Johnson*, 204 F.3d 168, 171 (5th Cir. 2000), a *showing* of innocence may, *see Gibson v. Klinger*, 232 F.3d 799, 808 (10th Cir. 2000); *Flanders v. Graves*, 299 F.3d 974, 978 (8th Cir. 2002). Note that, as previously discussed, the Eleventh Circuit has held that if a movant makes a *showing* of actual innocence, that showing overcomes the statute of limitations, and the court must consider the merits of the movant's claims. *Montano*, 398 F.3d at 1284.

(7) *the prison law library lacked legal materials in the movant's language, and the movant was unable to obtain translation services.* The circuits are split as to whether a prison law library's lack of legal materials in the prisoner's language, when combined with the prisoner's inability to obtain translation assistance before the one-year limitation deadline, could constitute extraordinary circumstances sufficient to allow for equitable tolling. The Second and Ninth Circuits have held that equitable tolling may be warranted in such circumstances. *See Diaz v. Kelly*, 515 F.3d 149, 154 (2d Cir. 2008); *Mendoza v. Carey*, 449 F.3d 1065, 1069 (9th Cir. 2006). The Tenth Circuit has expressly disagreed, concluding that a prisoner's limited proficiency in English does not constitute extraordinary circumstances. *See Yang v. Archuleta*, 525 F.3d 925, 929-30, (10th Cir. 2008).

§ 5.35. Equitable tolling and motions for an extension of time.

A federal court has jurisdiction to hear only live cases or controversies as delineated in Article III, Section 2, of the Constitution. This "case or controversy" requirement extends through all levels of federal judicial proceedings. *See Spencer v. Kemna*, 523 U.S. 1, 7, 118 S. Ct. 978, 983, 140 L. Ed. 2d 43 (1998).

In noncapital section 2255 proceedings, no "case or controversy" is before the court until an actual section 2255 motion is filed. *See Green v. United States*, 260 F.3d 78, 82–83 (2d Cir. 2001). As a result, the district court may not consider a motion requesting an extension of time to file a section 2255 motion unless an *actual motion* containing substantive claims for relief is filed with the request. *See id.* Where a motion that nominally seeks an extension of time is filed by a *pro se* litigant, and contains allegations sufficient to support a claim for relief, the district court is required to construe the motion as a substantive application for relief and then determine if it is timely. *See id.* In determining whether an extension of time is warranted, the court will consider whether "rare and exceptional" circumstances warrant equitably tolling the limitation period. *Id.*

Accordingly, if you wish to file a section 2255 motion but for some reason it is not yet complete as the one-year deadline approaches, your safest course is (1) to file an incomplete motion that contains all the claims you wish to include, and as much factual support as you have for each claim, and (2) to ask the court to grant you an extension of time to allow you to amend the incomplete motion, and allege "extraordinary circumstances" that prevented a complete motion from being filed on time. If an extension of time request is not accompanied by a substantive motion, the court will be unable to grant it.

IX. The Statute of Limitations and Amending a Section 2255 Motion

As discussed in greater detail in Chapter 12, a section 2255 motion may be amended or supplemented in the same manner as any other civil pleading under Federal Rule of Civil Procedure 15.[12] Civil Rule 15(a) provides for liberal amendment of original pleadings, stating that "[t]he court should freely give leave [to amend] when justice so requires." Fed. R. Civ. P. 15(a)(2). Section 2255's statute of limitations, however, complicates this liberal amendment process. Any new claim amending or supplementing the motion will be time-barred unless (1) it is itself independently timely because, as discussed earlier, it is filed within one year of one of the four triggering dates listed in section 2255(f), or (2) it "relates back" to the date of the original motion.

12. The text of Civil Rule 15 can be found in the Appendix to Chapter 12.

§ 5.36. The "relation-back" doctrine.

"'Relation back' causes an otherwise untimely claim to be considered timely by treating it as if it had been filed when the timely claims were filed." *Davenport v. United States*, 217 F.3d 1341, 1344 (11th Cir. 2000). Whether a claim relates back is controlled by Federal Rule of Civil Procedure 15(c). *See, e.g., id.*; *United States v. Thomas*, 221 F.3d 430, 436 (3d Cir. 2000); *Mederos*, 218 F.3d at 1254. Civil Rule 15(c) provides, in pertinent part: "An amendment to a pleading relates back to the date of the original pleading when: . . . the amendment asserts a claim or defense that arose out of the conduct, transaction, or occurrence set out—or attempted to be set out—in the original pleading." Fed. R. Civ. P. 15(c)(1)(B).

§ 5.37. New allegations in an amended motion will "relate back" only if they clarify a claim presented in the initial motion.

For any new allegations in an amended section 2255 motion to relate back under Civil Rule 15(c), they must clarify a claim presented in the initial motion. That is, the original motion and amendment must involve a "common core of operative facts." *Mayle v. Felix*, 545 U.S. 644, 664, 125 S. Ct. 2562, 2574, 162 L. Ed. 2d 582 (2005); *Thomas*, 221 F.3d at 436 (holding Civil Rule 15(c) "permit[s] an amendment to a petition to provide factual clarification or amplification after the expiration of the one-year period of limitations, as long as the petition itself was timely filed"); *Mederos*, 218 F.3d at 1254 ("Mederos's second motion satisfied the requirements to relate back to his initial motion, . . . as the second motion stated identical allegations as his initial motion.").

If the amendment depends on events that are separate both in time and type from the events upon which the original claims depended, it will not "relate back" to the timely filed initial motion, even though it arises from the same conviction and sentence. *See Mayle*, 545 U.S. at 649–50, 125 S. Ct. at 2566 (disallowing relation-back, where the claims presented in the original and amended pleadings were distinct under Civil Rule 15, in that one involved a Fifth Amendment challenge to the defendant's own pretrial statements, and the other involved a Confrontation Clause challenge to videotaped witness testimony); *Thomas*, 221 F.3d at 436 (relation back is not allowed where the amendment "seek[s] to add an entirely new claim or new theory of relief"); *United States v. Duffus*, 174 F.3d 333, 338 (3d Cir. 1999) ("A prisoner should not be able to assert a claim otherwise barred by the statute of limitations merely because he asserted a separate claim within the limitations period.").

§ 5.38. The safest course is to file a complete motion within one year of when the judgment of conviction became final under § 2255(f)(1).

Given the limited nature of the relation-back doctrine, the safest course is to file a timely and complete section 2255 motion containing all colorable claims within one year of when the judgment of conviction became final under § 2255(f)(1). Be sure to allot sufficient time prior to the filing of the motion to allow for the investigation and development of *all* potential claims so that they may be included in the initial, timely filed motion.

X. Appendix

A. Federal Rule of Civil Procedure 6 (2008)

**Rule 6. Computing and Extending Time;
Time for Motion Papers**

(a) Computing Time. The following rules apply in computing any time period specified in these rules or in any local rule, court order, or statute:

- **(1) Day of the Event Excluded.** Exclude the day of the act, event, or default that begins the period.
- **(2) Exclusions from Brief Periods.** Exclude intermediate Saturdays, Sundays, and legal holidays when the period is less than 11 days.
- **(3) Last Day.** Include the last day of the period unless it is a Saturday, Sunday, legal holiday, or—if the act to be done is filing a paper in court—a day on which weather or other conditions make the clerk's office inaccessible. When the last day is excluded, the period runs until the end of the next day that is not a Saturday, Sunday, legal holiday, or day when the clerk's office is inaccessible.
- **(4) "Legal Holiday" Defined.** As used in these rules, "legal holiday" means:
  - **(A)** the day set aside by statute for observing New Year's Day, Martin Luther King Jr.'s Birthday, Washington's Birthday, Memorial Day, Independence Day, Labor Day, Columbus Day, Veterans' Day, Thanksgiving Day, or Christmas Day; and
  - **(B)** any other day declared a holiday by the President, Congress, or the state where the district court is located.

(b) Extending Time.

(1) In General. When an act may or must be done within a specified time, the court may, for good cause, extend the time:

(A) with or without motion or notice if the court acts, or if a request is made, before the original time or its extension expires; or

(B) on motion made after the time has expired if the party failed to act because of excusable neglect.

(2) Exceptions. A court must not extend the time to act under Rules 50(b) and (d), 52(b), 59(b), (d), and (e), and 60(b), except as those rules allow.

(c) Motions, Notices of Hearing, and Affidavits.

(1) In General. A written motion and notice of the hearing must be served at least 5 days before the time specified for the hearing, with the following exceptions:

(A) when the motion may be heard ex parte;

(B) when these rules set a different time; or

(C) when a court order—which a party may, for good cause, apply for ex parte—sets a different time.

(2) Supporting Affidavit. Any affidavit supporting a motion must be served with the motion. Except as Rule 59(c) provides otherwise, any opposing affidavit must be served at least 1 day before the hearing, unless the court permits service at another time.

(d) Additional Time After Certain Kinds of Service. When a party may or must act within a specified time after service and service is made under Rule 5(b)(2)(C), (D), (E), or (F), 3 days are added after the period would otherwise expire under Rule 6(a).

B. Supreme Court Rule 13 (2008)

Rule 13. Review on Certiorari: Time for Petitioning

1. Unless otherwise provided by law, a petition for a writ of certiorari to review a judgment in any case, civil or criminal, entered by a state court of last resort or a United States court of appeals (including the United States Court of Appeals for the Armed Forces) is timely when it is filed with the Clerk of this Court within 90 days after the entry of the judgment. A petition for a writ of certiorari seeking review of a judgment of a lower state court that is subject to discretionary review by the state court of last resort is timely when it is filed with the Clerk within 90 days after entry of the order denying discretionary review.

2. The Clerk will not file any petition for a writ of certiorari that is jurisdictionally out of time. See, *e.g.*, 28 U.S.C. § 2101(c).

3. The time to file a petition for a writ of certiorari runs from the date of entry of the judgment or order sought to be reviewed, and not from the issuance date of the mandate (or its equivalent under local practice). But if a petition for rehearing is timely filed in the lower court by any party, or if the lower court appropriately entertains an untimely petition for rehearing, or *sua sponte* considers rehearing, the time to file the petition for a writ of certiorari for all parties (whether or not they requested rehearing or joined in the petition for rehearing) runs from the date of the denial of rehearing or, if rehearing is granted, the subsequent entry of judgment.

4. A cross-petition for a writ of certiorari is timely when it is filed with the Clerk as provided in paragraphs 1, 3, and 5 of this rule, or in Rule 12.5. However, a conditional cross-petition (which except for Rule 12.5 would be untimely) will not be granted unless another party's timely petition for a writ of certiorari is granted.

5. For good cause, a Justice may extend the time to file a petition for a writ of certiorari for a period not exceeding 60 days. An application to extend the time to file shall set out the basis for jurisdiction in this Court, identify the judgment sought to be reviewed, include a copy of the opinion and any order respecting rehearing, and set out specific reasons why an extension of time is justified. The application must be filed with the Clerk at least 10 days before the date the petition is due, except in extraordinary circumstances. For the time and manner of presenting the application, see Rules 21, 22, 30, and 33.2. An application to extend the time to file a petition for a writ of certiorari is not favored.

C. Federal Rule of Appellate Procedure 4(b) (2008)

Rule 4. Appeal as of Right—When Taken

* * *

(b) Appeal in a Criminal Case.

(1) Time for Filing a Notice of Appeal.

(A) In a criminal case, a defendant's notice of appeal must be filed in the district court within 10 days after the later of:

(i) the entry of either the judgment or the order being appealed; or

(ii) the filing of the government's notice of appeal.

(B) When the government is entitled to appeal, its notice of appeal must be filed in the district court within 30 days after the later of:

(i) the entry of the judgment or order being appealed; or

(ii) the filing of a notice of appeal by any defendant.

(2) Filing Before Entry of Judgment. A notice of appeal filed after the court announces a decision, sentence, or order—but before the entry of the judgment or order—is treated as filed on the date of and after the entry.

(3) Effect of a Motion on a Notice of Appeal.

(A) If a defendant timely makes any of the following motions under the Federal Rules of Criminal Procedure, the notice of appeal from a judgment of conviction must be filed within 10 days after the entry of the order disposing of the last such remaining motion, or within 10 days after the entry of the judgment of conviction, whichever period ends later. This provision applies to a timely motion:

(i) for judgment of acquittal under Rule 29;

(ii) for a new trial under Rule 33, but if based on newly discovered evidence, only if the motion is made no later than 10 days after the entry of the judgment; or

(iii) for arrest of judgment under Rule 34.

(B) A notice of appeal filed after the court announces a decision, sentence, or order—but before it disposes of any of the motions referred to in Rule 4(b)(3)(A)—becomes effective upon the later of the following:

(i) the entry of the order disposing of the last such remaining motion; or

(ii) the entry of the judgment of conviction.

(C) A valid notice of appeal is effective—without amendment—to appeal from an order disposing of any of the motions referred to in Rule 4(b)(3)(A).

(4) Motion for Extension of Time. Upon a finding of excusable neglect or good cause, the district court may—before or after the time has expired, with or without motion and notice—extend the time to file a notice of appeal for a period not to exceed 30 days from the expiration of the time otherwise prescribed by this Rule 4(b).

(5) Jurisdiction. The filing of a notice of appeal under this Rule 4(b) does not divest a district court of jurisdiction to correct a sentence under Federal Rule of Criminal Procedure 35(a), nor does the filing of a motion under 35(a) affect the validity of a notice of appeal filed before entry of the order disposing of the motion. The filing of a motion under Federal Rule of Criminal Procedure 35(a) does not suspend the time for filing a notice of appeal from a judgment of conviction.

(6) Entry Defined. A judgment or order is entered for purposes of this Rule 4(b) when it is entered on the criminal docket.

Part III:

Section 2255 Jurisdiction

Custody and Mootness

Contents

Introduction

§ 6.01. Custody and a live case or controversy are jurisdictional requirements.

A federal court may not grant section 2255 relief unless two interrelated requirements are met: (1) that the movant was "in custody" at the time the motion was filed, and (2) that the movant has been released from custody, that a live case or controversy remains, so that the case has not become moot.

I. A Section 2255 Movant Must Be "in Custody"

§ 6.02. A section 2255 movant must be "in custody" at the time the motion is filed.

To obtain section 2255 review by a federal court, the movant must be "[a] prisoner in custody under sentence of a court established by Act of Congress." § 2255(a). *Accord* Rule 1, Rules Governing § 2255 Proceedings. This is a jurisdictional requirement. *See Carafas v. LaVallee*, 391 U.S. 234, 238, 88 S. Ct. 1556, 1560, 20 L. Ed. 2d 554 (1968); *Heflin v. United States*, 358 U.S. 415, 418, 79 S. Ct. 451, 453, 3 L. Ed. 2d 407 (1959) ("§ 2255 is available only to attack a sentence under which a prisoner is in custody").

The "custody" requirement is satisfied if the movant is "in custody" at the time the motion is filed. *See Spencer v. Kemna*, 523 U.S. 1, 7, 118 S. Ct.

978, 983, 140 L. Ed. 2d 43 (1998).[1] That "is all the 'in custody' provision of 28 U.S.C. § [2255] requires." *Id.* Thus, "once the federal jurisdiction has attached in the District Court, it is not defeated by the release of the [movant] prior to completion of proceedings on such application." *Carafas*, 391 U.S. at 238, 88 S. Ct. at 1560.

II. Challenges to Sentences Not Being Served

Determining whether a movant meets section 2255's custody requirement can get complicated where the movant is serving consecutive sentences.

§ 6.03. A prisoner serving consecutive sentences is "in custody" under *all* of them.

For purposes of the custody requirement, "consecutive sentences should be treated as a continuous series," so that a prisoner "remains 'in custody' under *all* of his [consecutive] sentences until *all* are served." *Garlotte v. Fordice*, 515 U.S. 39, 40–41, 115 S. Ct. 1948, 1949, 132 L. Ed. 2d 36 (1995) (emphasis added); *see Peyton v. Rowe*, 391 U.S. 54, 67, 88 S. Ct. 1549, 1556, 20 L. Ed. 2d 426 (1968) (a "prisoner serving consecutive sentences is 'in custody' under any one of them."). Thus, a prisoner incarcerated under one conviction may file a section 2255 motion challenging a different conviction so long as the challenged conviction adds in some way to "the aggregate of the consecutive sentences" the movant eventually must serve. *Peyton*, 391 U.S. at 64–65, 88 S. Ct. at 1555.

§ 6.04. A prisoner serving consecutive sentences may challenge a future sentence.

Because a prisoner is "in custody" under each sentence in a continuous series of consecutive sentences, where a federal sentence runs consecutive to a state or federal sentence that the movant is already serving, the movant is considered to be "in custody" on the future federal sentence and may attack that sentence before completely serving the current sentence. *See* Rules Governing § 2255 Proceedings, Rule 1(b); *Peyton*, 391 U.S. at 64–65, 88 S. Ct. at 1555.

Indeed, given that the one-year statute of limitations for filing a section 2255 motion may elapse before the future federal sentence even begins

1. Although Spencer involved the custody requirement for state prisoners in habeas corpus proceedings under 28 U.S.C. § 2254, the same definition applies to section 2255 motions. *See* Advisory Committee Note to Rule 1, Rules Governing § 2255 Proceedings ("For a discussion of the 'custody' requirement and the intended scope of this inquiry, see advisory committee note to § 2254 Rule 1.").

to run,[2] a movant *must* attack that future federal sentence even if it has not yet begun to be served. *See Ospina v. United States*, 386 F.3d 750, 752 (6th Cir. 2004) (concluding that section 2255 movant serving a federal sentence consecutive to his state sentence was "in custody" during his state incarceration, and therefore his motion, filed within one year of the start of his federal sentence, was time-barred).

§ 6.05. A prisoner serving consecutive sentences is "in custody" under sentences fully served.

A movant who is serving some part of a series of consecutive sentences is also "in custody" under any sentences that have already expired, at least so long as invalidation of the expired sentence "would advance the date of [the movant's] eligibility for release from present incarceration." *Garlotte*, 515 U.S. at 47, 115 S. Ct. at 1952. Therefore, so long as an expired sentence "persists to postpone" the date for which she would be eligible for release under the unexpired sentences, a movant may file a section 2255 motion challenging the expired sentence. *Id.*, 515 U.S. at 41, 115 S. Ct. at 1949.

§ 6.06. A prisoner not serving consecutive sentences cannot challenge sentences fully served.

Unless the sentence being challenged is one of an aggregate of consecutive sentences, a prisoner is no longer "'in custody' under a conviction after the sentence imposed for it has fully expired." *Maleng v. Cook,* 490 U.S. 488, 492, 109 S. Ct. 1923, 1926, 104 L. Ed. 2d 540 (1989). That is, a section 2255 movant is not "in custody" under a conviction if the sentence imposed for that conviction was fully served at the time the motion was filed. *Id.*, 490 U.S. 490–91, 109 S. Ct. 1925. This is true even if that conviction was later used to enhance or lengthen a subsequent sentence imposed pursuant to a later conviction.

Moreover, a movant whose current sentence has been enhanced or lengthened by a prior conviction that has already been fully served may *not* use section 2255 to challenge the legality of the *current* sentence by arguing that the prior conviction was unlawful. Although a movant in this situation technically satisfies the "in custody" requirement, the Supreme Court, in *Daniels v. United States*, 532 U.S. 374, 382, 121 S. Ct. 1578, 1583, 149 L. Ed. 2d 590 (2001), held that if the prior conviction "is no longer open to direct or collateral attack in its own right because the defendant

2. The one-year statute of limitations applicable to section 2255 motions is discussed in Chapter 5.

failed to pursue those remedies while they were available (or because the defendant did so unsuccessfully), then that defendant is without recourse." Section 2255 cannot be used to attack the validity of the prior conviction, unless the prior conviction was secured in violation of the right to counsel. *Id.*, 532 U.S. at 382, 121 S. Ct. at 1583.

If, however, the prior conviction *is* still open to direct or collateral attack in its own right, and the prisoner successfully challenges that underlying conviction, then section 2255 *can* be used to attack the current sentence as wrongly enhanced by the now-invalidated prior conviction. *Id.*, 532 U.S. at 382, 121 S. Ct. at 1583.

III. Types of Restraint That Constitute Custody

"Custody" includes not only actual physical confinement, but other restrictions on a movant's liberty that arise from the conviction for a crime and are "not shared by the public generally." *Jones v. Cunningham*, 371 U.S. 236, 240, 83 S. Ct. 373, 376, 9 L. Ed. 2d 285 (1963). Following is an attempt to describe some of the types of restraint that have been found to satisfy the "custody" requirement. However, the boundaries of "custody" remain somewhat unclear, and you should consider this list a starting point, rather than a complete collection. *See* Advisory Committee Note to Rule 1, Rules Governing § 2254 Cases (made applicable to § 2255 proceedings by Advisory Committee Note to Rule 1, Rules Governing § 2255 Proceedings).

§ 6.07. "Custody" includes actual confinement.

The most common form of custody, of course, is actual incarceration pursuant to a criminal conviction. *See, e.g., Duncan v. Walker*, 533 U.S. 167, 176, 121 S. Ct. 2120, 2126, 150 L. Ed. 2d 251 (2001). "Custody" also includes involuntary commitment to a mental health facility, *id.*, 533 U.S. at 176, 121 S. Ct. at 2126; or confinement to a special penal facility, such as those for sexually violent predators, *Brock v. Weston*, 31 F.3d 887, 890 (9th Cir. 1994). A person held in immigration detention, however, is not "in custody" for the purpose of challenging a federal conviction or sentence under section 2255. *See United States v. Esogbue*, 357 F.3d 532, 534 (5th Cir. 2004); *Kandiel v. United States*, 964 F.2d 794, 796 (8th Cir. 1992).

§ 6.08. "Custody" also includes other restrictions on liberty.

"Custody," however, "is not restricted to situations in which the applicant is in actual, physical custody." *Jones*, 371 U.S. at 239, 83 S. Ct. at 375. Even if not physically confined, a movant may nonetheless be "in custody" if she has restrictions on her liberty as a result of her conviction for a crime, and those restrictions are "not shared by the public generally." *Id.*, 371 U.S. at 240, 83 S. Ct. at 376. For example, a movant satisfies the "custody" requirement if, at the time of filing the motion, she is:

(1) *serving a term of supervised release. See United States v. Cervini*, 379 F.3d 987, 989 n.1 (10th Cir. 2004), *cert. denied*, 544 U.S. 904, 125 S. Ct. 1592, 161 L. Ed. 2d 278 (2005); *Matus-Leva v. United States*, 287 F.3d 758, 761 (9th Cir. 2002); *United States v. Brown*, 117 F.3d 471, 475 (11th Cir. 1997).
(2) *on parole. See Jones*, 371 U.S. at 240–43, 83 S. Ct. at 376–77.
(3) *on probation. See United States v. Lopez*, 704 F.2d 1382, 1384 n.2 (5th Cir. 1983).
(4) *ordered to participate in certain rehabilitation programs. See Dow v. Circuit Court of the First Circuit,* 995 F.2d 922, 923 (9th Cir. 1993) (substance abuse program); *Barry v. Bergen County Probation Dept.*, 128 F.3d 152, 162 (3d Cir. 1997) (court-ordered community service); or
(5) *released on bail or bond or on her own recognizance. See Hensley v. Municipal Court*, 411 U.S. 345, 348–49, 93 S. Ct. 1571, 1573–74, 36 L. Ed. 2d 294 (1973) (release on own recognizance pending appeal); *Justices of Boston Municipal Court v. Lydon*, 466 U.S. 294, 300–02, 104 S. Ct. 1805, 1809–10, 80 L. Ed. 2d 311 (1984) (release on own recognizance pending trial); *Lefkowitz v. Newsome*, 420 U.S. 283, 286 n.2, 95 S. Ct. 886, 888 n.2, 43 L. Ed. 2d 196 (1975) (release on bail).

IV. Situations That Do Not Satisfy the Custody Requirement

Certain types of situations do *not* satisfy the custody requirement. These include:

(1) *payment of a fine or restitution.*[3] *See, e.g., United States v. Bernard*, 351 F.3d 360, 361 (8th Cir. 2003) (collecting restitution cases); *Obado v. New Jersey*, 328 F.3d 716, 718 (3d Cir. 2003) *(per curiam)* ("payment of restitution or a fine, absent more, is not the sort of 'significant restraint on liberty' contemplated in

3. Some courts have held that challenges to noncustodial punishments such as payment of a fine or an order of restitution are not cognizable in section 2255 proceedings. *See* Kaminski v. United States, 339 F.3d 84, 87–88 (2d Cir. 2003). Cognizability is discussed in Chapter 7. A writ of error *coram nobis*, however, may be used to challenge a restitution order or fine. *See id.* at 89–90; Barnickel v. United States, 113 F.3d 704, 706 (7th Cir. 1997). *Coram nobis* is discussed in Chapter 3.

the 'custody' requirement"); *United States v. Michaud*, 901 F.2d 5, 7 (1st Cir. 1990) *(per curiam)* ("A monetary fine is not a sufficient restraint on liberty to meet the 'in custody' requirement for § 2255 purposes.").

(2) *revocation of a license. See, e.g., Lefkowitz v. Fair*, 816 F.2d 17, 20 (1st Cir. 1987) (revocation of medical license); *Lillios v. New Hampshire*, 788 F.2d 60, 61 (1st Cir. 1986) *(per curiam)* (suspension of driver's license); *Ginsberg v. Abrams*, 702 F.2d 48, 48 (2d Cir. 1983) *(per curiam)* (revocation of license to practice law and disqualification as real estate broker and insurance agent).

(3) *registration as a sex offender. See Virsnieks v. Smith*, 521 F.3d 707, 718–20 (7th Cir. 2008) (collecting cases).

V. Mootness

If the movant has completely served his sentence, a question of constitutional dimension arises that is separate and distinct from the question of whether the movant meets the statutory "in custody" requirement. That constitutional question is one of mootness: does the movant's release from custody moot what was initially a live justiciable controversy? The answer: sometimes.

§ 6.09. A case is "moot" if there is no continuing injury.

A federal court has jurisdiction to hear only live cases or controversies as delineated in Article III, Section 2, of the Constitution. This "case or controversy" requirement extends through all levels of federal judicial proceedings, both trial and appellate. *Spencer*, 523 U.S. at 7, 118 S. Ct. at 983. "This means that, throughout the litigation, the plaintiff 'must have suffered, or be threatened with, an actual injury traceable to the defendant and likely to be redressed by a favorable judicial decision.'" *Id.* (quoting *Lewis v. Continental Bank Corp.*, 494 U.S. 472, 477, 110 S. Ct. 1249, 1253, 108 L. Ed. 2d 400 (1990)). Consequently, once the movant's sentence has expired, some concrete and continuing injury *other than* the now-completed incarceration (or parole or probation or supervised release)—"some 'collateral consequence' of the conviction—must exist if the suit is to be maintained." *Id.*, 523 U.S. at 7, 118 S. Ct. at 983.

§ 6.10. Expiration of movant's sentence does *not* moot an attack on the underlying conviction.

Where a section 2255 movant attacks his conviction, his motion is *not* mooted by the completion of his sentence prior to final adjudication of the motion. *See Carafas*, 391 U.S. at 237–38, 88 S. Ct. at 1559; *Spencer*, 523 U.S. at 8, 118 S. Ct. at 983. This is because the Supreme Court is willing to presume that a wrongful criminal conviction has collateral consequences that continue beyond the completion of the sentence. *Spencer*, 523 U.S. at 8, 118 S. Ct. at 983.

§ 6.11. Expiration of sentence moots a challenge that attacks *only* the sentence imposed.

Where a movant challenges *only* the sentence imposed following conviction, but not the underlying conviction itself, completion of the sentence renders the motion moot. *See Lane v. Williams*, 455 U.S. 624, 631, 102 S. Ct. 1322, 1326–27, 71 L. Ed. 2d 508 (1982).

Cognizable Claims

Contents

Introduction

§ 7.01. A wide range of claims is cognizable in section 2255 proceedings.

How do you determine whether a claim is cognizable under 28 U.S.C. § 2255? As discussed in Chapter 1, section 2255 was enacted solely to remedy problems arising from the mechanics of collateral proceedings brought by federal prisoners and was not intended to alter the scope of relief available under the traditional habeas corpus remedy. As a result, "the grounds for relief under § 2255 are equivalent to those encompassed by . . . the general federal habeas corpus statute, under which relief is available on the ground that '(a person) is in custody in violation of the Constitution or laws or treaties of the United States.'" *Davis v. United States*, 417 U.S. 333, 344, 94 S. Ct. 2298, 2304, 41 L. Ed. 2d 109 (1974) (citing 28 U.S.C. § 2254). Needless to say, this is a wide range of claims.

Moreover, section 2255 provides federal prisoners relief for additional types of claims: that the federal court acted outside its limited jurisdiction, that the sentence was "in excess of the maximum authorized by law," and that the conviction or sentence "is otherwise subject to collateral attack." *See* § 2255(a). As such, section 2255 relief is, in some ways, *broader* than the traditional habeas corpus remedy.

§ 7.02. This chapter and its appendix provide a broad outline of successful substantive claims.

Given the wide range of claims cognizable in section 2255 proceedings, and the variety of potential factual bases for each claim, it is impossible to create a complete list of the substantive grounds on which section 2255 relief may be granted. Rather than cataloging all possible section 2255 claims, this chapter attempts to provide a rough indication of the range and variety of substantive claims that have been successful in section 2255 proceedings. In addition, attached to this chapter is an Appendix that contains two case lists. The first lists all section 2255 decisions by the United States Supreme Court. The second lists *successful* published section 2255 cases in the federal courts of appeal since the adoption of the Sentencing Guidelines on November 1, 1987; that is, published cases where relief was granted or the case was remanded for an evidentiary hearing. A quick review of the cases in the Appendix should give you a better sense of the breadth of the section 2255 remedy.

You should be aware, however, that simply having a viable substantive claim is not enough to obtain section 2255 relief. First, a *timely* motion must be filed by a person *in custody* pursuant to a federal conviction and sentence. *See* Chapters 4–6. Second, in many cases, a number of procedural obstacles must also be surmounted before section 2255 relief may be had. Those obstacles are addressed in Chapters 8–11. Finally, if section 2255 relief is not available, it may be that some other federal postconviction remedy offers relief. Those alternative remedies are discussed in Chapter 3.

I. Cognizable Claims, Generally

§ 7.03. Statutory language.

Prisoners may move to "vacate, set aside or correct" a federal sentence under section 2255 on the grounds that "the sentence was imposed in violation of the Constitution or laws of the United States, or that the court was without jurisdiction to impose such a sentence, or that the sentence was in excess of the maximum authorized by law, or is otherwise subject to collateral attack." 28 U.S.C. § 2255(a). *See also* § 2255(b) ("the judgment was rendered without jurisdiction, or . . . the sentence imposed was not authorized by law or otherwise open to collateral attack, or . . . there has been such a denial or infringement of the constitutional rights of the prisoner as to render the judgment vulnerable to collateral attack"). The statutory language of section 2255 therefore recognizes four categories of claims: (1) the court lacked jurisdiction to render judgment, (2) the conviction or sentence is unconstitutional, (3) the conviction or sentence violates other federal law, or (4) the conviction or sentence is otherwise subject to collateral attack.

§ 7.04. "Fundamentality" requirement for nonjurisdictional and nonconstitutional claims.

Despite section 2255's statutory language, however, not all claims that fall into the latter two of these four categories are cognizable in section 2255 proceedings. For claims asserting a violation of federal law, or that the conviction or sentence was otherwise subject to collateral attack, the Supreme Court has read a "fundamentality" requirement into the statutory language. As a result, "an error which is neither jurisdictional nor constitutional" is not cognizable in section 2255 proceedings unless it is "a fundamental defect which inherently results in a complete miscarriage of justice," or "an omission inconsistent with the rudimentary demands of fair procedure." *Hill v. United States*, 368 U.S. 424, 428, 82 S. Ct. 468, 471, 7 L. Ed. 2d 417 (1962). Because of this fundamentality requirement, section 2255 relief generally is not available to correct mere "technical" violations of federal law.

For example, the Supreme Court has stated that, "as a general rule, . . . a court's failure to give a defendant advice required by the Federal Rules [of Criminal Procedure] is a sufficient basis for collateral relief only when the defendant is prejudiced by the court's error." *Peguero v. United States*, 526 U.S. 23, 27, 119 S. Ct. 961, 964, 143 L. Ed. 2d 18 (1999). In *Peguero*, the Supreme Court held that the district court's failure to advise the defendant of his right to appeal, as required by Federal Rule of Criminal Procedure 32(a)(2) was only a "technical" violation of the rule, and because the defendant could show no prejudice from the omission given that he was actually aware of his right to appeal at the time of his sentencing, the error was insufficient to justify section 2255 relief. *Id.*, 526 U.S. at 28, 119 S. Ct. at 964–65. Similarly, in *United States v. Timmreck*, 441 U.S. 780, 785, 99 S. Ct. 2085, 2088, 60 L. Ed. 2d 634 (1979), section 2255 relief was unavailable to a defendant who alleged only that the district court "'fail[ed] to comply with the formal requirements'" of Federal Rule of Criminal Procedure 11 by not advising him of a mandatory special parole term to which he was subject.

Consequently, movants seeking section 2255 relief for errors relating to a violation of the Federal Rules of Criminal Procedure—or any other error that is neither constitutional nor jurisdictional—must be sure to allege that the error was prejudicial in a way that rendered the proceedings fundamentally unfair. Otherwise, section 2255 relief will be unavailable.

II. Noncognizable Claims, Generally

§ 7.05. Few claims are not cognizable in section 2255 proceedings.

Because of the broad scope of the section 2255 remedy, the list of noncognizable claims is quite short. As discussed earlier, mere "technical" violations of federal law are not cognizable in section 2255 proceedings. Nor are challenges solely to noncustodial punishments, such as fines and restitution orders. Finally, section 2255 relief does not lie for claims that attack the *execution* of a federal sentence, rather than its *imposition*.

§ 7.06. Claims challenging noncustodial punishments are *not* cognizable under section 2255.

Because section 2255(a) affords relief only to those prisoners "claiming the right to be released" from custody,[1] it cannot be used to challenge noncustodial punishments—such as a fine or order of restitution. This is true whether or not the section 2255 motion also contains claims challenging the prisoner's sentence of incarceration. *See Kaminski v. United States*, 339 F.3d 84, 87–89 (2d Cir. 2003) (collecting cases).

§ 7.07. Claims attacking the execution of sentence are *not* cognizable under section 2255.

As discussed in Chapter 3, claims that attack the *execution* of a federal sentence by prison officials, rather than the imposition or terms of the sentence itself, are not cognizable in section 2255 proceedings. Such claims are, however, cognizable in a habeas corpus proceeding under 28 U.S.C. § 2241. Accordingly, a section 2241 petition for writ of habeas corpus, *not* a section 2255 motion to vacate sentence, should be used to attack such things as:

(1) *the denial of sentence credits for items such as good time or pretrial detention. See Reno v. Koray*, 515 U.S. 50, 52–53, 115 S. Ct. 2021, 2023, 132 L. Ed. 2d 46 (1995) (credit for pretrial detention in treatment center); *Rogers v. United States*, 180 F.3d 349, 358 & n.16 (1st Cir. 1999) (credit for time served in state prison); *Graham v. Lanfong*, 25 F.3d 203, 204 (3d Cir. 1994) (good time credits); *Bell*, 48 F.3d at 1043 (credit for time served under "no bond" order); *McClain v. Bureau of Prisons*, 9 F.3d 503, 504–05

1. The requirement that a section 2255 movant be "in custody" is discussed in Chapter 6.

(6th Cir. 1993) *(per curiam)* (credit for time spent in federal prison while on state parole).

(2) *transfers or other changes in the type of detention. See Rogers*, 180 F.3d at 357 (1st Cir. 1999) (failure to designate state prison as place of confinement); *Dunne v. Keohane*, 14 F.3d 335, 336–37 (7th Cir. 1994) (transfers between state and federal facilities); *United States v. Harris*, 12 F.3d 735, 736 (7th Cir. 1994) (disciplinary segregation); *United States v. Barth*, 28 F.3d 253, 256 (2d Cir. 1994) (commitment to another facility for psychiatric examination to assist with determination of competence); *United States v. Fuller*, 86 F.3d 105, 106–07 (7th Cir. 1996) (same).

(3) *prison disciplinary procedures. See Kingsley v. United States Bureau of Prisons*, 937 F.2d 26, 30 n.5 (2d Cir. 1991) (denial of right to call witnesses at disciplinary hearing).

(4) *immigration orders, e.g., INS v. St. Cyr*, 533 U.S. 289, 121 S. Ct. 2271, 150 L. Ed. 2d 347 (2001) (deportation/exclusion orders); *Zadvydas v. Davis*, 533 U.S. 678, 121 S. Ct. 2491, 150 L. Ed. 2d 653 (2001) (challenge to indefinite detention by immigration officials of person not likely to be deported). Note, however, that in May 2005, Congress passed the REAL ID Act, Pub. L. No. 109-13, Div. B, § 106, 119 Stat. 231, 310–11 (2005), which attempts to preclude the use of section 2241 as a means to obtain federal court review of immigration cases.

(5) *extradition to a foreign country. See In re Extradition of Drayer*, 190 F.3d 410, 412 n.2 (6th Cir. 1999); *Ludecke v. United States Marshal*, 15 F.3d 496, 497 (5th Cir. 1994); *Austin v. Healy*, 5 F.3d 598, 600–01 (2d Cir. 1993).

(6) *other detention orders issued by the executive branch. See Rasul v. Bush*, 542 U.S. 466, 124 S. Ct. 2686, 159 L. Ed. 2d 548 (2004) (challenges to legality of detention of foreign nationals captured by United States abroad and incarcerated at the Guantanamo Bay Naval Base, Cuba); *Hamdi v. Rumsfeld*, 542 U.S. 507, 124 S. Ct. 2633, 159 L. Ed. 2d 578 (2004) (habeas corpus available to review detention of an alleged "enemy combatant").

(7) *parole determinations. See Valona v. United States*, 138 F.3d 693, 694 (7th Cir. 1998); *Doganiere v. United States*, 914 F.2d 165, 169–70 (9th Cir. 1990).

III. The Court Lacked Jurisdiction to Render Judgment

Lack of jurisdiction is specifically mentioned in section 2255 as a ground for relief. *See* 28 U.S.C. § 2255(a) & (b); *see also United States v. Addonizio*,

442 U.S. 178, 185, 99 S. Ct. 2235, 2240, 60 L. Ed. 2d 805 (1979). Accordingly, claims that the district court acted outside its limited jurisdiction, that the indictment or information failed to charge an offense, or that the evidence was insufficient to support a jurisdictional element of the offense are all cognizable in section 2255 proceedings. Each will be discussed in turn.

§ 7.08. The court acted outside its limited jurisdiction.

If the district court acts outside its limited jurisdiction, section 2255 relief is available. *See Addonizio*, 442 U.S. at 185, 99 S. Ct. at 2240. For example, in *Bifulco v. United States*, 447 U.S. 381, 385–86, 400–01, 100 S. Ct. 2247, 2251, 2259, 65 L. Ed. 2d 205 (1980), the Court concluded that because 21 U.S.C. § 406 does not authorize imposition of a special parole term to be served upon completion of a term of imprisonment, movant, who was convicted under § 406 and sentenced to a special parole term, was entitled to section 2255 relief. *See also Smith v. United States*, 360 U.S. 1, 79 S. Ct. 991, 3 L. Ed. 2d 1041 (1959) (section 2255 relief warranted because Fifth Amendment requires that prisoner charged with crime that may be punished by death be prosecuted by indictment, and therefore, U.S. Attorney did not have authority to file information in instant case, and movant's waiver of indictment was not binding and did not confer power on the convicting court to hear the case); *United States v. DiPasquale*, 859 F.2d 9 (3d Cir. 1988) (granting section 2255 relief where district court was without power to impose pre-parole eligibility period that exceeded the limitation of ten years set forth in 18 U.S.C. § 4205(a)).

The court may also act outside of its jurisdiction in imposing sentencing enhancements under 21 U.S.C. § 851. If the government fails to comply with the procedural requirements of § 851 by not filing an information concerning the defendant's prior convictions at the requisite time, the court is without jurisdiction to use those prior convictions to enhance the defendant's sentence under § 851, and section 2255 relief is available. *See Harris v. United States*, 149 F.3d 1304, 1306–08 (11th Cir. 1998).

§ 7.09. The indictment or information failed to charge an offense.

Section 2255 relief will lie if the information or indictment failed to charge an offense, because the error is one that divests the court of jurisdiction. *See, e.g., United States v. Harper*, 901 F.2d 471, 472–73 (5th Cir. 1990).

§ 7.10. The evidence was insufficient to support a jurisdictional element of the offense.

If the evidence is insufficient to support the jurisdictional element of the offense, section 2255 relief is available. *See United States v. Ryan*, 227 F.3d 1058, 1061 (8th Cir. 2000) (granting section 2255 motion on claim that evidence was insufficient to satisfy 18 U.S.C. § 844(i)'s interstate commerce element); *United States v. Guess*, 203 F.3d 1143, 1147 (9th Cir. 2000) (determining that under *Bailey v. United States*, 516 U.S. 137, 116 S. Ct. 501, 133 L. Ed. 2d 472 (1995), there was insufficient evidence to support movant's conviction under 18 U.S.C. § 924(c)(1) for use of a firearm during and in relation to a drug trafficking offense, and granting section 2255 relief).

IV. The Conviction or Sentence Is Unconstitutional

Section 2255 relief is available to remedy a broad range of constitutional violations arising from the movant's conviction or sentence. This includes claims attacking misconduct by the government, arising from the denial of the Sixth Amendment right to counsel, relating to jury tampering, attacking the movant's guilty plea or sentence, and asserting a violation of double jeopardy.

§ 7.11. Claims attacking government misconduct.

Section 2255 relief is available where unconstitutional government misconduct tainted the movant's conviction or sentence. For example, in *United States v. Henry*, 447 U.S. 264, 100 S. Ct. 2183, 65 L. Ed. 2d 115 (1980), the Supreme Court granted section 2255 relief after it determined that a Sixth Amendment violation resulted from the district court's admission at trial of the testimony of an informant intentionally placed in the movant's cell pretrial by the government. Other section 2255 motions have been successful where:

(1) *the government failed to disclose material evidence. See Ferrera v. United States*, 456 F.3d 278, 297 (1st Cir. 2006) (affirming district court's grant of section 2255 relief on grounds that government violated due process by failing to disclose exculpatory evidence of a critical witness' recantation, where, absent prosecutorial misconduct, movant would not have pleaded guilty); *Conley v. United States*, 415 F.3d 183, 185 (1st Cir. 2005) (concluding government's

suppression of impeachment evidence violated Fifth Amendment, and affirming district court's grant of section 2255 relief); *United States v. Pelullo*, 105 F.3d 117, 122–24 (3d Cir. 1997) (concluding that government failed to disclose material impeachment evidence, in violation of *Brady v. Maryland*, 373 U.S. 83, 83 S. Ct. 1194, 10 L. Ed. 2d 215 (1963), and granting section 2255 relief).

(2) *the government knowingly presented falsified evidence or allowed it to go uncorrected when it appeared at trial. See United States v. Biberfeld*, 957 F.2d 98, 102–04 (3d Cir. 1992); *Humphrey v. United States*, 888 F.2d 1546, 1549–50 (11th Cir. 1989).

(3) *the government breached a plea agreement. See United States v. Al-Arian*, 514 F.3d 1184, 1191 (11th Cir. 2008); *United States v. De la Fuente*, 8 F.3d 1333, 1335 (9th Cir. 1993) (concluding that government breached plea agreement when it failed to recommend a sentence below the mandatory minimum, and granting section 2255 relief).

(4) *other government misconduct resulted in a miscarriage of justice. See Siddiqi v. United States*, 98 F.3d 1427, 1440 (2d Cir. 1999) (concluding that the prosecution's adoption of "shifting and at times misleading positions" that resulted in a conviction that "had no legitimate factual or legal basis" warranted section 2255 relief).

§ 7.12. Claims arising from the Sixth Amendment right to counsel.

Ineffective assistance of counsel, counsel's laboring under a conflict of interest, and the complete denial of counsel are all constitutionally based claims that are cognizable in section 2255 proceedings. Thus, section 2255 relief has been granted where counsel provided ineffective assistance:

(1) *in plea proceedings. See United States v. Gordon*, 156 F.3d 376, 381 (2d Cir. 1998) (counsel grossly underestimated movant's potential sentencing exposure); *United States v. Alvarez-Tautimez*, 60 F.3d 573, 577 (9th Cir. 1998) (counsel failed to move to withdraw movant's guilty plea following the grant of a codefendant's motion to suppress, where movant's plea had not yet been accepted by the district court, and movant therefore had an absolute right to withdraw it).

(2) *at trial. See United States v. Span*, 75 F.3d 1383, 1390 (9th Cir. 1996) (counsel failed to offer proper jury instructions on movant's only defense, and that defense had a strong likelihood of success); *Ward v. United States*, 995 F.2d 1317, 1318–19, 1322 (6th Cir. 1993) (to the detriment of his client, counsel opened the door to

the prosecution's introduction of otherwise inadmissible and damaging character evidence; made illogical and incomprehensible comments on the record; and acted with inappropriate hostility and paranoia).

(3) *at sentencing. See United States v. Franks*, 230 F.3d 811, 814–15 (5th Cir. 2000) (counsel failed to object to erroneous enhancement); *Prou v. United States*, 199 F.3d 37, 48–49 (1st Cir. 1999) (counsel failed to object to government's untimely filing of 21 U.S.C. § 851 enhancement); *United States v. Granados*, 168 F.3d 343, 346 (8th Cir. 1999) (counsel failed to object to information in pre-sentence report that increased scope of relevant conduct beyond that in plea agreement).

(4) *on appeal. See Rodriguez v. United States*, 395 U.S. 327, 328–29, 89 S. Ct. 1715, 1716–17, 23 L. Ed. 2d 340 (1969) (failure to file notice of appeal); *Hernandez v. United States*, 202 F.3d 486, 489 (2d Cir. 2000) (failure to file timely notice of appeal); *McHale v. United States*, 175 F.3d 115, 119 (2d Cir. 1999) (although appeal was properly filed, counsel failed to timely file record on appeal or briefing, which resulted in dismissal of appeal); *Brown v. United States*, 167 F.3d 109, 111 (2d Cir. 1999) (failure to raise on appeal obviously winning argument).

(5) *in failing to investigate adequately. See United States v. Kauffman*, 109 F.3d 186, 190–91 (3d Cir. 1997) (counsel failed to conduct any investigation into an insanity defense after receiving a letter from a psychiatrist who concluded, based on an interview with the defendant immediately following his arrest, that the defendant was manic and psychotic at the time of the crime); *United States v. Gray*, 878 F.3d 702, 711–14 (3d Cir. 1989) (counsel failed to conduct any pretrial investigation, failed to hire an investigator to conduct such investigation, and failed to contact potential witnesses).

Section 2255 relief is also available where counsel was laboring under an actual conflict of interest. *See, e.g., United States v. Cook*, 45 F.3d 388, 393, 396 (10th Cir. 1995) (granting section 2255 motion where court order required defense counsel to advise government witness that her decision not to testify against counsel's client would violate her plea agreement); *United States v. Fulton*, 5 F.3d 605, 610–11 (2d Cir. 1993) (granting section 2255 relief on claim that movant's trial counsel labored under conflict of interest after government witness alleged that trial counsel was engaged in drug trafficking related to the charge for which movant was on trial).

Finally, a section 2255 movant may also obtain relief where counsel was denied altogether. *See, e.g., United States v. Behrens*, 375 U.S. 162,

84 S. Ct. 295, 11 L. Ed. 2d 224 (1963) (granting section 2255 relief where district court imposed sentence in absence of movant and counsel); *United States v. Russell*, 205 F.3d 768, 772 (5th Cir. 2000) (granting section 2255 relief where defendant was unrepresented during two days of trial); *United States v. Moore*, 159 F.3d 1154, 1159–60 (9th Cir. 1998) (holding trial counsel's irreconcilable conflict with movant resulted in denial of counsel); *United States v. Fuller*, 941 F.2d 993, 994 (9th Cir. 1991) (movant was denied counsel during plea negotiations).

§ 7.13. Double jeopardy claims.

Section 2255 movants have obtained relief on double jeopardy claims. *See, e.g., United States v. Silvers*, 90 F.3d 95, 101 (4th Cir. 1996); *Brown v. United States*, 34 F.3d 990, 990–91 (10th Cir. 1994).

§ 7.14. Jury tampering claims.

Movants have also obtained section 2255 relief on claims that a codefendant tampered with the jury. *See United States v. Dutkel*, 192 F.3d 893, 898–99 (9th Cir. 1999); *United States v. Cheek*, 94 F.3d 136, 144 (4th Cir. 1996).

§ 7.15. Constitutional claims relating to guilty pleas.

A federal defendant who has pleaded guilty or *nolo contendere* cannot obtain section 2255 relief on any claim alleging that a violation of rights, constitutional or otherwise, occurred *prior* to the plea. *Tollett v. Henderson*, 411 U.S. 258, 267, 93 S. Ct. 1602, 1608, 36 L. Ed. 2d 235 (1973).[2] A guilty plea does not, however, preclude challenges to the validity of the plea itself. As such, convictions obtained by means of a guilty plea have been successfully attacked in section 2255 proceedings where the movant has shown that:

(1) *the plea was induced by threats or promises. See Machibroda v. United States*, 368 U.S. 487, 493, 82 S. Ct. 510, 513, 7 L. Ed. 2d 473 (1962); *Fontaine v. United States*, 411 U.S. 213, 214–15, 93 S. Ct. 1461, 1462–63, 36 L. Ed. 2d 169 (1973); *United States v. Wright*, 43 F.3d 491, 497–99 (10th Cir. 1994) (threats to prosecute a third party).

(2) *the government breached a plea agreement. See United States v. Taylor*, 77 F.3d 368, 370–71 (11th Cir. 1996); *De la Fuente*, 8 F.3d at 1335.

2. The implicit waiver of section 2255 relief by means of a plea of guilty or *nolo contendere* is discussed in Chapter 9.

(3) *the district court initiated or participated in plea negotiations. See United States v. Garfield*, 987 F.2d 1424, 1426–27 (9th Cir. 1993).

(4) *the plea was otherwise not knowing and voluntary. See United States v. Guerra*, 94 F.3d 989, 995 (5th Cir. 1996) (district court misinformed movant as to possible maximum sentence he could have received); *Tress v. United States*, 87 F.3d 188, 189–90 (7th Cir. 1996) (district court failed to advise movant of his right to appeal his sentence, and there is no evidence that movant learned of his right to appeal from another source); *United States v. Neely*, 38 F.3d 458, 460–61 (9th Cir. 1994) (district court failed to inform movant, before accepting plea, that his federal sentence could be served consecutively to any state sentence subsequently imposed); *United States v. Roberts*, 5 F.3d 365, 369–70 (9th Cir. 1993) (district court failed to advise movant of a term of supervised release).

§ 7.16. Constitutional claims relating to sentencing.

A due process claim that the movant's sentence was based in part on false information in the pre-sentence report is cognizable in section 2255 proceedings. *See Shukwit v. United States*, 973 F.2d 903, 904 (11th Cir. 1992).

V. The Conviction or Sentence Violates Federal Law

Federal courts have also granted section 2255 relief to movants who have demonstrated that their conviction or sentence violated federal law. That violation may be due to intervening changes in the substantive law or intervening amendments to the Sentencing Guidelines, or because the district court simply imposed a sentence not otherwise authorized by federal law. Remember, however, that section 2255 relief is available for such claims only so long as the violation of federal law was "a fundamental defect which inherently results in a complete miscarriage of justice," or "an omission inconsistent with the rudimentary demands of fair procedure." *Hill*, 368 U.S. at 428, 82 S. Ct. at 471.

§ 7.17. Intervening changes in the substantive law.

Changes in the substantive law since the time of conviction and sentence may provide a basis for section 2255 relief. *See Davis*, 417 U.S. at 346–47, 94 S. Ct. at 2305. For example, many federal prisoners obtained section 2255 relief following the Supreme Court's decision in *Bailey v. United States*, 516 U.S. 137, 116 S. Ct. 501, 133 L. Ed. 2d 472 (1995), which changed the understanding of the term "use" in 18 U.S.C. § 924(c). *See, e.g., United States v. Johnson*, 260 F.3d 919, 920–21 (8th Cir. 2001); *United States v. Guess*, 203 F.3d 1143, 1146 (9th Cir. 2000).

Indeed, intervening Supreme Court decisions have formed the basis for section 2255 relief in a number of circumstances. *See Davis*, 417 U.S. at 341–46, 94 S. Ct. at 2302–05 (granting section 2255 relief because movant established that his conviction and punishment were for an act that was held not criminal under law as interpreted by intervening decision); *United States v. Brown*, 117 F.3d 471, 479–80 (11th Cir. 1997) (granting section 2255 relief after concluding that in light of the Supreme Court's decision in *Ratzlaf v. United States*, 510 U.S. 135, 114 S. Ct. 655, 126 L. Ed. 2d 615 (1994), which held that knowledge of illegality is an essential element of the crime of currency structuring, a guilty plea to that crime based upon pre-*Ratzlaf* law to the contrary was invalid because not knowing and voluntary); *United States v. Ross*, 40 F.3d 144, 145–46 (7th Cir. 1994) (granting section 2255 relief where intervening decision in *Staples v. United States*, 511 U.S. 600, 114 S. Ct. 1793, 128 L. Ed. 2d 608 (1994), made clear that the jury at movant's trial was erroneously instructed with respect to an element of the offense).

§ 7.18. Intervening amendments to the Sentencing Guidelines.

A post-sentencing amendment by the United States Sentencing Commission to a Sentencing Guideline or its comments warrant section 2255 relief if the amendment "clarifies" the guideline or comment in place at the time of the original sentencing. *See United States v. Marmolejos*, 140 F.3d 488, 489 (3d Cir. 1998); *Isabel v. United States*, 980 F.2d 60, 62–63 (1st Cir. 1992).

§ 7.19. The sentence was imposed in violation of federal law.

Section 2255 motions have been successful where the district court imposed a sentence that was not authorized under federal law; *see Bifulco*, 447 U.S. at 385, 400–01, 100 S. Ct. at 2251, 2259 (supervised parole term not authorized). Section 2255 relief has also been granted where the district court entered a written judgment that imposed a penalty greater than that announced orally. *See United States v. DeMartino*, 112 F.3d 75, 78 (2d Cir. 1997).

VI. The Conviction or Sentence Is Otherwise Subject to Collateral Attack

Section 2255 expressly provides for relief where the conviction or sentence "is otherwise subject to collateral attack." § 2255(a). In such circumstances, relief is available "where 'the alleged error constituted a fundamental defect which inherently results in a complete miscarriage of justice.'" *Siddiqi*, 98 F.3d at 1438 (quoting *Reed v. Farley*, 512 U.S. 339, 354, 114 S. Ct. 2291, 2300, 129 L. Ed. 2d 277 (1994)). This catch-all provision allows section 2255 relief in circumstances where the movant's sentence was based on misinformation, such as invalid prior convictions, and also in those rare circumstances where no specific right or law was violated, but the circumstances simply constitute a miscarriage of justice.

§ 7.20. The sentence is based on misinformation, including invalid prior convictions.

A federal sentence may be "otherwise subject to collateral attack," and section 2255 provides a remedy, where that sentence is based on misinformation, such as an invalid prior conviction. Indeed, federal prisoners who have successfully attacked prior convictions used to calculate their criminal history or enhance their sentence have obtained section 2255 relief. *See United States v. Tucker*, 404 U.S. 443, 92 S. Ct. 589, 30 L. Ed. 2d 592 (1972) (granting section 2255 relief where sentence was based at least in part on misinformation—three prior felony convictions, two of which were constitutionally invalid because movant was not represented by counsel in violation of *Gideon v. Wainwright*, 372 U.S. 335, 83 S. Ct. 792, 9 L. Ed. 2d 799 (1963)); *United States v. Pettiford*, 101 F.3d 199, 200 (1st Cir. 1996) (reducing movant's sentence on the ground that the enhancement under the Armed Career Criminal Act, 18 U.S.C. § 924(e)(1), was no longer applicable following the state court's post-sentencing vacation of eight of nine convictions used to enhance movant's federal sentence); *United States v. Cox*, 83 F.3d 336, 339 (10th Cir. 1996) (concluding that district court should have granted section 2255 relief and reopened movant's sentence after he successfully attacked several prior convictions used to calculate his criminal history).

§ 7.21. The conviction or sentence constituted a miscarriage of justice.

Finally, section 2255 also provides a remedy in those rare circumstances where no specific right or law was violated, but the circumstances simply constituted a miscarriage of justice. For example, in *Siddiqi*, the Second

Circuit determined that section 2255 relief was warranted in the unique circumstances of that case. 98 F.3d at 1438. There, "[t]he shifting nature of the government's case," from one theory of guilt during the presentation of evidence, to another in summation at trial, to yet another on appeal, "materially impeded the effective presentation of a defense during trial by misleading defense counsel as to the government's theory of guilt," and "enabled the government to obtain a conviction from the jury on a factual theory that was put forth for the first time in summation and had no foundation in fact." *Id.* As such, the court determined, movant's trial and post-trial proceedings "did not meet the rudimentary demands of fair procedure," and "constituted a miscarriage of justice" and section 2255 relief was warranted. *Id.*

VII. Appendix

A. Section 2255 Decisions, United States Supreme Court

(1948 to June 30, 2008)

United States v. Santos, ___ U.S. ___, 128 S. Ct. 2020, 170 L. Ed. 2d 912 (June 2, 2008) (upholding grant of section 2255 relief upon conclusion that the word "proceeds" as used in 18 U.S.C. §§ 1956(a)(1)(A)(i) and (h) applies only to criminal "profits" and not merely to criminal "receipts.").

Dodd v. United States, 545 U.S. 353, 125 S. Ct. 2478, 162 L. Ed. 2d 343 (2005) (under section 2255(f)(3), the one-year limitation period for filing motion to vacate based on right that was newly recognized by the Supreme Court runs from the date on which the Supreme Court initially recognized the right asserted, not from the date on which the right asserted was made retroactively applicable to cases on collateral review).

Johnson v. United States, 544 U.S. 295, 125 S. Ct. 1571, 161 L. Ed. 2d 542 (2005) (although the vacatur of movant's prior state convictions is a matter of fact, which could start renewed one-year limitations period for motion to vacate under section 2255(f)(4), and movant's receipt of notice of order vacating his prior state court conviction triggered limitations period, section 2255(f)(4) also requires that movant act with due diligence in attacking prior state court convictions, with that diligence measured from the date the prior convictions were used to enhance the federal sentence; here, because movant waited three years after entry of judgment to seek vacatur, he failed to fulfill the due diligence requirement).

Castro v. United States, 540 U.S. 375, 124 S. Ct. 786, 157 L. Ed. 2d 778 (2003) ("when a court recharacterizes a *pro se* litigant's motion as a first § 2255 motion . . . the district court must notify the *pro se* litigant that it intends to recharacterize the pleading, warn the litigant that this recharacterization means that any subsequent § 2255 motion will be subject to the restrictions on 'second or successive' motions, and provide the litigant an opportunity to withdraw the motion or to amend it so that it contains all the § 2255 claims he believes he has. If the court fails to do so, the motion cannot be considered to have become a § 2255 motion for purposes of applying to later motions the law's 'second or successive' restrictions").

Massaro v. United States, 538 U.S. 500, 123 S. Ct. 1690, 155 L. Ed. 2d 714 (2003) (federal defendant may always raise ineffective assistance of counsel claim in section 2255 proceeding, even though defendant could have, but did not, raise claim on direct appeal).

Clay v. United States, 537 U.S. 522, 123 S. Ct. 1072, 155 L. Ed. 2d 88 (2003) (for purposes of starting clock on section 2255's one-year limitation period under section 2255(f)(1), a judgment of conviction becomes final when the time expires for filing a petition for writ of *certiorari* contesting the appellate court's affirmation of the conviction).

Daniels v. United States, 532 U.S. 374, 121 S. Ct. 1578, 149 L. Ed. 2d 590 (2001) (a section 2255 movant whose current sentence has been enhanced or lengthened by a prior conviction may not use section 2255 to challenge the legality of the *current* sentence by arguing that the prior conviction was unlawful: if the prior conviction "is no longer open to direct or collateral attack in its own right because the defendant failed to pursue those remedies while they were available (or because the defendant did so unsuccessfully), then that defendant is without recourse," unless the prior conviction was secured in violation of the right to counsel; if, however, the prior conviction *is* still "open to direct or collateral attack in its own right," and the prisoner successfully challenges that underlying conviction, then section 2255 can be used to attack the current sentence as enhanced by the now-invalidated prior conviction).

Glover v. United States, 531 U.S. 198, 121 S. Ct. 696, 148 L. Ed. 2d 604 (2001) (an increase in movant's sentence from 6 to 21 months as a result of counsel's error constituted prejudice required for establishing ineffective assistance of counsel under *Strickland v. Washington*, 466 U.S. 668, 104 S. Ct. 2052, 80 L. Ed. 2d 674 (1984); indeed, "any amount of actual jail time has Sixth Amendment significance").

United States v. Johnson, 529 U.S. 53, 120 S. Ct. 1114, 146 L. Ed. 2d 39 (2000) (even though movant convicted for multiple felonies had two of his convictions declared invalid and, as a result, had served too much prison time, 18 U.S.C. § 3624(e) precluded excess prison time from being credited to the supervised release term, and movant's supervised release term began to run on date he was actually released from prison, not date on which he should have been released).

Peguero v. United States, 526 U.S. 23, 119 S. Ct. 961, 143 L. Ed. 2d 18 (1999) (as a general rule, a court's failure to give a federal defendant advice required by the Federal Rules of Criminal Procedure does not form a basis for section 2255 relief unless that defendant was prejudiced by the court's error; here, district court's failure to advise movant of his right to appeal does not entitle him to section 2255 relief as movant was already aware of his right to appeal and therefore court's violation of rule did not prejudice him).

Hohn v. United States, 524 U.S. 236, 118 S. Ct. 1969, 141 L. Ed. 2d 242 (1998) (where both the district court and the court of appeals deny a certificate of appealability as to all issues, a petition for writ of *certiorari* may be filed in the United States Supreme Court seeking review of that denial).

Bousley v. United States, 523 U.S. 614, 118 S. Ct. 1604, 140 L. Ed. 2d 828 (1998) (rule of *Teague v. Lane*, 489 U.S. 288, 109 S. Ct. 1060, 103 L. Ed. 2d 334 (1989)—that a new rule of criminal procedure is generally not applicable in cases that became final before the new rule was announced—is inapplicable to situations where the Court decides the meaning of a criminal statute enacted by Congress; here, remanding section 2255 case for evidentiary hearing on whether movant can establish actual innocence so that his procedurally defaulted claim under *Bailey v. United States*, 516 U.S. 137, 116 S. Ct. 501, 133 L. Ed. 2d 472 (1995), may be considered on the merits).

United States v. Bagley, 473 U.S. 667, 105 S. Ct. 3375, 87 L. Ed. 2d 481 (1985) (exculpatory evidence is "material" for purposes of *Brady v. Maryland*, 373 U.S. 83, 83 S. Ct. 1194, 10 L. Ed. 2d 215 (1963), and requires reversal of conviction, only if there is reasonable probability that, had evidence been disclosed to defense, result of proceeding would have been different).

United States v. Benchimol, 471 U.S. 453, 105 S. Ct. 2103, 85 L. Ed. 2d 462 (1985) *(per curiam)* (government, which agreed to make recommendation as to sentence as part of plea bargain, was not required to explain its reasons or to make its recommendation "enthusiastically").

United States v. Cronic, 466 U.S. 648, 104 S. Ct. 2039, 80 L. Ed. 2d 657 (1984) (right to the effective assistance of counsel is "the right of the accused to require the prosecution's case to survive the crucible of meaningful adversarial testing. When a true adversarial criminal trial has been conducted—even if defense counsel may have made demonstrable errors—the kind of testing envisioned by the Sixth Amendment has occurred. But if the process loses its character as a confrontation between adversaries, the constitutional guarantee is violated." Here, the fact that counsel was given only 25 days to prepare for trial, that counsel was young and inexperienced in criminal matters, that charges were complex and grave, and that some witnesses were not easily accessible did not provide basis for finding *per se* ineffectiveness).

United States v. Frady, 456 U.S. 152, 168, 102 S. Ct. 1584, 1594, 71 L. Ed. 2d 816 (1982) (if a section 2255 movant could have raised a claim at trial or on direct appeal but did not do so, section 2255 relief on that claim is completely barred by the judicially created "procedural default" doctrine unless the movant can demonstrate "cause" for the failure to raise the claim at the proper time and actual "prejudice").

United States v. Henry, 447 U.S. 264, 100 S. Ct. 2183, 65 L. Ed. 2d 115 (1980) (granting section 2255 relief on movant's claim that his Sixth Amendment right to counsel was violated when the district court allowed introduction of the testimony of an informant the government had intentionally placed in movant's cell pretrial in order to elicit incriminating information from movant, where movant did not learn that the cellmate was a paid informant until after the completion of direct appeal).

Bifulco v. United States, 447 U.S. 381, 100 S. Ct. 2247, 65 L. Ed. 2d 205 (1980) (concluding that 21 U.S.C. § 406 does not authorize imposition of a special parole term to be served upon completion of a term of imprisonment, and granting section 2255 relief to movant who was convicted under § 406 and sentenced to special parole term).

United States v. Addonizio, 442 U.S. 178, 99 S. Ct. 2235, 60 L. Ed. 2d 805 (1979) (movant's allegation that a post-sentencing change in the policies of the U.S. Parole Commission had prolonged his actual imprisonment beyond the period intended by the sentencing judge does not support section 2255 relief from the original sentence: while the section 2255 remedy is "comprehensive, it does not encompass all claimed errors in conviction and sentencing;" although section 2255 relief is available where the movant "alleges a lack of jurisdiction or constitutional error, . . . an error of law does not provide a basis for collateral attack unless the claimed error constituted 'a fundamental defect which inherently results in a complete miscarriage of justice.'" The claimed error here—that the judge was incorrect in his assumptions about the future course of parole proceedings—did not infect the proceedings "with any error of fact or law of the 'fundamental' character that renders the entire proceeding irregular or invalid," and therefore section 2255 relief is unavailable).

United States v. Timmreck, 441 U.S. 780, 99 S. Ct. 2085, 60 L. Ed. 2d 634 (1979) (section 2255 relief is unavailable to movant who alleged only a "technical violation" of Federal Rule of Criminal Procedure 11—movant alleged only that district court failed to comply with formal requirements of Rule 11 by not advising him of a mandatory special parole term to which he was subject, but did not allege that he was actually unaware of special parole term or that, if he had been properly advised by the judge, he would not have pleaded guilty; in addition, claim could have been raised on direct appeal, but was not, and "there is no basis here for allowing collateral attack 'to do service for an appeal'").

Dorszynski v. United States, 418 U.S. 424, 94 S. Ct. 3042, 41 L. Ed. 2d 855 (1974) (granting section 2255 relief on movant's claim that the district court was without jurisdiction to impose sentence because it failed to make a specific finding that the 19-year-old movant would not derive benefits from treatment under the Federal Youth Corrections Act, 18 U.S.C. § 5005).

Davis v. United States, 417 U.S. 333, 94 S. Ct. 2298, 41 L. Ed. 2d 109 (1974) (although general rule is that a section 2255 proceeding may not be used to relitigate questions that have already been raised and considered on direct appeal, where there has been an intervening change in the law—"'if new law has been made . . . since the trial and appeal'"—then the fact that the issue was raised and rejected on direct appeal does not preclude movant from securing relief under section 2255; here, movant is entitled to section 2255 relief because his conviction and punishment were for an act that was held not criminal under law as interpreted by intervening decision).

Marshall v. United States, 414 U.S. 417, 94 S. Ct. 700, 38 L. Ed. 2d 618 (1974) (concluding that the provisions of the Narcotic Rehabilitation Act of 1966, which excludes addicts with two or more prior felony convictions from discretionary rehabilitative commitment, did not deny section 2255 movant due process or equal protection of the law).

Davis v. United States, 411 U.S. 233, 93 S. Ct. 1577, 36 L. Ed. 2d 216 (1973) (waiver standard set forth in Federal Rule of Criminal Procedure 12(b)(2) governs an untimely claim of grand jury discrimination made on collateral review; here, movant waived right to obtain section 2255 relief on discrimination claim, where he failed to attack the grand jury's composition at all prior stages of the proceedings and made no showing of "cause" that would provide relief from the waiver).

Fontaine v. United States, 411 U.S. 213, 93 S. Ct. 1461, 36 L. Ed. 2d 169 (1973) (concluding that section 2255 relief is available to remedy a coerced guilty plea, and remanding for evidentiary hearing on movant's claim that his guilty plea was induced by a combination of fear, coercive police tactics, and illness, including mental illness).

United States v. Tucker, 404 U.S. 443, 92 S. Ct. 589, 30 L. Ed. 2d 592 (1972) (granting section 2255 relief from sentence where sentence was based at least in part on two prior felony convictions that were constitutionally invalid because movant was not represented by counsel in violation of *Gideon v. Wainwright*, 372 U.S. 335 (1963)).

Williams v. United States, 401 U.S. 646, 91 S. Ct. 1148, 28 L. Ed. 2d 388 (1971) (concluding that *Chimel v. California*, 395 U.S. 752, 89 S. Ct. 2034, 23 L. Ed. 2d 685 (1969), which narrowed the scope of permissible searches incident to arrest, should not be applied retroactively either on direct review or in section 2255 proceedings, and denying section 2255 relief to movant whose search antedated *Chimel*).

Mackey v. United States, 401 U.S. 667, 91 S. Ct. 1160, 28 L. Ed. 2d 404 (1971) (concluding that two Supreme Court decisions—together holding that a statutory requirement to register and file gambling tax returns compelled self-incrimination, and compelled statements were not admissible in prosecution's case-in-chief—did not apply retroactively to allow movant section 2255 relief from his conviction for evading payment of income taxes by willfully preparing false tax returns).

Brady v. United States, 397 U.S. 742, 90 S. Ct. 1463, 25 L. Ed. 2d 747 (1970) (movant's plea of guilty was not rendered involuntary because of possible fear of death penalty if case were tried to jury, and section 2255 relief is unwarranted, where movant was advised by competent counsel and tendered his plea after his codefendant, who had already given a confession, and became available to testify against movant).

Bryson v. United States, 396 U.S. 64, 90 S. Ct. 355, 24 L. Ed. 2d 264 (1969) (constitutionality of statute that precluded unions from participating in proceedings conducted by the National Labor Relations Board (NLRB) unless each union officer filed a "non-Communist" affidavit was irrelevant to validity of movant's conviction for making fraudulent statements to the government when he falsely denied his affiliation with the Communist party in an affidavit filed with the NLRB, and therefore afforded no basis for section 2255 relief).

Rodriguez v. United States, 395 U.S. 327, 89 S. Ct. 1715, 23 L. Ed. 2d 340 (1969) (granting section 2255 relief on movant's claim that counsel was constitutionally ineffective for failing to file a notice of appeal after movant requested that he do so).

Halliday v. United States, 394 U.S. 831, 89 S. Ct. 1498, 23 L. Ed. 2d 16 (1969) *(per curiam)* (concluding that *McCarthy v. United States*, 394 U.S. 459, 89 S. Ct. 1166, 22 L. Ed. 2d 418 (1969)—which holds that a defendant must be afforded an opportunity to plead anew when a guilty plea is accepted in violation of Federal Rule of Criminal Procedure 11—should not be applied retroactively, and denying section 2255 relief to movant whose plea was entered before that decision).

Kaufman v. United States, 394 U.S. 217, 89 S. Ct. 1068, 22 L. Ed. 2d 227 (1960) (claim of unconstitutional search and seizure under the Fourth Amendment is cognizable in section 2255 proceedings).

United States v. Ewell, 383 U.S. 116, 86 S. Ct. 773, 15 L. Ed. 2d 627 (1966) (reversing circuit court's grant of section 2255 relief and concluding that passage of 19 months between original arrests of movants and hearings on later indictments did not itself demonstrate violation of Sixth Amendment right to speedy trial).

United States v. Tateo, 377 U.S. 463, 84 S. Ct. 1587, 12 L. Ed. 2d 448 (1964) (reversing grant of section 2255 relief and concluding that movant's retrial following guilty plea was not barred by double jeopardy even though plea was entered after prosecution had commenced before a jury).

United States v. Behrens, 375 U.S. 162, 84 S. Ct. 295, 11 L. Ed. 2d 224 (1963) (granting section 2255 relief where district court modified original oral sentencing order and fixed movant's final sentence in absence of movant and counsel).

Andrews v. United States, 373 U.S. 334, 83 S. Ct. 1236, 10 L. Ed. 2d 383 (1963) (where the district court has granted § 2255 relief and its order requires a retrial or resentencing of the movant, that order is not considered to be a "final" order, and no appeal will be permitted until the district court has completed the further proceedings contemplated by its order).

Sanders v. United States, 373 U.S. 1, 83 S. Ct. 1068, 10 L. Ed. 2d 148 (1963) (section 2255 was not intended to change the judicially evolved law governing second or successive habeas corpus proceedings, accordingly, "controlling weight may be given to denial of a prior application for federal habeas corpus or § 2255 relief only if (1) the same ground presented in the subsequent application was determined adversely to the applicant on the prior application, (2) the prior determination was on the merits, and (3) the ends of justice would not be served by reaching the merits of the subsequent application").

Machibroda v. United States, 368 U.S. 487, 82 S. Ct. 510, 7 L. Ed. 2d 473 (1962) (concluding section 2255 relief is available to attack a guilty plea if plea is induced by promises or threats that deprive it of the character of a voluntary act, and remanding for an evidentiary hearing to determine whether movant's plea was involuntary because induced by promises made by the prosecutor as to the length of the sentences that would be imposed).

Mitchell v. United States, 368 U.S. 439, 82 S. Ct. 462, 7 L. Ed. 2d 429 (1962) *(per curiam)* (summarily vacating denial of *pro se* section 2255 motion, and remanding for consideration of motion by district court as a motion for new trial on the ground of newly discovered evidence).

Hill v. United States, 368 U.S. 424, 82 S. Ct. 468, 7 L. Ed. 2d 417 (1962) (as it is an error "which is neither jurisdictional nor constitutional [and] [i]t is not a fundamental defect which inherently results in a complete miscarriage of justice, nor an omission inconsistent with the rudimentary demands of fair procedure," failure of district court to comply with Federal Rule of Criminal Procedure requiring court to allow defendant to allocute at sentencing does not furnish grounds for section 2255 relief).

Smith v. United States, 360 U.S. 1, 79 S. Ct. 991, 3 L. Ed. 2d 1041 (1959) (section 2255 relief warranted because Fifth Amendment requires that prisoner charged with crime that may be punished by death be prosecuted by indictment, and therefore, U.S. Attorney did not have authority to file information in instant case, and waivers made by movant of indictment, counsel, and venue were not binding and did not confer power on the convicting court to hear the case).

Heflin v. United States, 358 U.S. 415, 79 S. Ct. 451, 3 L. Ed. 2d 407 (1959) (motion to vacate sentence is not a proceeding in the original prosecution, but an independent civil suit; section 2255 "is available only to attack a sentence under which a prisoner is in custody").

Ladner v. United States, 358 U.S. 169, 79 S. Ct. 209, 3 L. Ed. 2d 199 (1958) (considering appropriate construction of statute penalizing assault on a federal officer, and determining that single discharge of a shotgun would constitute only single violation of statute even though more than one officer was injured thereby).

Gore v. United States, 357 U.S. 386, 78 S. Ct. 1280, 2 L. Ed. 2d 1405 (1958) (reconsidering and adhering to *Blockburger v. United States*, 284 U.S. 299, 52 S. Ct. 180, 76 L. Ed. 2d 306 (1932), and concluding that movant was correctly sentenced for three distinct offenses notwithstanding the fact that the violations were all committed in a single act of selling illicit drugs).

Prince v. United States, 352 U.S. 322, 77 S. Ct. 403, 1 L. Ed. 2d 370 (1957) (considering appropriate construction of Federal Bank Robbery Act, and concluding that when Congress amended act to make not only robbery but also entry for such purpose a crime, it intended that no additional punishment for entry to commit robbery should be imposed).

Pollard v. United States, 352 U.S. 354, 77 S. Ct. 481, 1 L. Ed. 2d 393 (1957) (in a criminal case, "final judgment" means sentence, and a void order purporting permanently to suspend sentence is neither a final order nor a valid judgment; whether delay in completing a prosecution amounts to an unconstitutional deprivation of the right to speedy trial depends on the circumstances, and the delay may not be purposeful or oppressive; here, movant was not denied right to speedy trial by court's imposition of valid formal judgment committing movant to prison nearly two years after entry of invalid original order of probation, which was entered when movant was absent from the courtroom; error in the course of a prosecution resulting in a conviction calls for correction of the error, not release of the accused).

United States v. Morgan, 346 U.S. 502, 74 S. Ct. 247, 98 L. Ed. 2d 248 (1954) (granting *coram nobis* relief and vacating federal conviction on grounds that defendant was not provided legal representation at taking of plea; holding that the common law writ of *coram nobis* could be used by a former federal prisoner to collaterally attack his conviction, where section 2255 relief was not available because he was no longer in custody: "The contention is made that section 2255 . . . should be construed to cover the entire field of remedies in the nature of *coram nobis* in federal courts. We see no compelling reason to reach that conclusion.").

Tinder v. United States, 345 U.S. 565, 73 S. Ct. 911, 97 L. Ed. 1250 (1953) (concluding movant was improperly convicted of felony under mail theft statute where indictment charged only a misdemeanor, and granting section 2255 relief).

United States v. Hayman, 342 U.S. 205, 72 S. Ct. 263, 96 L. Ed. 2d 232 (1952) (appeal from an order denying a section 2255 motion is governed by the civil rules applicable to appeals from final judgments in habeas corpus actions, and therefore appeal brought within 60 days of date of entry of such order is timely; section 2255's substantive scope is the same as that of the traditional habeas corpus remedy and as such, is constitutional; where movant alleged that lawyer who represented him at trial suffered from irreconcilable conflict of interest resulting from his concurrent representation of principal witness against movant, issues raised by motion were not determinable by "files and records" in trial court, and trial court was required to issue order to show cause on government, to grant a prompt hearing on the motion, to determine the issues, and to make findings of fact and conclusions of law with respect to the motion; the word "hearing" as used in section 2255 refers to traditional judicial proceedings, and therefore the *ex parte* hearing held by the trial court outside movant's presence was insufficient; trial court must issue order to secure prisoner's presence at hearing, and issuance of such an order to obtain presence of prisoner incarcerated in Western District of Washington for hearing in Southern District of California was within jurisdiction of trial court; in adopting section 2255, Congress did not adopt the common law procedures governing *coram nobis* petitions, which allowed for *ex parte* proceedings; movant need not be produced in every section 2255 proceeding, but where there are substantial issues of fact as to events in which movant participated, the trial court should hold a hearing and secure movant's presence).

B. Section 2255 Decisions, United States Court of Appeal Published Section 2255 Decisions

From November 1, 1987 (Date of Adoption of the Sentencing Guidelines) to June 30, 2008 Where Relief Was Granted or the Case Was Remanded for an Evidentiary Hearing

Benitez v. United States, 521 F.3d 625 (6th Cir. 2008) (concluding district court's failure to inquire into movant's dissatisfaction with his retained counsel violated movant's Sixth Amendment right to counsel, and remanding for consideration of whether movant was entitled to equitable tolling to overcome fact that motion was filed two days late).

Suggs v. United States, 513 F.3d 675 (7th Cir. 2008) (concluding movant was denied the effective assistance of counsel where appellate counsel failed to raise meritorious sentencing issue on appeal, and granting section 2255 relief).

United States v. Culverhouse, 507 F.3d 888 (5th Cir. 2007) (remanding for evidentiary hearing to determine whether defense counsel (1) suffered from a conflict of interest when, prior to movant's guilty plea, he simultaneously represented movant and codefendant, where codefendant provided information to investigators that was beneficial to himself but detrimental to movant, and (2) was ineffective for failing to object adequately at sentencing to district court's erroneous relevant conduct finding).

Thompson v. United States, 504 F.3d 1203 (11th Cir. 2007) (concluding counsel was ineffective in failing to consult adequately with movant as to whether movant wished to appeal, and granting section 2255 relief).

United States v. Shedrick, 493 F.3d 292 (3d Cir. 2007) (concluding counsel was ineffective in failing to file a notice of appeal after movant requested that he do so, granting section 2255 relief, vacating movant's sentence and remanding to district court with instructions to re-enter sentence so that movant has opportunity to appeal).

Watson v. United States, 493 F.3d 960 (8th Cir. 2007) (remanding section 2255 motion for an evidentiary hearing on the question of whether counsel was ineffective in failing to file a notice of appeal after movant requested that he do so).

United States v. Poindexter, 492 F.3d 263 (4th Cir. 2007) (remanding section 2255 motion for an evidentiary hearing on the question of whether counsel was ineffective in failing to file a notice of appeal after movant requested that he do so).

United States v. Price, 491 F.3d 613 (7th Cir. 2007) (in response to prisoner's section 2255 motion asserting that his appellate counsel was ineffective in failing to file a petition for writ of *certiorari* on direct appeal, court concludes that counsel violated prisoner's statutory right to counsel under the Criminal Justice Act, recalled its mandate on direct appeal, and appointed new counsel for purposes of filing a *certiorari* petition for prisoner), cert. denied, 128 S. Ct. 669, 169 L. Ed. 2d 525 (2007).

United States v. Tapp, 491 F.3d 263 (5th Cir. 2007) (remanding section 2255 motion for an evidentiary hearing on the question of whether counsel was ineffective in failing to file a notice of appeal after movant requested that he do so).

Valentine v. United States, 488 F.3d 325 (6th Cir. 2007) (remanding for evidentiary hearing to resolve whether government offered movant a plea that his lawyer essentially prevented him from accepting), cert. denied, 128 S. Ct. 2944 (2008).

Owens v. United States, 483 F.3d 48 (1st Cir. 2007) (remanding for evidentiary hearing on movant's claims that counsel's failure to inform him of his right to testify at trial constituted ineffective assistance of counsel, and that district court's decision to clear the courtroom of spectators—including movant's family—during jury selection violated movant's Sixth Amendment right to a public trial).

United States v. Nicholson, 475 F.3d 241 (4th Cir. 2007) (determining that trial counsel's simultaneous representation of movant and person who threatened to kill movant was an actual conflict of interest and remanding for an evidentiary hearing on whether counsel's conflict adversely impacted his performance at movant's sentencing proceedings).

Ferrera v. United States, 456 F.3d 278 (1st Cir. 2006) (affirming district court's grant of section 2255 relief on grounds that government violated due process by failing to disclose exculpatory evidence of a critical witness's recantation, where, absent prosecutorial misconduct, movant would not have pleaded guilty).

Campusano v. United States, 442 F.3d 770 (2d Cir. 2006) (remanding section 2255 motion for an evidentiary hearing on the question of whether counsel was ineffective in failing to file a notice of appeal after movant requested that he do so).

Gomez-Diaz v. United States, 433 F.3d 788 (11th Cir. 2005) (remanding section 2255 motion for evidentiary hearing on question of whether trial counsel was ineffective in failing to file notice of appeal after movant requested that he do so, notwithstanding the fact that movant signed appeal waiver).

United States v. Booth, 432 F.3d 542 (3d Cir. 2005) (remanding section 2255 motion for an evidentiary hearing on whether trial counsel was ineffective for failing to inform movant of possibility of open plea to both charges where movant rejected plea offer that required him to testify against others in exchange for the dismissal of one of two counts, and open plea would have resulted in significantly shorter sentence under Sentencing Guidelines).

Galviz Zapata v. United States, 431 F.3d 395 (2d Cir. 2005) (remanding section 2255 motion for an evidentiary hearing to determine whether counsel failed to consult with movant about an appeal).

Conley v. United States, 415 F.3d 183 (1st Cir. 2005) (concluding government's suppression of impeachment evidence violated Fifth Amendment, and affirming district court's grant of section 2255 relief).

United States v. Holmes, 413 F.3d 770 (8th Cir. 2005) (granting section 2255 relief after concluding that prosecutor's remarks in closing argument—that movant and defense counsel were colluding to fool the jurors and distract them from important evidence—violated due process).

United States v. Herrerra, 412 F.3d 577 (5th Cir. 2005) (remanding section 2255 motion for evidentiary hearing on whether trial counsel misadvised movant about his possible sentencing exposure and whether movant relied on that misrepresentation in rejecting government's plea offer).

United States v. Holder, 410 F.3d 651 (10th Cir. 2005) (remanding section 2255 motion for an evidentiary hearing on whether trial counsel's failure to call only two witnesses to shooting was sound trial strategy).

United States v. McCoy, 410 F.3d 124 (3d Cir. 2005) (remanding section 2255 motion for an evidentiary hearing on whether counsel's decision—to enter into a stipulation that relieved government of its burden of having to prove movant's knowledge and intent—was "strategic").

Cirilo-Munoz v. United States, 404 F.3d 527 (1st Cir. 2005) (granting section 2255 relief on claim that appellate counsel was ineffective in failing to challenge official victim sentencing enhancement).

United States v. Jones, 403 F.3d 604 (8th Cir. 2005) (granting section 2255 relief on claim that counsel provided ineffective assistance by not challenging indictment as multiplicitous).

United States v. Garrett, 402 F.3d 1262 (10th Cir. 2005) (remanding section 2255 motion for an evidentiary hearing on whether counsel was ineffective in failing to file a notice of appeal after movant asked him to do so, notwithstanding movant's appellate waiver).

Rivera Alicea v. United States, 404 F.3d 1 (1st Cir. 2005) (remanding section 2255 motion for evidentiary hearing on whether counsel was ineffective in failing to call at trial two witnesses who would have testified that the government's key witness admitted to them that he was going to lie on the witness stand).

Ballard v. United States, 400 F.3d 404 (6th Cir. 2005) (granting section 2255 relief on movant's claim that her appellate counsel provided ineffective assistance by not arguing on appeal that district court's sentencing of movant based on a judicial determination that her role in conspiracy involved cocaine violated *Apprendi v. New Jersey*, 530 U.S. 466, 120 S. Ct. 2348, 147 L. Ed. 2d 435 (2000), where movant was convicted under general verdict form that did not distinguish whether her part in the drug conspiracy involved transporting cocaine or marijuana).

United States v. Montano, 398 F.3d 1276 (11th Cir. 2005) (concluding that a showing of actual innocence "serves to lift the procedural bar caused by [movant's] failure timely to file his § 2255 motion," and remanding for consideration of whether movant has demonstrated his actual innocence of "use" of a firearm in violation of 18 U.S.C. § 924(c)).

Mateo v. United States, 398 F.3d 126 (1st Cir. 2005) (affirming district court's grant of section 2255 relief and reduction of movant's federal sentence, where movant obtained state court orders undermining the state conviction that had been used to enhance his original federal sentence).

United States v. Rashad, 396 F.3d 398 (D.C. Cir 2005) (remanding section 2255 motion raising claim that trial counsel was ineffective in failing to advise movant that he could obtain reduction for acceptance of responsibility simply by pleading guilty).

LoCascio v. United States, 395 F.3d 51 (2d Cir. 2005) (remanding section 2255 motion for evidentiary hearing on whether defense counsel suffered a conflict of interest due to codefendant John Gotti's intercession directly with movant's counsel without movant's knowledge, and gaining control of movant's defense by threatening to kill movant's counsel).

United States v. Davies, 394 F.3d 182 (3d Cir. 2005) (concluding movant demonstrated his actual innocence of a violation of 18 U.S.C. § 844(i) because no reasonable juror would have concluded that the local church he stood convicted of burning had the requisite nexus to interstate commerce, and therefore movant overcame the procedural default of his claim attacking his guilty plea as not supported by an adequate factual basis, and remanding section 2255 motion for further consideration).

United States v. Hilliard, 392 F.3d 981 (8th Cir. 2004) (concluding trial counsel was ineffective for filing an out-of-time motion for new trial, particularly after being reminded by district court judge to check the time requirements for such motions, and affirming district court's grant of section 2255 relief).

Owens v. United States, 387 F.3d 607 (4th Cir. 2004) (concluding trial counsel was ineffective in failing to move to suppress woefully inadequate search warrant, where motion "would have been granted and [movant] would have been acquitted," and granting section 2255 relief).

United States v. Hilton, 386 F.3d 13 (1st Cir. 2004) (affirming district court's grant of section 2255 relief to movant convicted of violation of Child Pornography Prevention Act, where, on direct appeal, movant's challenges to constitutionality of act and sufficiency of the evidence were rejected by the court of appeals, but those issues were later resolved in his favor by the Supreme Court in *Ashcroft v. Free Speech Coalition*, 535 U.S. 234, 122 S. Ct. 1389, 152 L. Ed. 2d 493 (2002)).

Waucaush v. United States, 380 F.3d 251 (6th Cir. 2004) (after concluding that movant was actually innocent of conspiring to violate RICO because his activities did not affect interstate commerce, and therefore the court could address movant's procedurally defaulted claim attacking the voluntariness of his plea, determining that movant's plea was not intelligently made when it was entered with a misunderstanding as to the scope of the affecting interstate commerce requirement, and granting section 2255 relief).

United States v. Howard, 381 F.3d 873 (9th Cir. 2004) (remanding section 2255 motion for evidentiary hearing on claim that counsel was ineffective in allowing movant to plead guilty at time he was under influence of powerful narcotic painkiller).

Ballinger v. United States, 379 F.2d 427 (7th Cir. 2004) (remanding section 2255 motion for evidentiary hearing to determine whether, in light of *Jones v. United States*, 529 U.S. 848, 120 S. Ct. 1904, 146 L. Ed. 2d 902 (2000), counsel was ineffective in failing to raise a jurisdictional challenge to movant's arson charges as having an insufficient impact on interstate commerce).

United States v. Eakman, 378 F.3d 294 (3d Cir. 2004) (concluding that movant's challenge to his sentence as invalid because the district court mistakenly believed that the Bureau of Prisons had discretion to place movant in a halfway house, when, in fact, BOP lacked such authority, could be raised in a section 2255 motion, and remanding claim for an evidentiary hearing).

United States v. Grammas, 376 F.3d 433 (5th Cir. 2004) (concluding that counsel's erroneous advice concerning movant's potential sentence exposure should he go to trial rather than plead guilty was deficient performance under *Strickland v. Washington*, 466 U.S. 668, 104 S. Ct. 2052, 80 L. Ed. 2d 674 (1984), and remanding section 2255 motion for evidentiary hearing to determine if that deficient performance prejudiced movant).

Hall v. United States, 371 F.3d 969 (7th Cir. 2004) (remanding section 2255 motion for evidentiary hearing to determine whether trial counsel labored under a conflict of interest resulting from his representation of an informant who provided information to the FBI regarding the drug activities of movant's coconspirator).

Jansen v. United States, 369 F.3d 237 (3d Cir. 2004) (concluding that trial counsel's representation of movant charged with possession with intent to distribute drugs was deficient, where, at sentencing, counsel failed to argue that the drugs movant held for his personal use should not be included in the computation of his base offense level, and remanding section 2255 motion for a determination of the amount of drugs, if any, movant possessed for his personal use).

United States v. White, 366 F.3d 291 (4th Cir. 2004) (remanding section 2255 motion for evidentiary hearing on movant's allegations that the government made him an oral promise that his plea was conditional, thereby permitting him to appeal denial of the suppression motion).

United States v. Battles, 362 F.3d 1195 (9th Cir. 2004) (remanding section 2255 motion to allow district court to determine whether movant is entitled to equitable tolling of statute of limitations due to counsel's refusal to provide movant with his trial transcripts).

United States v. Reinhart, 357 F.3d 521 (4th Cir. 2004) (granting section 2255 relief after concluding that appellate counsel was ineffective for failing to raise the claim that a coconspirator's sexual exploitation of two minors in a videotape that was created before movant entered into the conspiracy could not be used to establish movant's base offense level, where, had counsel raised the issue, it would have been successful, and resulted in a five-year reduction of movant's sentence).

Alaniz v. United States, 351 F.3d 365 (8th Cir. 2003) (granting section 2255 relief after concluding that appellate counsel was ineffective for failing to appeal district court's aggregation of movant's uncharged methamphetamine sales with his charged marijuana trafficking, resulting in the imposition of a 20-year mandatory minimum sentence, where, without the aggregation, movant's Sentencing Guidelines range was 210 to 262 months).

United States v. Conley, 349 F.3d 837 (5th Cir. 2003) (granting section 2255 relief after concluding that movant should have been sentenced under general conspiracy statute, not harsher conspiracy provision of money laundering statute, and counsel was ineffective for failing to object to error at sentencing or raise issue on appeal, where error resulted in movant receiving 120-month sentence when, had he been properly sentenced, his maximum sentence would have been 60 months).

Smith v. United States, 348 F.3d 545 (6th Cir. 2003) (remanding section 2255 motion for evidentiary hearing on whether counsel was ineffective for failing to advise movant to accept government's plea offer).

United States v. Smack, 347 F.3d 533 (3d Cir. 2003) (concluding counsel's performance was deficient where he stipulated for purposes of sentencing to the highest drug quantity discussed in reverse sting buy, and remanding section 2255 motion for evidentiary hearing on whether counsel's deficient performance prejudiced movant).

United States v. Snitz, 342 F.3d 1154 (10th Cir. 2003) (concluding that counsel was ineffective in failing to file appeal when requested to do so by movant, and granting section 2255 relief).

United States v. Skurdal, 341 F.3d 921 (9th Cir. 2003) (concluding that movant was denied the effective assistance of appellate counsel where counsel failed to file a proper *Anders* brief in support of his motion to be relieved of his appointment to represent movant on direct appeal, and therefore movant demonstrated cause and prejudice for the failure to raise the issues presented in his section 2255 motion on direct appeal, and remanding motion for consideration of movant's claims on the merits).

United States v. Horey, 333 F.3d 1185 (10th Cir. 2003) (concluding that counsel's failure to object to the application of inapplicable career offender enhancement was constitutionally ineffective, and granting section 2255 relief).

Griffin v. United States, 330 F.3d 733 (6th Cir. 2003) (determining that counsel's performance was deficient for failing to communicate plea offer to movant, and remanding section 2255 motion for evidentiary hearing on whether movant would have accepted offer had it been communicated to him).

United States v. Leonti, 326 F.3d 1111 (9th Cir. 2003) (remanding section 2255 motion for evidentiary hearing on whether counsel was constitutionally ineffective by failing to represent movant during period of time, prior to sentencing, when movant was attempting to cooperate with government in order to obtain downward departure for substantial assistance).

Pham v. United States, 317 F.3d 178 (2d Cir. 2003) (remanding section 2255 motion for hearing on whether trial counsel rendered ineffective assistance when he failed to convey a plea offer to movant).

Johnson v. United States, 313 F.3d 815 (2d Cir. 2002) (granting section 2255 relief on movant's claim that counsel was ineffective in failing to object to the miscalculation of movant's base offense level under applicable Application Note to Sentencing Guidelines).

United States v. Bass, 310 F.3d 321 (5th Cir. 2002) (determining that insufficient evidence supported movant's conviction for engaging in a continuing criminal enterprise (CCE), and granting section 2255 relief on claim that appellate counsel was ineffective in failing to raise sufficiency of the evidence issue on appeal).

United States v. Wiseman, 297 F.3d 975 (10th Cir. 2002) (after declining to raise procedural default *sua sponte,* and determining that sentencing relief under *Castillo v. United States*, 530 U.S. 120, 120 S. Ct. 2090, 147 L. Ed. 2d 94 (2000), is not barred by *Teague v. Lane*, 489 U.S. 288, 109 S. Ct. 1060, 103 L. Ed. 2d 334 (1989), granting section 2255 relief under *Castillo* as to one count).

Cox v. United States, 294 F.3d 959 (8th Cir. 2002) (granting section 2255 relief on movant's claim that appellate counsel was ineffective in failing to file a promised petition for writ of *certiorari*).

United States v. Booze, 293 F.3d 516 (D.C. Cir. 2002) (determining that movant's allegations—that counsel was ineffective in grossly underestimating movant's sentencing exposure when advising movant to reject government's plea offer—require an evidentiary hearing, and remanding section 2255 motion to allow district court to determine whether government actually made alleged plea offer).

United States v. Stricklin, 290 F.3d 748 (5th Cir. 2002) (granting section 2255 relief on movant's claim that counsel was ineffective in failing to object to the drug quantity that was used in the calculation of his base offense level, and remanding for resentencing).

Tse v. United States, 290 F.3d 462 (1st Cir. 2002) (remanding section 2255 motion for evidentiary hearing on movant's claim that trial counsel was ineffective in advising movant regarding the potential consequences of rejecting the government's plea offer).

United States v. Day, 285 F.3d 1167 (9th Cir. 2002) (remanding section 2255 motion for determination of whether counsel's performance was deficient in misadvising movant that he could only raise entrapment defense if he went to trial, where by going to trial, movant lost three-point sentencing reduction for acceptance of responsibility).

Garcia v. United States, 278 F.3d 134 (2d Cir. 2002) (granting section 2255 relief where counsel incorrectly advised movant that no appeal could be filed because movant had filed an appellate waiver, and the district court confirmed that incorrect advice).

United States v. Johnson, 260 F.3d 919 (8th Cir. 2001) (affirming district court's grant of section 2255 relief on movant's claim that his guilty plea to the charge that he used a firearm within the meaning of 18 U.S.C. § 924(c) was invalid after *Bailey v. United States*, 516 U.S. 137, 116 S. Ct. 501, 133 L. Ed. 2d 472 (1995), where movant overcame procedural default by showing his actual innocence of the § 924(c) charge, as well as more serious charges foregone by the government in the course of plea bargaining).

Hughes v. United States, 258 F.3d 453 (6th Cir. 2001) (concluding that counsel was ineffective in failing to strike a juror who stated expressly on *voir dire* that she did not think she could be fair, and as juror was not rehabilitated by counsel or the court, actual bias of the juror was established, and section 2255 relief required).

Bruce v. United States, 256 F.3d 592 (7th Cir. 2001) (remanding section 2255 motion for evidentiary hearing on whether counsel was ineffective in failing to adequately assess potential alibi witnesses).

Solis v. United States, 252 F.3d 289 (3d Cir. 2001) (remanding section 2255 motion for evidentiary hearing on claim that movant instructed counsel to file a direct appeal, but counsel failed to do so).

United States v. Apker, 241 F.3d 1060 (8th Cir. 2001) (remanding section 2255 motion to determine if movant can demonstrate actual innocence sufficient to overcome procedural default of his claim under *Bailey v. United States*, 516 U.S. 137, 116 S. Ct. 501, 133 L. Ed. 2d 472 (1995)).

United States v. Christakis, 238 F.3d 1164 (9th Cir. 2001) (remanding section 2255 motion for evidentiary hearing to determine whether counsel's representation of unindicted coconspirator during time counsel also represented movant was an actual conflict of interest).

Koskela v. United States, 235 F.3d 1148 (8th Cir. 2001) (remanding section 2255 motion for evidentiary hearing on whether counsel rendered ineffective assistance of counsel by not presenting alibi defense and alibi witnesses).

Armiente v. United States, 234 F.3d 820 (2d Cir. 2000) (remanding section 2255 motion for evidentiary hearing to determine whether trial counsel, who, at the time he was representing movant, was under criminal investigation by the same U.S. Attorney's office that was also prosecuting movant, labored under an actual conflict of interest).

Lipson v. United States, 233 F.3d 942 (7th Cir. 2000) (remanding section 2255 motion for evidentiary hearing to determine whether counsel deferred to wishes of codefendant in not seeking plea agreement for movant, and whether, if counsel did so, the actions resulted from a conflict of interest).

United States v. Hayes, 231 F.3d 1132 (9th Cir. 2000) (granting section 2255 relief and remanding for a new trial because movant was not made aware of dangers and disadvantages of self-representation, as is required for a valid waiver of counsel).

United States v. Witherspoon, 231 F.3d 923 (4th Cir. 2000) (remanding section 2255 motion for evidentiary hearing on claim that counsel was ineffective in failing to file notice of appeal requested by movant).

United States v. Franks, 230 F.3d 811 (5th Cir. 2000) (granting section 2255 relief on claim counsel was ineffective in failing to object to the sentencing judge's erroneous enhancement of movant's sentence).

United States v. Ryan, 227 F.3d 1058 (8th Cir. 2000) (determining that *Jones v. United States*, 529 U.S. 848, 120 S. Ct. 1904, 146 L. Ed. 2d 902 (2000), applies retroactively to cases on collateral review, and granting section 2255 relief on claim that evidence was insufficient to satisfy 18 U.S.C. § 844(i)'s interstate commerce element).

Jones v. United States, 224 F.3d 1251 (11th Cir. 2000) (granting section 2255 relief on movant's claim that counsel rendered ineffective assistance by failing to move for suppression of wiretap evidence based on the government's delay in sealing the tapes, and by failing to object to movant's illegal general sentence).

Olden v. United States, 224 F.3d 561 (6th Cir. 2000) (concluding that counsel's absences during critical stages of trial resulted in unconstitutional denial of movant's right to counsel, and granting section 2255 relief).

DeRoo v. United States, 223 F.3d 919 (8th Cir. 2000) (determining section 2255 motion was not barred by waiver in plea agreement, and granting sentencing relief because movant was improperly sentenced under Armed Career Criminal Act).

United States v. Baird, 218 F.3d 221 (3d Cir. 2000) (remanding for an evidentiary hearing to determine whether counsel was ineffective in failing to object at sentencing to the use of incriminating statements made by movant as part of a cooperation agreement with the government, where those statements were immunized by the Sentencing Guidelines).

United States v. Halter, 217 F.3d 551 (8th Cir. 2000) (determining movant showed his actual innocence of more serious charges dismissed as part of his plea negotiations sufficient to overcome his procedural default, concluding movant's pre-*Bailey v. United States*, 516 U.S. 137, 116 S. Ct. 501, 133 L. Ed. 2d 472 (1995) guilty plea to the charge of using and carrying a firearm in violation of 18 U.S.C. § 924(c) was constitutionally defective, and granting section 2255 relief).

United States v. Mannino, 212 F.3d 835 (3d Cir. 2000) (granting section 2255 relief and ordering resentencing after concluding that appellate counsel was ineffective in failing to raise on direct appeal meritorious claim that district court had incorrectly attributed to movant the total drug amount distributed throughout entirety of conspiracy rather than making an individualized determination, and relying on ineffectiveness of appellate counsel to find also that movant demonstrated cause and prejudice sufficient to overcome failure to present sentencing issue on direct appeal).

United States v. Phillips, 210 F.3d 345 (5th Cir. 2000) (granting section 2255 relief on movant's claim that appellate counsel was ineffective for failing to raise on appeal meritorious challenge to obstruction of justice enhancement).

United States v. Jackson, 209 F.3d 1103 (9th Cir. 2000) (remanding section 2255 motion for evidentiary hearing on claim of juror bias, where juror received threatening phone call during trial that juror thought was from movant or codefendant).

Amiel v. United States, 209 F.3d 195 (2d Cir. 2000) (remanding section 2255 motion for evidentiary hearing on counsel's conflict of interest, where counsel's fee was paid by codefendant's mother).

United States v. Chancon-Palomares, 208 F.3d 1157 (9th Cir. 2000) (remanding section 2255 motion for evidentiary hearing to determine whether counsel was ineffective in advising movant to reject government's plea offer).

United States v. Russell, 205 F.3d 768 (5th Cir. 2000) (granting section 2255 relief where counsel was absent from two days of movant's trial, and movant did not affirmatively waive counsel's presence).

United States v. Guess, 203 F.3d 1143 (9th Cir. 2000) (determining that under *Bailey v. United States*, 516 U.S. 137, 116 S. Ct. 501, 133 L. Ed. 2d 472 (1995), there was insufficient evidence to support movant's conviction under 18 U.S.C. § 924(c)(1) for use of a firearm during and in relation to a drug trafficking offense, and granting section 2255 relief).

Hernandez v. United States, 202 F.3d 486 (2d Cir. 2000) (granting section 2255 relief upon concluding that counsel's failure to file appeal requested by movant was ineffective assistance of counsel).

Prou v. United States, 199 F.3d 37 (1st Cir. 1999) (because trial counsel was ineffective in failing to object to government's untimely filing of 21 U.S.C. § 851(a)(1) enhancement—an enhancement that doubles the mandatory minimum sentence for distribution of a controlled substance if defendant has prior felony drug conviction—section 2255 movant established cause and prejudice for failure to raise enhancement issue on direct appeal, and granting section 2255 relief).

United States v. Walker, 198 F.3d 811 (11th Cir. 1999) (affirming district court's grant of section 2255 relief and vacating sentence enhanced under Armed Career Criminal Act, 18 U.S.C. § 924(e), where one of three convictions on which enhancement was based had later been vacated in state habeas action).

Latorre v. United States, 193 F.3d 1035 (8th Cir. 1999) (remanding section 2255 motion for evidentiary hearing on whether movant can establish actual innocence so that his procedurally defaulted claim under *Bailey v. United States*, 516 U.S. 137, 116 S. Ct. 501, 133 L. Ed. 2d 472 (1995), may be considered on the merits).

Hohn v. United States, 193 F.3d 921 (8th Cir. 1999) (remanding section 2255 motion for evidentiary hearing on whether movant can establish actual innocence so that his procedurally defaulted claim under *Bailey v. United States*, 516 U.S. 137, 116 S. Ct. 501, 133 L. Ed. 2d 472 (1995), may be considered on the merits).

United States v. Dutkel, 192 F.3d 893 (9th Cir. 1999) (remanding section 2255 motion for evidentiary hearing to determine whether government can demonstrate that movant was not prejudiced by codefendant's tampering with jury during joint trial).

United States v. Garth, 188 F.3d 99 (3d Cir. 1999) (remanding section 2255 motion for evidentiary hearing on whether movant can establish actual innocence so that his procedurally defaulted claim under *Bailey v. United States*, 516 U.S. 137, 116 S. Ct. 501, 133 L. Ed. 2d 472 (1995), may be considered on the merits).

Johnson v. United States, 186 F.3d 876 (8th Cir. 1999) (remanding section 2255 motion for evidentiary hearing on whether movant can establish actual innocence so that his procedurally defaulted claim under *Bailey v. United States*, 516 U.S. 137, 116 S. Ct. 501, 133 L. Ed. 2d 472 (1995), may be considered on the merits).

Soto v. United States, 185 F.3d 48 (2d Cir. 1999) (remanding section 2255 motion for evidentiary hearing as to whether district court's failure to inform movant of his right to appeal was harmless).

United States v. Romero, 183 F.3d 1145 (9th Cir. 1999) (concluding, in light of *Bailey v. United States*, 516 U.S. 137, 116 S. Ct. 501, 133 L. Ed. 2d 472 (1995), that there was insufficient evidence to support movant's conviction under 18 U.S.C. § 924(c)(1) for using a firearm during and in relation to a drug trafficking offense, and granting section 2255 relief).

Smith v. United States, 182 F.3d 1023 (8th Cir. 1999) (remanding section 2255 motion for evidentiary hearing on whether counsel was ineffective for failing to object to movant's appearance at trial in orange prison garb).

Arredondo v. United States, 178 F.3d 778 (6th Cir. 1999) (remanding for evidentiary hearing on whether a section 2255 movant who received minimum mandatory 20-year sentence under 21 U.S.C. § 841(b)(1)(A)(1) was denied the effective assistance of counsel at sentencing, where counsel failed to object to statement in pre-sentence report that movant was responsible for one to three kilograms of heroin, the report itself recited no specific facts about movant's conduct that would lead one to conclude that he was responsible for any particular amount, and even calculations by the government did not reach the one-kilogram level necessary to justify the 20-year sentence received).

McHale v. United States, 175 F.3d 115 (2d Cir. 1999) (concluding appellate counsel who timely filed notice of appeal was ineffective in failing to perfect appeal, and granting section 2255 relief).

United States v. Harfst, 168 F.3d 398 (10th Cir. 1999) (remanding section 2255 case for evidentiary hearing on whether counsel was ineffective for failing to rebut assertion in pre-sentence report that movant was a "single participant in a single occurrence crime" and in failing to seek sentence reduction under U.S.S.G. § 3B1.2 on the basis of movant's minor or minimal participation in the offense).

United States v. Granados, 168 F.3d 343 (8th Cir. 1999) (granting section 2255 relief on claim that counsel was ineffective for failing to object to pre-sentence report that attributed 5 to 15 kilograms of cocaine to movant, where government had entered in plea agreement in which it agreed that the scope of relevant conduct was limited to 3.5 to 5 kilograms; as a result of the failure to object, movant was sentenced to serve an additional 40 to 50 months under the Sentencing Guidelines).

Brown v. United States, 167 F.3d 109 (2d Cir. 1999) (concluding appellate counsel was ineffective in failing to challenge obviously deficient reasonable doubt instructions, and granting section 2255 relief).

United States v. Alvarez-Tautimez, 160 F.3d 573 (9th Cir. 1998) (granting section 2255 relief on claim that trial counsel was ineffective in failing to move to withdraw movant's guilty plea following the grant of a codefendant's motion to suppress, where movant's plea had not yet been accepted by the district court, and movant therefore had an absolute right to withdraw it).

United States v. Moore, 159 F.3d 1154 (9th Cir. 1998) (concluding trial counsel's irreconcilable conflict with movant resulted in denial of counsel, and granting section 2255 relief).

United States v. Gordon, 156 F.3d 376 (2d Cir. 1998) (affirming district court's grant of section 2255 relief after concluding that counsel was ineffective for grossly underestimating movant's potential sentencing exposure, and where, but for counsel's inaccurate advice, movant would have pursued plea negotiations).

United States v. Mejia-Mesa, 153 F.3d 925 (9th Cir. 1998) (remanding section 2255 motion for evidentiary hearing on whether government failed to comply with its obligation to turn over exculpatory evidence under *Brady v. Maryland*, 373 U.S. 83, 83 S. Ct. 1194, 10L. Ed. 2d 215 (1963) showing that vessel carrying cocaine for which movant was prosecuted was outside United States waters at the time it was seized).

Harris v. United States, 149 F.3d 1304 (11th Cir. 1998) (granting section 2255 relief on claim that district court lacked jurisdiction to enhance movant's sentence with prior conviction where government failed to comply with procedural requirements of 21 U.S.C. § 851(a)(1)).

United States v. Hellbusch, 147 F.3d 782 (8th Cir. 1998) (remanding section 2255 case for evidentiary hearing on whether movant can establish actual innocence so that his procedurally defaulted claim under *Bailey v. United States*, 516 U.S. 137, 116 S. Ct. 501, 133 L. Ed. 2d 472 (1995), may be considered on the merits).

United States v. Marmolejos, 140 F.3d 488 (3d Cir. 1998) (granting section 2255 relief based on retroactively applicable post-sentence amendment to the Application Notes of U.S.S.G. § 2D1.1).

United States v. Gobert, 139 F.3d 436 (5th Cir. 1998) (concluding, in light of *Bailey v. United States*, 516 U.S. 137, 116 S. Ct. 501, 133 L. Ed. 2d 472 (1995), that there was insufficient evidence to support movant's conviction under 18 U.S.C. § 924(c)(1) for using a firearm during and in relation to a drug trafficking offense, and granting section 2255 relief).

United States v. Jacobs, 136 F.3d 1187 (8th Cir. 1998) (vacating movant's sentence and remanding to allow consideration of whether an explicitly retroactive amendment to the Sentencing Guidelines affects movant's offense level).

United States v. Brown, 117 F.3d 471 (11th Cir. 1997) (concluding that under *Ratzlaf v. United States*, 510 U.S. 135, 114 S. Ct. 655, 126 L. Ed. 2d 615 (1994), which held that knowledge of illegality is an essential element of the crime of currency structuring, a guilty plea to that crime based upon pre-*Ratzlaf* law to the contrary was invalid because not knowing and voluntary, and granting section 2255 relief).

United States v. Carter, 117 F.3d 262 (5th Cir. 1997) (concluding, in light of *Bailey v. United States*, 516 U.S. 137, 116 S. Ct. 501, 133 L. Ed. 2d 472 (1995), that there was insufficient evidence to support movant's conviction under 18 U.S.C. § 924(c)(1) for using a firearm during and in relation to a drug trafficking offense, and granting section 2255 relief).

Stanback v. United States, 113 F.3d 651 (7th Cir. 1997) (concluding, in light of *Bailey v. United States*, 516 U.S. 137, 116 S. Ct. 501, 133 L. Ed. 2d 472 (1995), that there was insufficient evidence to support movant's conviction under 18 U.S.C. § 924(c)(1) for using or carrying a firearm during and in relation to a drug trafficking offense, and granting section 2255 relief).

Lee v. United States, 113 F.3d 73 (7th Cir. 1997) (concluding, in light of *Bailey v. United States*, 516 U.S. 137, 116 S. Ct. 501, 133 L. Ed. 2d 472 (1995), that there was insufficient evidence to support movant's conviction under 18 U.S.C. § 924(c)(1) for using a firearm during and in relation to a drug trafficking offense, and affirming the district court's grant of section 2255 relief).

United States v. McPhail, 112 F.3d 197 (5th Cir. 1997) (concluding, in light of *Bailey v. United States*, 516 U.S. 137, 116 S. Ct. 501, 133 L. Ed. 2d 472 (1995), that there was insufficient evidence to support movant's conviction under 18 U.S.C. § 924(c)(1) for using or carrying a firearm during and in relation to a drug trafficking offense, and granting section 2255 relief).

United States v. DeMartino, 112 F.3d 75 (2d Cir. 1997) (concluding district court erred in entering a written judgment that provided for a penalty greater than that imposed by the sentence announced orally, and granting section 2255 relief).

Valente v. United States, 111 F.3d 290 (2d Cir. 1997) (although plea agreement signed by movant contained appellate waiver, remanding section 2255 motion for evidentiary hearing as to whether movant knowingly and voluntarily waived the right to appeal where the district court did not ask movant at the plea proceeding whether he had read agreement or his lawyer had explained its meaning, movant had only a fifth-grade education, and the waiver of the right to appeal was not mentioned at plea hearing).

Griffin v. United States, 109 F.3d 1217 (7th Cir. 1997) (remanding section 2255 motion for an evidentiary hearing on whether counsel was ineffective in failing to prosecute movant's direct appeal, and in convincing movant to agree to dismiss his direct appeal and file instead a motion under Federal Rule of Criminal Procedure 35—a motion that can be filed only by the government).

United States v. Kauffman, 109 F.3d 186 (3d Cir. 1997) (granting section 2255 relief on claim that counsel was ineffective in failing to conduct any investigation into an insanity defense where counsel received a letter from a psychiatrist who concluded, based on an interview with movant immediately following his arrest, that the movant was manic and psychotic at the time of the crime; had counsel investigated, he would have uncovered substantial psychiatric evidence indicating that an insanity defense was viable).

United States v. Pelullo, 105 F.3d 117 (3d Cir. 1997) (concluding that government failed to disclose material impeachment evidence, in violation of *Brady v. Maryland*, 373 U.S. 83, 83 S. Ct. 1194, 10L. Ed. 2d 215 (1963), and granting section 2255 relief).

United States v. Pettiford, 101 F.3d 199 (1st Cir. 1996) (affirming district court's grant of section 2255 relief and reducing movant's sentence on the ground that the enhancement under the Armed Career Criminal

Act, 18 U.S.C. § 924(e)(1), was no longer applicable following the state court's post-sentencing vacation of eight of nine convictions used to enhance movant's federal sentence).

Siddiqi v. United States, 98 F.3d 1427 (2d Cir. 1996) (concluding that movant's conviction "had no legitimate factual or legal basis and that, but for the conduct of the prosecution in adopting shifting and at times misleading positions, no conviction would have been obtained or successfully defended on appeal," and granting section 2255 relief to remedy this miscarriage of justice).

United States v. Morrison, 98 F.3d 619 (D.C. Cir. 1996) (concluding, in light of *Bailey v. United States*, 516 U.S. 137, 116 S. Ct. 501, 133 L. Ed. 2d 472 (1995), that there was insufficient evidence to support movant's conviction under 18 U.S.C. § 924(c)(1) for using or carrying a firearm during and in relation to a drug trafficking offense, and granting section 2255 relief).

United States v. Guerra, 94 F.3d 989 (5th Cir. 1996) (granting section 2255 relief on claim that movant's guilty plea was not knowing and voluntary where the district court misinformed movant as to the possible maximum sentence he faced).

United States v. Cheek, 94 F.3d 136 (4th Cir. 1996) (granting section 2255 relief where codefendant, who was tried jointly with movant, attempted to bribe juror).

United States v. Silvers, 90 F.3d 95 (4th Cir. 1996) (concluding that district court's reimposition of sentences that movant had already fully served violates double jeopardy, and granting section 2255 relief).

Tress v. United States, 87 F.3d 188 (7th Cir. 1996) (granting section 2255 relief where district court failed to advise movant of his right to appeal his sentence, and there was no evidence that movant learned of his right to appeal from another source).

Manko v. United States, 87 F.3d 50 (2d Cir. 1996) (holding that district court erred in concluding Federal Rule of Evidence 408 required exclusion of evidence relating to movant's civil settlement with the Internal Revenue Service during his criminal trial on tax fraud charges, and remanding section 2255 motion for an evidentiary hearing to determine whether the exclusion of this evidence warranted new trial).

United States v. Cox, 83 F.3d 336 (10th Cir. 1996) (concluding that district court should have granted section 2255 relief and reopened movant's sentence after he successfully attacked several prior convictions used to calculate his criminal history).

United States v. Smith, 77 F.3d 511 (D.C. Cir. 1996) (concluding that government violated *Brady v. Maryland*, 373 U.S. 83, 83 S. Ct. 1194 10L. Ed. 2d 215 (1963), by failing to disclose plea agreement to dismiss charges against government witness, and granting section 2255 relief).

United States v. Garcia, 77 F.3d 274 (9th Cir. 1996) (concluding, in light of *Bailey v. United States*, 516 U.S. 137, 116 S. Ct. 501, 133 L. Ed. 2d 472 (1995), that there was insufficient evidence to support movant's conviction under 18 U.S.C. § 924(c)(1) for using a firearm during and in relation to a drug trafficking offense, and granting section 2255 relief).

United States v. Span, 75 F.3d 1383 (9th Cir. 1996) (concluding trial counsel was ineffective for failing to offer proper jury instructions on movant's only defense, where that defense had a strong likelihood of success, and granting section 2255 relief).

United States v. Kissick, 69 F.3d 1048 (10th Cir. 1995) (remanding for evidentiary hearing to determine whether movant was improperly classified as a "career offender" under U.S.S.G. § 4B1.2; if movant was wrongly classified as a "career offender," counsel's failure to object on "dead bang winner" issue was ineffective assistance of counsel sufficient to establish cause and prejudice for movant's failure to raise claim on direct appeal).

Montemoino v. United States, 68 F.3d 416 (11th Cir. 1995) (where counsel failed to file an appeal following a guilty plea, remanding section 2255 motion for evidentiary hearing to determine whether movant asked counsel to file an appeal).

United States v. Kelly, 62 F.3d 1215 (9th Cir. 1995) (concluding that movant was not a previously convicted felon as defined by 18 U.S.C. § 921(a)(20) because his right to possess a firearm had been restored under state law, and remanding section 2255 motion for evidentiary hearing on whether counsel was ineffective in advising movant to plead guilty to being a felon in possession of a firearm).

United States v. Nagib, 56 F.3d 798 (7th Cir. 1995) (granting section 2255 relief on claim that appellate counsel was ineffective in failing to appeal in a timely manner, despite instructions from movant to do so).

United States v. Dashney, 52 F.3d 298 (10th Cir. 1995) (remanding section 2255 motion for district court to consider whether, in light of *Ratzlaf v. United States*, 510 U.S. 135, 114 S. Ct. 655, 126 L. Ed. 2d 615 (1994)—which held that knowledge of illegality is an essential element of the crime of currency structuring—movant's conviction to that crime based upon pre-*Ratzlaf* law to the contrary was invalid).

United States v. Cook, 49 F.3d 663 (10th Cir. 1995) (remanding section 2255 motion to allow district court to determine whether DL-methamphetamine should be considered "pure" methamphetamine for purposes of U.S.S.G. § 2D1.1(c) note * (1989 version), and if not, whether counsel was ineffective in failing to object to pre-sentence report's calculation of movant's base offense level based upon "pure" methamphetamine).

United States v. Cook, 45 F.3d 388 (10th Cir. 1995) (granting section 2255 relief on movant's claim that trial counsel labored under a conflict of interest when the district court ordered counsel to advise movant's codefendant to comply with plea agreement; appellate counsel's failure to raise the meritorious conflict issue on direct appeal was ineffective assistance of counsel; therefore, movant established cause and prejudice, allowing consideration of the claim on the merits).

United States v. Wright, 43 F.3d 491 (10th Cir. 1994) (remanding section 2255 motion for evidentiary hearing to determine whether the government threatened to indict movant's family members, and if so, whether movant's guilty plea was involuntary because movant was induced by those threats).

United States v. Ross, 40 F.3d 144 (7th Cir. 1994) (granting section 2255 relief where the intervening decision in *Staples v. United States*, 511 U.S. 1124, 114 S. Ct. 2129, 128 L. Ed. 2d 860 (1994), made clear that the jury at movant's trial was erroneously instructed with respect to an element of the offense).

United States v. Neely, 38 F.3d 458 (9th Cir. 1994) (concluding that movant's guilty plea was not voluntary because the district court failed to inform movant, before accepting plea, that his federal sentence could be served consecutively to any state sentence subsequently imposed, and granting section 2255 relief).

Soto v. United States, 37 F.3d 252 (7th Cir. 1994) (remanding section 2255 motion for evidentiary hearing to resolve whether, in light of movant's counsel's failure to perceive that the government's theory that movant had engaged in single long-term drug conspiracy was mistaken, counsel was ineffective in not discouraging movant from pleading guilty, where the guilty plea exposed movant to minimum mandatory sentence).

Brown v. United States, 34 F.3d 990 (10th Cir. 1994) (concluding district court violated double jeopardy when it failed to merge movant's two counts for sentencing because they were based upon a single criminal episode, and granting section 2255 relief).

Castillo v. United States, 34 F.3d 443 (7th Cir. 1994) (remanding section 2255 motion for evidentiary hearing to determine whether movant's command of English is such that his waiver of his right to be represented by a lawyer other than his codefendant's counsel was knowing and voluntary).

Quintero v. United States, 33 F.3d 1133 (9th Cir. 1994) (remanding section 2255 case for evidentiary hearing as to whether conflict of interest affected counsel's performance where counsel, who was retained by unknown third parties to defend movant in drug conspiracy case involving large quantities of cocaine, urged movant to reject plea agreement rather than become a "snitch").

United States v. Smith, 32 F.3d 194 (5th Cir. 1994) (granting section 2255 relief where intervening decision in *Gozlon-Peretz v. United States*, 498 U.S. 395, 111 S. Ct. 840, 112 L. Ed. 2d 919 (1991), made clear that movant should have been sentenced to a term of supervised release instead of special parole).

Peavy v. United States, 31 F.3d 1341 (6th Cir. 1994) (remanding section 2255 motion for evidentiary hearing as to whether movant's plea was involuntary because induced by unfulfilled promises by government agents that if he cooperated, the prosecutor would seek reduction of his sentence).

Bemis v. United States, 30 F.3d 220 (1st Cir. 1994) (remanding section 2255 motion for evidentiary hearing on whether movant's plea was involuntary because induced by a promise made as part of his plea agreement, and later reneged upon by the government, to recommend movant's entry into the Federal Witness Protection Program).

Pelaez v. United States, 27 F.3d 219 (6th Cir. 1994) (concluding that district erred in not retroactively applying *Crosby v. United States*, 506 U.S. 255, 113 S. Ct. 748, 122 L. Ed. 2d 25 (1993), and granting section 2255 relief on movant's claim that he could not be tried in absentia because he was not present at the beginning of trial).

Castellanos v. United States, 26 F.3d 717 (7th Cir. 1994) (granting section 2255 relief on claim that movant was deprived of right to counsel where appellate counsel failed to perfect an appeal after movant requested that an appeal be filed).

United States v. Maybeck, 23 F.3d 888 (4th Cir. 1994) (overlooking procedural default and granting section 2255 relief after concluding that movant's prior criminal history had been mischaracterized without objection at the time of sentencing, and that he was actually innocent of being a career offender as defined in U.S.S.G. § 4B1.1).

Stoia v. United States, 22 F.3d 766 (7th Cir. 1994) (remanding section 2255 motion for evidentiary hearing as to whether retained trial counsel operated under a conflict of interest by declining to file motions or appear at trial for fear of being found to have violated plea agreement counsel entered into with U.S. Attorney's office).

Gall v. United States, 21 F.3d 107 (6th Cir. 1994) (granting section 2255 relief after concluding that district court's restitution order was in error because (1) a defendant cannot be ordered to pay restitution for losses arising from crimes other than those for which he was actually charged and convicted, and (2) the costs to the government for investigating and prosecuting an offense are not losses for which restitution may be ordered under the Victim and Witness Protection Act).

United States v. Blaylock, 20 F.3d 1458 (9th Cir. 1994) (remanding section 2255 motion for evidentiary hearing on movant's allegations that trial counsel was ineffective in failing to inform movant that the government had made a plea offer).

Frazer v. United States, 18 F.3d 778 (9th Cir. 1994) (remanding section 2255 motion for evidentiary hearing on movant's allegations that counsel was ineffective for calling movant a "stupid nigger son of a bitch" and threatening to provide substandard representation if movant chose to exercise his right to trial).

Mathews v. United States, 11 F.3d 583 (6th Cir. 1993) (relying on intervening decision in *United States v. Dunnigan*, 507 U.S. 87, 113 S. Ct. 1111, 112 L. Ed. 2d 445 (1993), to grant section 2255 relief on claim that district court erred in deferring to jury's verdict against movant in assessing obstruction of justice enhancement based on movant's trial testimony).

United States v. De la Fuente, 8 F.3d 1333 (9th Cir. 1993) (concluding that government breached plea agreement when it failed to recommend a sentence below the mandatory minimum, and granting section 2255 relief; appellate counsel's failure to raise meritorious breach issue was ineffective assistance of counsel, providing cause and prejudice allowing consideration of claim on merits).

United States v. Fulton, 5 F.3d 605 (2d Cir. 1993) (granting section 2255 relief on claim that movant's trial counsel labored under conflict of interest after government witness alleged that trial counsel was engaged in drug trafficking related to the charge for which movant was on trial).

United States v. Roberts, 5 F.3d 365 (9th Cir. 1993) (granting section 2255 relief on claim that district court violated Federal Rule of Criminal Procedure 11 when it failed to advise movant of a term of supervised release at plea hearing).

Ratliff v. United States, 999 F.2d 1023 (6th Cir. 1993) (concluding that district court's restitution order was in error because the costs to the government for investigating and prosecuting an offense are not losses for which restitution may be ordered under the Victim and Witness Protection Act, and granting section 2255 relief).

Neary v. United States, 998 F.2d 563 (8th Cir. 1993) (granting section 2255 relief on claim that movant's sentence was unlawfully enhanced by a prior conviction despite the government's failure to comply with 21 U.S.C. § 851(a)(1), where counsel was ineffective in advising movant to waive the government's noncompliance with § 851(a)(1) and in not appealing the unlawfully enhanced sentence; also, remanding for evidentiary hearing on claim that counsel was ineffective for failing to appeal a two-level enhancement of movant's base offense level for obstruction of justice).

Ward v. United States, 995 F.2d 1317 (6th Cir. 1993) (determining that trial counsel was ineffective and granting section 2255 relief where, to the detriment of his client, counsel opened the door to the prosecution's introduction of otherwise inadmissible character evidence; made illogical and incomprehensible comments on the record; and acted with inappropriate hostility and paranoia towards the government).

West v. United States, 994 F.2d 510 (8th Cir. 1993) (remanding section 2255 case for evidentiary hearing on movant's allegations that trial counsel was ineffective in failing to object to not receiving the pre-sentence report more than ten days before the sentencing hearing, and in failing to object to all of the errors movant noted in the report).

United States v. Horodner, 993 F.2d 191 (9th Cir. 1993) (granting section 2255 relief after concluding that two separate convictions for possession of the same firearm on two separate dates violated double jeopardy).

Risher v. United States, 992 F.2d 982 (9th Cir. 1993) (after determining that counsel's failure to advise movant before he entered his guilty plea of the likelihood that he might be sentenced under the Sentencing Guidelines constituted deficient performance under *Strickland v. Washington*, 466 U.S. 668 (1984), remanding section 2255 motion for evidentiary hearing on whether counsel's actions prejudiced movant).

United States v. Peak, 992 F.2d 39 (4th Cir. 1993) (granting section 2255 relief on claim that counsel was ineffective in failing to file a notice of appeal despite request from movant to do so).

United States v. Garfield, 987 F.2d 1424 (9th Cir. 1993) (granting section 2255 relief on movant's claims that district court improperly participated in plea negotiations in violation of Federal Rule of Criminal Procedure 11(e)(1), and improperly failed to make adequate findings regarding disputed information in the pre-sentence report as required by Federal Rule of Criminal Procedure 32(c)(3)(D)).

United States v. Gipson, 985 F.2d 212 (5th Cir. 1993) (concluding that movant was denied the effective assistance of counsel where counsel failed to inform movant of time limit for filing appeal and failed to file appeal on movant's behalf within limit, and granting section 2255 relief).

Isabel v. United States, 980 F.2d 60 (1st Cir. 1992) (granting section 2255 relief in light of post-sentence amendment to the application notes of U.S.S.G. § 3C1.1, where the amendment "clarified" the existing application note, rather than effecting a substantive change in the law).

United States v. Whalen, 976 F.2d 1346 (10th Cir. 1992) (remanding section 2255 motion for evidentiary hearing on movant's allegations that his guilty plea was involuntary because induced by the government's threats to prosecute his wife).

Shukwit v. United States, 973 F.2d 903 (11th Cir. 1992) (remanding section 2255 motion to allow district court to make findings as to movant's factual challenge to the pre-sentence report under Federal Rule of Criminal Procedure 32(c)(3)(D) and determine whether movant was sentenced based on factually inaccurate information).

United States v. Day, 969 F.2d 39 (3d Cir. 1992) (remanding section 2255 motion for evidentiary hearing on movant's allegations that counsel was ineffective by grossly underestimating movant's potential sentencing exposure, and that but for counsel's inaccurate advice, movant would have accepted plea offer).

Kingsley v. United States, 968 F.2d 109 (1st Cir. 1992) (remanding section 2255 motion for evidentiary hearing to determine whether government breached plea agreement by reneging on its promise to undertake all reasonable steps to collect debts owed to movant who was convicted of tax evasion, where monies collected from those debts were to be applied against movant's tax liability).

United States v. Martin, 965 F.2d 839 (10th Cir. 1992) (concluding that counsel's dual representation of movant and his codefendant created an actual conflict of interest that affected counsel's representation of movant, and affirming district court's grant of section 2255 relief).

Bonneau v. United States, 961 F.2d 17 (1st Cir. 1992) (granting section 2255 relief where appellate counsel failed to perfect an appeal after movant requested that an appeal be filed).

United States v. Biberfeld, 957 F.2d 98 (3d Cir. 1992) (remanding section 2255 case for evidentiary hearing on movant's claim that the government knowingly presented perjured testimony).

United States v. Garcia, 956 F.2d 41 (4th Cir. 1992) (granting section 2255 relief and concluding that government breached plea agreement that movant would not be required to cooperate with law enforcement, where government subpoenaed movant to testify before grand jury).

Moore v. United States, 950 F.2d 656 (10th Cir. 1991) (remanding section 2255 case for evidentiary hearing on movant's claim that his trial counsel, whose fees were paid for by a third party who was implicated in the drug conspiracy pursuant to which movant was convicted, labored under a conflict of interest).

Anderson v. United States, 948 F.2d 704 (11th Cir. 1991) (remanding section 2255 motion for consideration of movant's allegations that trial counsel was ineffective for failing to request a competency hearing, where records show that movant is serving his sentence at a federal psychiatric facility).

United States v. Fuller, 941 F.2d 993 (9th Cir. 1991) (concluding movant's guilty plea was involuntary because she was denied the right to counsel during plea negotiations, and granting section 2255 relief).

United States v. Briggs, 939 F.2d 222 (5th Cir. 1991) (remanding section 2255 motion for evidentiary hearing on whether movant's plea was involuntary because she did not understand that the crime to which she was pleading guilty did not encompass her conduct).

Murchu v. United States, 926 F.2d 50 (1st Cir. 1991) (remanding section 2255 motion to allow consideration of whether district court violated Federal Rule of Criminal Procedure 11(e) by initiating and participating in plea discussions).

Hernandez-Hernandez v. United States, 904 F.2d 758 (1st Cir. 1990) (remanding section 2255 motion for evidentiary hearing to determine whether movant's plea was unknowing and involuntary because induced by counsel's misrepresentation of movant's possible sentencing exposure).

Costo v. United States, 904 F.2d 344 (6th Cir. 1990) (concluding that movant's sentence violated double jeopardy, and granting section 2255 relief where he was sentenced on two counts—distribution and attempted distribution of cocaine—that were all part of the same transaction).

United States v. Bruno, 903 F.2d 393 (5th Cir. 1990) (granting section 2255 relief in light of intervening decision in *McNally v. United States*, 483 U.S. 350, 107 S. Ct. 2875, 97 L. Ed. 2d 292 (1987), which repudiated intangible rights theory on which movant's convictions for fraud had been premised).

Rosenwald v. United States, 898 F.2d 585 (7th Cir. 1990) (remanding section 2255 motion for evidentiary hearing to determine whether counsel was laboring under a conflict of interest because counsel was simultaneously representing movant and government's chief witness on unrelated civil matter).

Humphrey v. United States, 888 F.2d 1546 (11th Cir. 1989) (remanding section 2255 motion for evidentiary hearing to determine whether falsified evidence was used against movant at trial).

United States v. Birdwell, 887 F.2d 643 (5th Cir. 1989) (remanding section 2255 motion for evidentiary hearing to determine whether movant's guilty plea was involuntary because induced by a plea bargain with state authorities, which was incorporated into movant's federal plea bargain, and state authorities breached agreement).

Callanan v. United States, 881 F.2d 229 (6th Cir. 1989) (granting section 2255 relief in light of intervening decision in *McNally v. United States*, 483 U.S. 350, 107 S. Ct. 2875, 97 L. Ed. 2d 292 (1987), which repudiated intangible rights theory on which movant's convictions for fraud had been premised).

United States v. Gray, 878 F.3d 702 (3d Cir. 1989) (concluding that trial counsel was ineffective in failing to conduct any pretrial investigation, failing to hire an investigator to conduct such investigation, and failing to contact potential witnesses, and granting section 2255 relief).

United States v. Flenory, 876 F.2d 10 (3d Cir. 1989) (remanding section 2255 motion for consideration of movant's claim that the government breached plea agreement).

Toulabi v. United States, 875 F.2d 122 (7th Cir. 1989) (granting section 2255 relief in light of intervening Supreme Court decision in *McNally v. United States*, 483 U.S. 350, 107 S. Ct. 2875, 97 L. Ed. 2d 292 (1987), which repudiated intangible rights theory on which movant's convictions for fraud had been premised).

United States v. Burrows, 872 F.2d 915 (9th Cir. 1989) (remanding section 2255 motion for evidentiary hearing as to whether counsel was ineffective for failing to investigate a mental health defense and for failing to present evidence regarding movant's mental state at trial).

United States v. Weintraub, 871 F.2d 1257 (5th Cir. 1989) (concluding that impeachment evidence that would have allowed movant to challenge the only evidence presented at trial as to the amount of narcotics sold was improperly withheld in violation of *Brady v. Maryland*, 373 U.S. 83, 83 C. Ct. 1194, 10 L. Ed. 2d. 215 (1963), and granting section 2255 relief).

Nevarez-Diaz v. United States, 870 F.2d 417 (7th Cir. 1989) (granting section 2255 relief after concluding that movant's guilty plea hearing was defective because movant did not understand the nature of the charges against him).

United States v. Mitchell, 867 F.2d 1232 (9th Cir. 1989) (granting section 2255 relief in light of intervening decision in *McNally v. United States*, 483 U.S. 350, 107 S. Ct. 2875, 97 L. Ed. 2d 292 (1987), which repudiated intangible rights theory on which movant's convictions for fraud had been premised).

United States v. Espinoza, 866 F.2d 1067 (9th Cir. 1989) (remanding section 2255 motion for evidentiary hearing as to whether movant's guilty plea was involuntary because induced by counsel's representations that movant would receive a certain sentence).

United States v. Pogue, 865 F.2d 226 (10th Cir. 1989) (remanding section 2255 motion for evidentiary hearing to determine whether movant's guilty plea was involuntary because he was not informed by the district court, prior to entering his plea, of the possibility that restitution could be ordered, and court later ordered restitution of $1.75 million).

Brunelle v. United States, 864 F.2d 64 (8th Cir. 1988) (affirming district court's grant of section 2255 relief based on government's breach of plea agreement).

Magnuson v. United States, 861 F.2d 166 (7th Cir. 1988) (granting section 2255 relief in light of intervening decision in *McNally v. United States*, 483 U.S. 350, 107 S. Ct. 2875, 97 L. Ed. 2d 292 (1987), which repudiated intangible rights theory on which movants' convictions for fraud had been premised).

United States v. DiPasquale, 859 F.2d 9 (3d Cir. 1988) (granting section 2255 relief where district court erred in imposing preparole eligibility period that exceeds the limitation of ten years set forth in 18 U.S.C. § 4205(a)).

United States v. Dawson, 857 F.2d 923 (3d Cir. 1988) (remanding section 2255 motion for evidentiary hearing as to whether counsel was ineffective for failing to interview prospective witnesses).

Montgomery v. United States, 853 F.2d 83 (2d Cir. 1988) (concluding that movant's guilty plea was accepted by the district court without an adequate factual basis, in violation of Federal Rule of Criminal Procedure 11(f), and granting section 2255 relief).

United States v. Estrada, 849 F.2d 1304 (10th Cir. 1988) (remanding section 2255 motion for evidentiary hearing to determine whether movant's guilty plea was involuntary because coerced by actions of both prosecutor and defense attorney).

United States v. Shelton, 848 F.2d 1485 (10th Cir. 1988) (granting section 2255 relief in light of intervening decision in *McNally v. United States*, 483 U.S. 350, 107 S. Ct. 2875, 97 L. Ed. 2d 292 (1987), which repudiated intangible rights theory on which movant's convictions for fraud had been premised).

Ward v. United States, 845 F.2d 1459 (7th Cir. 1988) (affirming district court's grant of section 2255 relief in light of intervening Supreme Court decision in *McNally v. United States*, 483 U.S. 350, 107 S. Ct. 2875, 97 L. Ed. 2d 292 (1987), which repudiated intangible rights theory on which movant's convictions for fraud had been premised).

Valladares v. United States, 841 F.2d 1089 (11th Cir. 1988) (remanding section 2255 motion for consideration of movant's claim that he was denied a fair trial because an interpreter was not present the first day of trial).

Part IV:

Obstacles to Relief

Claims Previously Raised on Direct Appeal

Contents

I. General Rule

§ 8.01. A section 2255 motion may not relitigate issues raised and rejected on direct appeal.

Generally, a section 2255 proceeding may not be used to relitigate questions that already have been raised and considered on direct appeal. *See, e.g., United States v. Sanin*, 252 F.3d 79, 83 (2d Cir. 2001) *(per curiam)*; *United States v. Wiley*, 245 F.3d 750, 752 (8th Cir. 2001); *Jones v. United States*, 178 F.3d 790, 796 (6th Cir. 1999). This is simply an application of the traditional "law of the case" doctrine to section 2255 proceedings.

II. Exceptions

There are, however, two limited exceptions to the general rule stated in Section I. A claim already litigated on direct appeal may be relitigated in a section 2255 motion if (1) there has been an intervening change in the law or (2) the movant is actually innocent.

§ 8.02. Relitigation is allowed if there has been an intervening change in the law.

Where there has been an intervening change in the law—"if new law has been made . . . since the trial and appeal"—then the fact that a legal issue was raised and rejected on direct appeal does not preclude a movant from securing relief under section 2255. *Davis v. United States*, 417 U.S. 333, 342, 94 S. Ct. 2298, 2303, 41 L. Ed. 2d 109 (1974) (internal quotation marks omitted). *See Jones*, 178 F.3d at 796.

§ 8.03. *Teague v. Lane* may bar relief on a claim based on an intervening change in the law.

Even though an intervening change in the law allows a section 2255 motion to be used to relitigate an issue already rejected on direct appeal, that does not necessarily mean that section 2255 relief is available on all such claims. In *Teague v. Lane*, 489 U.S. 288, 109 S. Ct. 1060, 103 L. Ed. 2d 334 (1989), the Supreme Court greatly limited the relief available in collateral proceedings where there has been an intervening change in the law. Indeed, section 2255 relief on any claim based on a new rule of criminal procedure promulgated because the case was on direct review is likely barred under *Teague*. *Teague* is discussed in Chapter 10.

§ 8.04. Relitigation is allowed if the movant is actually innocent.

Relitigation in a section 2255 motion of claims previously considered on direct appeal is also allowed where there is new and convincing evidence that the movant is "actually innocent." *See, e.g., Wiley*, 245 F.3d at 752. The showing of "actual innocence" necessary to allow the relitigation of claims rejected on appeal is the same as that required to excuse a procedural default. *See id.* Just what constitutes "actual innocence" is discussed in Chapter 9.

Procedural Default and Waiver

Contents

Introduction

§ 9.01. A prisoner may waive the right to section 2255 relief in various ways.

As discussed in Chapter 8, a section 2255 motion may not be used to relitigate issues already raised and rejected on appeal, unless certain exceptions apply. The converse is also true: a section 2255 motion generally may not be used to litigate—for the first time—claims that *could have been* raised earlier in the proceedings, but were not. This implied waiver of claims forms the basis for the "procedural default" doctrine. A plea of guilty or *nolo contendere* may also either implicitly or expressly waive the right to raise certain claims in a section 2255 motion. This chapter discusses the various ways in which a federal prisoner can waive the right to section 2255 relief.

I. The Procedural Default Doctrine

§ 9.02. A section 2255 motion may not relitigate issues that could have been, but were not, raised earlier in the proceedings unless the movant can show cause and prejudice or a miscarriage of justice.

In general, if a section 2255 movant could have raised a claim on direct appeal but did not do so, section 2255 relief on that claim is deemed waived—barred by the judicially created "procedural default" doctrine. *See United States v. Frady*, 456 U.S. 152, 168, 102 S. Ct. 1584, 1594, 71 L. Ed. 2d 816 (1982). A claim is "procedurally defaulted" if it is the type of claim that "can be fully and completely addressed on direct review based on the record created" in the trial court, but was not raised on direct appeal. *Bousley v. United States*, 523 U.S. 614, 622, 118 S. Ct. 1604, 1611, 140 L. Ed. 2d 828 (1998).

The procedural default doctrine's effect is harsh. It completely bars relief on a defaulted claim unless the movant can demonstrate either (1) "cause" for the failure to raise the claim at the proper time and actual "prejudice," *Frady*, 456 U.S. at 168, 102 S. Ct. at 1594, or (2) that the denial of relief would be a "fundamental miscarriage of justice," *Murray v. Carrier*, 477 U.S. 478, 495–96, 106 S. Ct. 2639, 2649, 91 L. Ed. 2d 397 (1986). These hurdles are intentionally high ones to surmount, as the Supreme Court has concluded that respect for the finality of judgments demands that "a collateral challenge may not do service for an appeal," except in exceptional circumstances. *See Frady*, 456 U.S. at 165, 102 S. Ct. at 1593.

§ 9.03. The procedural default doctrine does *not* apply to extra-record claims.

Note, however, that the procedural default doctrine applies only to claims that *could* have been raised at trial or on direct appeal. It does not apply to claims that require development of facts outside the trial record. *See Bousley*, 523 U.S. at 621, 118 S. Ct. at 1610 (recognizing an "exception to the procedural default rule for claims that could not be presented without further factual development"). For example, in *Waley v. Johnston*, 316 U.S. 101, 104, 62 S. Ct. 964, 966, 86 L. Ed. 1302 (1942) *(per curiam),* the Supreme Court held that procedural default did not bar a federal prisoner's claim that his guilty plea had been coerced by government threats, because the facts were "dehors the record and their effect on the judgment was not open to consideration and review on appeal."

§ 9.04. The procedural default doctrine *never* applies to a claim of ineffective assistance of counsel, even if that claim could have been raised on appeal.

In *Massaro v. United States*, 538 U.S. 500, 123 S. Ct. 1690, 155 L. Ed. 2d 714 (2003), the Supreme Court extended the exception for outside-the-record claims even farther. *Massaro* held that the procedural default doctrine *never* bars a claim of ineffective assistance of counsel raised in a section 2255 proceeding, even if that claim could have been, but was not, raised on direct appeal. *Id.*, 538 U.S. at 503–04, 123 S. Ct. at 1693. For this reason, you should consider whether an ineffective assistance of counsel claim may provide an avenue by which to litigate those record-based claims that might otherwise be barred by the procedural default doctrine. For example, a meritorious claim not presented on appeal might be raised in a section 2255 motion as a claim of ineffective assistance of appellate counsel. *See, e.g., Cirilo-Munoz v. United States*, 404 F.3d 527, 530 (1st Cir. 2005).

II. Government Waiver and *Sua Sponte* Invocation by the Court

§ 9.05. The government may waive a procedural default either expressly or implicitly.

Because of the procedural default doctrine's harsh results—the complete loss of a potentially meritorious claim—and because it is *very* difficult to prove the "cause and prejudice" and "miscarriage of justice" exceptions, you should first consider whether the government has waived the default.

The procedural default doctrine is not jurisdictional, but an affirmative defense. *Trest v. Cain*, 522 U.S. 87, 89, 118 S. Ct. 478, 480, 139 L. Ed. 2d 444 (1997). As such, the government may waive its application expressly. *See Pierce v. United States*, 976 F.2d 369, 370 n.1 (7th Cir. 1992) *(per curiam)*.

The government may also implicitly waive the application of procedural default by failing to raise it at the appropriate time: "procedural default is normally a 'defense' that the [government] is 'obligated to raise' and 'preserv[e]' if it is not to 'lose the right to assert the defense thereafter.'" *Trest*, 522 U.S. at 89, 118 S. Ct. at 480 (*quoting Gray v. Netherland*, 518 U.S. 152, 166, 116 S. Ct. 2074, 2082, 135 L. Ed. 2d 457 (1996)). Thus, the government may "lose the right" to assert that a claim is barred by procedural default if it does not raise the defense in proceedings before the district court, *see, e.g., United States v. Guess*, 203 F.3d 1143, 1145–46 (9th Cir. 2000); *United States v. Drobny*, 955 F.2d 990, 995 (5th Cir. 1992); *United States v. Hall*, 843 F.2d 408, 410 (10th Cir. 1988), or fails to assert it on appeal, *see Buggs v. United States*, 153 F.3d 439, 444 (7th Cir. 1998). Moreover, even if the government asserts in its response to a section 2255 motion that a claim is procedurally defaulted, it may nonetheless waive the default if it does not renew its default argument in its objections to a magistrate judge's proposed findings and recommendations. *See United States v. Kallestad*, 236 F.3d 225, 227 (5th Cir. 2000).[1]

§ 9.06. Even if the government waives application of a procedural default, the court may invoke it *sua sponte*.

A waiver by the government of the procedural default defense does not necessarily mean that the court will reach the merits of the claim. Federal courts may invoke a procedural bar *sua sponte* if the movant has notice of the court's intention to apply the bar, and a reasonable opportunity to argue against it. *See Oakes v. United States*, 400 F.3d 92, 97–99 (1st Cir. 2005) (collecting cases).

III. "Cause and Prejudice"

§ 9.07. A procedurally defaulted claim will be considered on its merits if the movant can demonstrate "cause *and* prejudice."

If a claim is procedurally defaulted, and the government has not waived application of the default, the default will be excused—and the claim considered on its merits—if the movant can establish "cause and prejudice." The phrase "cause and prejudice" is conjunctive, meaning that a movant must establish *both* "cause" for the default *and* resultant "prejudice" before a procedural default is excused. *Smith v. Murray*, 477 U.S. 527, 533, 106 S. Ct. 2661, 2666, 91 L. Ed. 2d 434 (1986); *Francis v. Henderson*, 425 U.S. 536, 542, 96 S. Ct. 1708, 1711, 48 L. Ed. 2d 149 (1976).

A. Cause

§ 9.08. "Cause" exists if some objective factor external to the defense impeded compliance with the procedural rule.

"'Cause' is a legitimate excuse for the default." *Thomas v. Lewis*, 945 F.2d 1119, 1123 (9th Cir. 1991). Ordinarily, "cause" exists to excuse a procedural default if "the prisoner can show that some objective factor external to the defense impeded counsel's efforts to comply with the . . . procedural rule." *Murray v. Carrier*, 477 U.S. at 488, 106 S. Ct. at 2645. The exter-

1. Procedures governing magistrate judge practice in section 2255 proceedings are discussed in Chapter 14.

nal impediment "must have *prevented* petitioner from raising the claim." *McCleskey v. Zant*, 499 U.S. 467, 497, 111 S. Ct. 1454, 1472, 113 L. Ed. 2d 517 (1991) (emphasis added); *Murray*, 477 U.S. at 492, 106 S. Ct. at 2648 ("cause for a procedural default . . . ordinarily requires a showing of some external impediment *preventing* counsel from constructing or raising the claim") (emphasis added).

§ 9.09. A novel legal claim may constitute cause.

"[A] claim that 'is so novel that its legal basis is not reasonably available to counsel' may constitute cause for a procedural default." *Bousley*, 523 U.S. at 622, 118 S. Ct. at 1611 (quoting *Reed v. Ross*, 468 U.S. 1, 16, 104 S. Ct. 2901, 2910, 82 L. Ed. 2d 1 (1984)). Thus, cause may be established if the legal basis for the claim was not previously available because the new precedent on which the movant relies:

(1) "explicitly overrule[s]" a prior Supreme Court decision. *Reed*, 468 U.S. at 17, 104 S. Ct. at 2911;
(2) "'overtur[ns] a longstanding and widespread practice to which [the Supreme Court] has not spoken, but which a near-unanimous body of lower court authority has expressly approved.'" *Id.*, 468 U.S. at 17, 104 S. Ct. at 2911 (quoting *United States v. Johnson*, 457 U.S. 537, 551, 102 S. Ct. 2579, 2588, 73 L. Ed. 2d 202 (1982)); or,
(3) "'disapprov[es] a practice [the Supreme] Court arguably has sanctioned in prior cases.'" *Reed*, 468 U.S. at 17, 104 S. Ct. at 2911 (quoting *Johnson*, 457 U.S. at 551, 102 S. Ct. at 2588).

The novelty doctrine, however, does not provide "cause" for a procedural default where existing Supreme Court precedent lays the basis for the defaulted claim, and the claim was pressed by other defendants and ruled on by the lower courts. *See Reed*, 468 U.S. at 19, 104 S. Ct. at 2912; *Bousley*, 523 U.S. at 622–23, 118 S. Ct. at 1611 (novelty doctrine does not provide cause where, at the time of the default, "the Federal Reporters were replete with cases involving [identical] challenges").

Unfortunately, the extent to which a novel legal claim may excuse a procedural default has been greatly circumscribed by the non-retroactivity doctrine established in *Teague v. Lane*, 489 U.S. 288, 109 S. Ct. 1060, 103 L. Ed. 2d 334 (1989). "Application of the cause and prejudice standard . . . does not mitigate the force of *Teague v. Lane*, which prohibits, with certain exceptions, the retroactive application of new law to claims raised" in collateral proceedings. *McCleskey*, 499 U.S. at 495, 111 S. Ct. at 1470–71 (internal citation omitted). As such, a movant who argues "cause" based on the novelty of a legal claim may find that any relief on the merits is barred by *Teague*. Chapter 10 discusses *Teague* in greater detail.

§ 9.10. Cause exists if the factual basis for the claim was not previously available.

"Cause" is also present if the "factual . . . basis for a claim was not reasonably available to counsel" at the time of the procedural default. *Murray*, 477 U.S. at 488, 106 S. Ct. at 2645. *See Perkins v. LeCureux*, 58 F.3d 214, 218 (6th Cir. 1995) ("cause" established where factual basis for claim that judge improperly considered racial factors at sentencing did not become apparent until judge testified at evidentiary hearing in codefendant's federal habeas corpus proceeding); *Carnine v. United States*, 974 F.2d 924, 927–28 (7th Cir. 1992) ("cause" established where claim did not arise until after time for direct appeal had run). If counsel only suspects that the factual basis for the claim exists at the time of the default, then that claim is not reasonably available to counsel and "cause" exists for the failure to raise it: "[m]ere speculation" and "suspicion" do not "suffice to impose a duty on counsel to advance a claim for which they have no evidentiary support." *Strickler v. Greene*, 527 U.S. 263, 286, 119 S. Ct. 1936, 1950–51, 144 L. Ed. 2d 286 (1999).

Nonetheless, the facts that were previously unavailable must be critical to the establishment of the claim. That the movant "did not possess, or could not have reasonably obtained, certain evidence fails to establish cause if other known or discoverable evidence could have supported the claim in any event." *McCleskey*, 499 U.S. at 497, 111 S. Ct. at 1472.

§ 9.11. Cause exists if government interference made compliance with the procedural rule impossible.

Cause is also satisfied if interference by governmental officials made compliance with the procedural rule impracticable. See *Strickler*, 527 U.S. at 283 & n.24, 119 S. Ct. at 1949 & n.24 (cause established where prosecutor withheld exculpatory evidence, counsel reasonably relied on prosecutor's open-file policy, and government asserted that petitioner had "everything known to the government"); *Banks v. Dretke*, 540 U.S. 668, 691, 124 S. Ct. 1256, 1272, 157 L. Ed. 2d 1166 (2004) ("a petitioner shows 'cause' when the reason for his failure to develop facts [at the appropriate time] was the State's suppression of the relevant evidence"); *Amadeo v. Zant*, 486 U.S. 214, 223, 108 S. Ct. 1771, 1777, 100 L. Ed. 2d 249 (1988) (cause demonstrated where evidence revealing claim "was concealed by county officials and therefore was not reasonably available to petitioner's lawyers"); *United States v. Wright*, 43 F.3d 491, 497–500 (10th Cir. 1994) (movant had "cause" for failing to challenge guilty plea on direct appeal because of prosecutor's threat to indict movant's family).

§ 9.12. Ineffective assistance of counsel may also establish cause for a default.

If the default took place at a stage of the proceedings at which the movant was constitutionally entitled to counsel, ineffective assistance of counsel that violates the Sixth Amendment is cause for the default. *See Murray*, 477 U.S. at 488, 106 S. Ct. at 2645; *Coleman v. Thompson*, 501 U.S. 722, 752, 111 S. Ct. 2546, 2566, 115 L. Ed. 2d 640 (1991). Similarly, cause is established if counsel suffered a conflict of interest that rises to the level of a constitutional violation. *See Hollis v. Davis*, 941 F.2d 1471, 1478–79 (11th Cir. 1991) (cause established where counsel failed to object to discriminatory peremptory challenges "out of fear for his own practice and reputation"); *Riner v. Owens*, 764 F.2d 1253, 1257 (7th Cir. 1985) (cause established where counsel who represented codefendants failed to "appeal issues stemming from the defendants' conflicting defenses because to do so might cast doubt on the effectiveness or propriety of the attorney's dual representation at trial").

In contrast, counsel ignorance, inadvertence, or tactical error short of that which is constitutionally ineffective is not cause for procedural default. *See Murray*, 477 U.S. at 487, 106 S. Ct. at 2644–45; *Reed v. Ross*, 468 U.S. at 14, 104 S. Ct. at 2909.

B. Prejudice

§ 9.13. In addition to "cause," a movant must also show *actual* "prejudice."

To establish prejudice sufficient to excuse a procedural default, the movant bears "the burden of showing, not merely that the errors at his trial created a *possibility* of prejudice, but that they worked to his *actual* and substantial disadvantage, infecting his entire trial with error of constitutional dimensions." *Frady*, 456 U.S. at 170, 102 S. Ct. at 1596 (emphasis in original). Under *Frady*, "prejudice" is established if the movant demonstrates "that there is a reasonable probability that the result of the [proceeding] would have been different" absent the error. *Strickler*, 527 U.S. at 289, 119 S. Ct. at 1952 (internal quotation marks omitted).

Importantly, this prejudice calculus does not involve an inquiry into the strength of the evidence against the defendant. In *Strickler*, the lower court found no prejudice because "the record contained ample, independent evidence of guilt." *Id.*, 527 U.S. at 290, 114 S. Ct. at 1952. The Supreme Court labeled the use of such a standard "incorrect." *Id.*, 527 U.S.

at 290, 114 S. Ct. at 1952. Rather, the Court stated, "[t]he question is not whether the defendant would more likely than not have received a different verdict with the evidence, but whether in its absence he received a fair trial, understood as a trial resulting in a verdict worthy of confidence.'" *Id.*, 527 U.S. at 289–90, 114 S. Ct. at 1952 (quoting *Kyles v. Whitley*, 514 U.S. 419, 434, 115 S. Ct. 1555, 1566, 131 L. Ed. 2d 490 (1995)).

For this reason, the showing of prejudice required to excuse a procedural default parallels the showing required to demonstrate prejudice under *Strickland v. Washington*, 466 U.S. 668, 104 S. Ct. 2052, 80 L. Ed. 2d 674 (1984), or materiality under *Brady v. Maryland,* 373 U.S. 83, 83 S. Ct. 1194, 10 L. Ed. 2d 215 (1963). For example, to establish a claim of ineffective assistance of counsel under *Strickland*, "prejudice" must be shown—that is, that "there is a reasonable probability that, but for counsel's unprofessional errors, the result of the proceeding would have been different." *See Strickland*, 466 U.S. at 694, 104 S. Ct. at 2068. For this reason, where a movant asserts that ineffective assistance of counsel establishes "cause" for a procedural default, a showing of *Strickland* prejudice satisfies the "prejudice" required to excuse the default. *See Prou v. United States*, 199 F.3d 37, 49 (1st Cir. 1999) ("Given the striking linguistic parallel [between them], we conclude that the *Frady* and *Strickland* prejudice standards are one and the same."); *Mincey v. Head*, 206 F.3d 1106, 1147 n.86 (11th Cir. 2000). The same is true when the prosecution's suppression of evidence in violation of *Brady* is asserted as cause for the failure to raise the claim earlier: "prejudice within the compass of the 'cause and prejudice' requirement exists when the suppressed evidence is 'material' for *Brady* purposes." *Banks*, 540 U.S. at 691, 124 S. Ct. at 1272.

IV. Fundamental Miscarriage of Justice and Actual Innocence

§ 9.14. A procedurally defaulted claim will be considered on its merits if the movant can demonstrate "actual innocence."

In addition to "cause and prejudice," there is a second exception to the procedural default rule: where "a fundamental miscarriage of justice" has occurred, a defaulted claim will be considered on its merits. *Murray*, 477 U.S. at 495–96, 106 S. Ct. at 2649. As the Supreme Court has explained, "the principles of comity and finality that inform the concepts of cause and prejudice 'must yield to the imperative of correcting a fundamentally unjust incarceration.'" *Id.*, 477 U.S. at 495, 106 S. Ct. at 2649 (quoting *Engle v. Issac*, 456 U.S. 107, 135, 102 S. Ct. 1558, 1576, 71 L. Ed. 2d 783

(1982)). Although the contours of the fundamental miscarriage of justice standard are not well defined, it is clear that a movant meets this standard by showing "actual innocence." *Murray*, 477 U.S. at 496, 106 S. Ct. at 2649. *Accord Schlup v. Delo*, 513 U.S. 298, 321, 115 S. Ct. 851, 864, 130 L. Ed. 2d 808 (1995).

§ 9.15. Showing required to demonstrate "actual innocence" following trial.

To demonstrate "actual innocence," a movant who was convicted following trial "must establish that, in light of new evidence, 'it is more likely than not that no reasonable juror would have found petitioner guilty beyond a reasonable doubt.'" *House v. Bell*, 547 U.S. 518, 536–37, 126 S. Ct. 2064, 2076–77,1 65 L. Ed. 2d 1 (2006) (quoting *Schlup*, 513 U.S. at 327, 115 S. Ct. at 867). "To be credible," a gateway innocence claim requires "new reliable evidence—whether it be exculpatory scientific evidence, trustworthy eyewitness accounts, or critical physical evidence—that was not presented at trial." *Schlup*, 513 U.S. at 324, 115 S. Ct. at 865. However, the court's analysis "is not limited to such evidence." *House*, 547 U.S. at 537, 126 S. Ct. at 2077. Rather, the court "must consider all the evidence, old and new, incriminating and exculpatory, without regard to whether it would necessarily be admitted under rules of admissibility that would govern at trial." *Id.*, 547 U.S. at 538, 126 S. Ct. at 2077 (internal quotation marks omitted). Then, "[b]ased on this total record, the court must make 'a probabilistic determination about what reasonable, properly instructed jurors would do.'" *House*, 547 U.S. at 538, 126 S. Ct. at 2077 (quoting *Schlup*, 513 U.S. at 329, 115 S. Ct. at 868). If the movant can demonstrate that, in light of the new evidence, no reasonable juror would find him guilty beyond a reasonable doubt, then he has met his burden of showing "actual innocence" and the court may consider any and all defaulted claims on the merits. *House*, 547 U.S. at 537, 126 S. Ct. at 2077.

§ 9.16. Showing required to demonstrate "actual innocence" following a guilty plea.

The showing of actual innocence required following a guilty plea is slightly different. "In cases where the Government has foregone more serious charges in the course of plea bargaining, petitioner's showing of actual innocence must also extend to those charges." *Bousley*, 523 U.S. at 624, 118 S. Ct. at 1612. The government is permitted to introduce any admissible evidence of movant's guilt, whether or not that evidence was presented in the plea colloquy. *Id.*, 523 U.S. at 624, 118 S. Ct. at 1612. The movant bears the burden of establishing that, in light of all the evidence available, it is more likely than not that no reasonable juror would have convicted him of any charge. *Id.*, 523 U.S. at 624, 118 S. Ct. at 1612.

§ 9.17. There is a split in the circuits as to whether one can be "actually innocent" of a noncapital sentence.

In capital cases, a defendant may also be "actually innocent" of a death sentence—that is, of the aggravating circumstances that rendered the defendant eligible for the death penalty. *See Dretke v. Haley*, 541 U.S. 386, 393, 124 S. Ct. 1847, 1852, 158 L. Ed. 2d 659 (2004) (citing *Sawyer v. Whitley*, 505 U.S. 333, 112 S. Ct. 2514, 120 L. Ed. 2d 269 (1992)). There is, however, a split in the circuits "regarding the availability and scope of the actual innocence exception in the noncapital sentencing context." *Dretke*, 541 U.S. at 392, 124 S. Ct. at 1851 (collecting cases). The Supreme Court granted *certiorari* in *Dretke* to resolve this split, but did not reach the question for jurisprudential reasons. *See* 541 U.S. at 393–94, 124 S. Ct. at 1852. Certainly, until the Supreme Court makes clear the extent to which one can be actually innocent of a noncapital sentence, movants should argue that the actual innocence exception applies in the noncapital sentencing context.

V. Waiver by Plea or Plea Agreement

Procedural default is not the only way a section 2255 movant may waive the consideration of a claim. A plea of guilty or *nolo contendere* also implicitly waives certain claims. Moreover, section 2255 rights may also be waived in a plea agreement.

§ 9.18. A plea of guilty or *nolo contendere* waives some section 2255 claims.

A federal defendant who has pleaded guilty or *nolo contendere* is prevented from raising in a section 2255 motion any nonjurisdictional claim alleging that a violation of rights, constitutional or otherwise, occurred *prior* to the plea. *See Tollett v. Henderson*, 411 U.S. 258, 267, 93 S. Ct. 1602, 1608, 36 L. Ed. 2d 235 (1973). Thereby precluded, for example, is any claim of double jeopardy, *see United States v. Broce*, 488 U.S. 563, 573–74, 109 S. Ct. 757, 764–65, 102 L. Ed. 2d 927 (1989), regarding an illegal search or seizure, *see United States v. Johnson*, 634 F.2d 385, 386 (8th Cir. 1980) *(per curiam),* or involving the right to a speedy trial, *see United State's v. Bohn*, 956 F.2d 208, 209 (9th Cir. 1992) *(per curiam).*

This does not mean, however, that section 2255 relief is entirely precluded by a guilty plea. Chapter 7 discusses in greater detail those claims cognizable in a section 2255 proceeding even though the movant pleaded guilty or *nolo contendere*. For example, a guilty plea waives only *non*jurisdictional defenses. A defendant who has pleaded guilty may still obtain section 2255 relief on a claim alleging that the district court lacked jurisdiction. *See* § 7.08. In addition, a plea does not waive challenges to the validity of the plea itself, and convictions obtained by means of a guilty plea have been successfully attacked in section 2255 proceedings where the movant has shown that (1) the plea was induced by threats or promises, (2) the government breached a plea agreement, (3) the district court initiated or participated in plea negotiations, or (4) the plea was otherwise not knowing and voluntary. *See* § 7.15. Moreover, a plea does not waive section 2255 relief on a claim that counsel provided ineffective assistance in plea proceedings. *See* § 7.12. Finally, a plea does not waive the ability to seek section 2255 relief on claims of error arising *after* the plea, such as errors at sentencing. *See* §§ 7.16–7.21.

§ 9.19. Section 2255 rights may also be waived in a plea agreement.

A federal defendant may also waive the right to section 2255 relief in a plea agreement. A plea agreement that waives the right to section 2255 relief is generally enforceable. *See, e.g., Williams v. United States*, 396 F.3d 1340, 1342 (11th Cir.) (collecting cases), *cert. denied,* 546 U.S. 902, 126 S. Ct. 246, 163 L. Ed. 2d 226 (2005). Such waivers, however, are not absolute. The decision to be bound by the provisions of the agreement, including the waiver provisions, must be knowing and voluntary. *See id.*; *United States v. Cockerham*, 237 F.3d 1179, 1182–83 (10th Cir. 2001); *DeRoo v. United States*, 223 F.3d 919, 923 (8th Cir. 2000). Moreover, defendants cannot waive their right to seek relief from an illegal sentence, such as one that exceeds the statutory maximum, *DeRoo*, 223 F.3d at 923, or was imposed in violation of the terms of the agreement, *id.*, or is based upon an impermissible factor such as race, *Cockerham*, 237 F.3d at 1182.

Dismissal of a section 2255 motion on the basis of waiver is also inappropriate if the motion includes a claim of ineffective assistance of counsel relating to the negotiation of, and entry into, the plea agreement and waiver. *Cockerham*, 237 F.3d at 1187; *DeRoo*, 223 F.3d at 923–24. "[J]ustice dictates that a claim of ineffective assistance of counsel in connection with the negotiation of a cooperation agreement cannot be barred by the agreement itself—the very product of the alleged ineffectiveness." *DeRoo*, 223 F.3d at 924 (internal quotation marks omitted).

Finally, the language of the plea agreement must be consulted to determine whether it indeed contains an express waiver of section 2255 rights, and the scope of that waiver. If the plea agreement specifies only that no *appeal* will be taken, it does not waive the right to bring a section 2255 motion. *See United States v. Benboe*, 157 F.3d 1181, 1183 (9th Cir. 1998). Similarly, if the plea agreement only expressly waives any section 2255 challenge to the *sentence*, it does not foreclose a challenge to the movant's plea. *See Bridgeman v. United States*, 229 F.3d 589, 591–92 (7th Cir. 2000).

CHAPTER 10

Retroactive Application of a New Rule: *Teague v. Lane*

Contents

Introduction

§ 10.01. *Teague*'s nonretroactivity doctrine.

In *Teague v. Lane*, 489 U.S. 288, 109 S. Ct. 1060, 103 L. Ed. 2d 334 (1989), the Supreme Court dramatically narrowed the habeas corpus remedy by creating a new framework to be used in determining whether a rule of criminal procedure announced in a United States Supreme Court decision should be applied retroactively to cases on collateral review. "Under the *Teague* framework, an old rule applies both on direct and collateral review, but a new rule is generally applicable only to cases that are still on direct review." *Whorton v. Bockting*, 549 U.S. 406, 127 S. Ct. 1173, 1180, 167 L. Ed. 2d 1 (2007) (citing *Griffith v. Kentucky*, 479 U.S. 314, 107 S. Ct. 708, 93 L. Ed. 2d 649 (1987)). For cases that are on collateral review when the Supreme Court announces a "new" rule of criminal procedure, that "new" rule applies only in two very limited circumstances, which are explained in greater detail later.

§ 10.02. You must assume that *Teague* applies in section 2255 cases.

The Supreme Court has never expressly held that *Teague*'s nonretroactivity doctrine applies to section 2255 motions,[1] but the courts of appeal

1. In *Bousley v. United States*, 523 U.S. 614, 619–20, 118 S. Ct. 1604, 1609–10, 140 L. Ed. 2d 828 (1998), a section 2255 proceeding, *amicus curiae* "urge[d] [the Court] to apply the rule of *Teague*," but the Court declined to do so because the rule at issue was neither "new" nor one of "criminal procedure." *See also Danforth v. Minnesota*, ___ U.S. ___, 128 S. Ct. 1029, 1034 n.4, 169 L. Ed. 2d 859 (2008) (expressly declining to consider question).

to consider the question agree that it does. *See United States v. Sanchez-Cervantes*, 282 F.3d 664, 667 & n.9 (9th Cir. 2002) (collecting cases). As a result, you must assume that the question of whether *Teague* bars relief may be raised at some point in any section 2255 proceeding.

I. Preliminary Considerations

The requirements for application of the *Teague* doctrine will be discussed later in this chapter. But first, here are some preliminary things to keep in mind:

§ 10.03. *Teague*'s effect on the pleadings.

Tempting as it might be to assert that the movant's claims are "novel" or controlled by a "ground-breaking" Supreme Court case that came down last month, such monikers are a red flag to the government and the court that the claim implicates *Teague*. *See Breard v. Greene*, 523 U.S. 371, 377, 118 S. Ct. 1352, 1355, 140 L. Ed. 2d 529 (1998) (assuming that petitioner's argument—that his claims "were so novel that he could not have discovered them earlier"—was true, "such novel claims would be barred on [collateral] review under *Teague*.") Be wary, too, of characterizing claims as requiring an expansion of existing precedent or resolution of an unsettled question of law. If possible, allege in your section 2255 motion and argue throughout the proceedings that all the court need do is to apply well-established law to a nonexceptional fact pattern.

§ 10.04. *Teague*'s effect on *certiorari* proceedings.

Teague's bar to the creation of new rules of criminal procedure in collateral proceedings also affects *certiorari* proceedings following direct appeal. Because *Teague* likely precludes section 2255 relief on any rule promulgated after the movant's direct appeal was completed, it may be in the movant's interest to file a petition for writ of *certiorari* to extend the period of direct review. By doing so, the movant will obtain the benefit of any new rules announced during the time period that elapses between affirmance on direct appeal and the completion of *certiorari* proceedings.

In addition, *Teague* alters somewhat the usual appellate practice of narrowing issues for presentation in a petition for writ of *certiorari*. Serious consideration should be given to raising on *certiorari* every potentially meritorious "novel" claim for which section 2255 relief might be barred by *Teague*.

§ 10.05. *Teague* is an affirmative defense.

The *Teague* doctrine is not jurisdictional and, accordingly, may be waived by the government if not asserted in a timely manner. *See, e.g., Caspari v. Bohlen*, 510 U.S. 383, 389, 114 S. Ct. 948, 953, 127 L. Ed. 2d 236 (1994). However, the government's failure to raise *Teague* does not preclude the court from applying it *sua sponte:* "a federal court may, *but need not,* decline to apply *Teague* if the [government] does not argue it." *Caspari*, 510 U.S. at 389, 114 S. Ct. at 953 (emphasis added); *see United States v. Ishmael* 343 F.3d 741, 743 (5th Cir. 2003) (applying *Teague sua sponte*).

§ 10.06. *Teague* is not a two-way street.

Because many decisions issued by the Supreme Court in recent years have restricted rather than expanded rights, some prisoners have attempted to use the *Teague* doctrine to avoid retroactive application of damaging new cases. In *Lockhart v. Fretwell*, 506 U.S. 364, 372–73, 113 S. Ct. 838, 844, 122 L. Ed. 2d 180 (1993), however, the Supreme Court stated that *Teague* does *not* bar retroactive application of *restrictions* of rights; only the retroactive broadening of such rights. A leading commentator has stated that in *Lockhart*, the Court expressed the view that *Teague* "is a one-way street that denies habeas corpus petitioners the benefit of favorable new rules but does not exempt petitioners from new rules that narrow the rights of criminal defendants." 2 J. Liebman & R. Hertz, *Federal Habeas Corpus Practice and Procedure* § 25.8, at 1247 (5th ed. 2001). *See also Gilmore v. Taylor*, 508 U.S. 333, 342, 113 S. Ct. 2112, 2117, 124 L. Ed. 2d 306 (1993) (retroactively applying "new rule" notwithstanding *Teague*, because rule "did not work a change in the law favoring criminal defendants.")

§ 10.07. Timing and *Teague*.

Teague opined that the question of whether relief is barred by the *Teague* doctrine must be addressed as a "threshold" matter *before* the court addresses the merits of the claim. *Teague*, 489 U.S. at 300, 109 S. Ct. at 1070. Applicability of the *Teague* bar, however, generally should not be decided until *after* the court considers other matters that are antecedent to a decision on the merits, such as whether the movant is "in custody," and whether a claim is procedurally defaulted.[2] *See Lambrix v. Singletary*, 520 U.S. 518, 524, 117 S. Ct. 1517, 1523, 137 L. Ed. 2d 771 (1997); *Daniels v. United States*, 254 F.3d 1180, 1189 n.2 (10th Cir. 2001).

---

2. The requirement that a section 2255 movant be "in custody" is discussed in Chapter 6; procedural default is discussed in Chapter 9.

II. *Teague*'s Four-Part Inquiry

§ 10.08. A four-step analysis must be undertaken to see if *Teague* bars relief.

Under *Teague*, "unless they fall within an exception to the general rule, new constitutional rules of criminal procedure will not be applicable to those cases which have become final before the new rules are announced," 489 U.S. at 310, 109 S. Ct. at 1075. Accordingly, a four-step analysis must be undertaken to determine whether the *Teague* nonretroactivity doctrine bars relief.

First, "because *Teague* by its terms applies only to procedural rules," the court must determine if the rule on which the movant relies is one of substance or procedure. *Bousley*, 523 U.S. at 620, 118 S. Ct. at 1610. Second, if the rule is one of criminal procedure, "the court must ascertain the date on which the defendant's conviction and sentence became final for *Teague* purposes." *Caspari*, 510 U.S. at 390, 114 S. Ct. at 953. Third, the court must determine whether the rule is "new"; that is, it must survey the legal landscape at the time the movant's conviction became final and determine whether a court at that time would have felt compelled by existing precedent to apply the rule the movant propounds. *Id.*, 510 U.S. at 390, 114 S. Ct. at 953. Fourth, if the court concludes the rule the movant seeks is both one of criminal procedure and "new," then the court must determine whether either of the two *Teague* exceptions applies. *Id.*, 510 U.S. at 390, 114 S. Ct. at 953. If the rule in question is a new rule of criminal procedure and neither of the exceptions applies, then relief is barred by *Teague*.

III. What Constitutes a "New Rule of Criminal Procedure"?

§ 10.09. Is the rule one of "criminal procedure"?

Teague bars only the retroactive application of new rules "*of criminal procedure*." *Teague*, 489 U.S. at 310, 109 S. Ct. at 1075 (emphasis added). Because "*Teague* by its terms applies only to procedural rules . . . [t]his distinction between substance and procedure is an important one." *Bousley*, 523 U.S. at 620, 118 S. Ct. at 1610. For example, every court of appeals to consider the question has determined that the Supreme Court's decision in *United States v. Booker*, 543 U.S. 220, 125 S. Ct. 738, 160 L. Ed. 2d 621 (2005), created a new rule of criminal procedure that does not apply retroactively in collateral proceedings. *See, e.g., Never Misses A Shot v. United States*, 413 F.3d 781, 783–84 (8th Cir. 2005) (collecting cases).

In contrast, *Teague* does not bar relief if the rule in question is one of substantive criminal law: *Teague* "is inapplicable to the situation in which [the Supreme] Court decides the meaning of a criminal statute enacted by Congress." *Bousley*, 523 U.S. at 620, 118 S. Ct. at 1610. For example, because the Supreme Court announced a new rule of *substantive* law in its decision in *Richardson v. United States*, 526 U.S. 813, 119 S. Ct. 1707, 143 L. Ed. 2d 985 (1999),[3] *Teague* did not bar the retroactive application of *Richardson* in section 2255 proceedings. *See United States v. Barajas-Diaz*, 313 F.3d 1242, 1245 (10th Cir. 2002) (collecting cases).

IV. Finality

§ 10.10. *Teague* bars reliance on any rule that arose after "finality."

Under *Teague*, a movant may not rely on any new rules of criminal procedure that arise after the date his conviction and sentence became "final," unless one of the two exceptions to *Teague* applies. The date of finality is therefore critical to the application of the *Teague* bar. Before filing a section 2255 motion, you should determine the date on which the movant's conviction became final, and, where possible, root all claims raised in the motion firmly in precedent that existed prior to that date.

§ 10.11. "Finality" is the conclusion of direct appeal, or the time for seeking an appeal.

A conviction and sentence become "final" for purposes of *Teague* "when the availability of direct appeal . . . has been exhausted and the time for filing a petition for writ of *certiorari* has elapsed or a timely filed petition has finally been denied." *Caspari*, 510 U.S. at 390, 114 S. Ct. at 953. Thus, for a federal prisoner who files a petition for writ of *certiorari* following affirmance on direct appeal, finality occurs when the United States Supreme Court either denies *certiorari* or issues a decision on the merits. If no *certiorari* petition is filed, the date of "finality" is when the 90-day period for filing a *certiorari* petition expires. If no appeal is filed, then finality occurs ten days after the entry of judgment, when the time to file

3. In *Richardson*, the Court determined that to support a conviction for engaging in a continuing criminal enterprise, in violation of 21 U.S.C. § 848, the jury "must unanimously agree not only that the defendant committed some 'continuing series of violations' but also that the defendant committed each of the individual 'violations' necessary to make up that 'continuing series.'" 526 U.S. at 815, 119 S. Ct. at 1709 (quoting § 848(c)).

a notice of appeal has expired. *See Never Misses a Shot*, 413 F.3d at 782; *United States v. Bellamy*, 411 F.3d 1182, 1186 (10th Cir. 2005).

V. Is the Rule "New"?

§ 10.12. *Teague* bars only the retroactive application of "new" rules of criminal procedure.

Even if the rule upon which movant relies is a rule of criminal procedure *and* the rule arose after the movant's conviction became final, *Teague* still will not bar relief unless the rule is also "new." Just what constitutes a "new rule" for purposes of *Teague* is not always clear. The Supreme Court has "offered various formulations" defining a "new rule." *Gilmore v. Taylor*, 508 U.S. 333, 340, 113 S. Ct. 2112, 2116, 124 L. Ed. 2d 306 (1993). Recently, however, the Supreme Court has stated the analysis to be undertaken as follows: the court must survey the legal landscape as of the date of finality and determine whether the rule "was *dictated* by then-existing precedent—whether, that is, the unlawfulness of [the movant's] conviction was apparent to all reasonable jurists." *Lambrix*, 520 U.S. at 527–28, 117 S. Ct. at 1525 (emphasis in original). *See Whorton*, 127 S. Ct. at 1181 (a "new rule" is defined as a rule that was not dictated by precedent existing at the time the defendant's conviction became final). If not, then the rule is "new," and *Teague* bars relief unless the rule falls within one of the two *Teague* exceptions.

VI. Exceptions to the Application of *Teague*

There are two *Teague* exceptions—two circumstances in which a new rule expanding procedural protections for criminal defendants may be applied in section 2255 proceedings, even if the movant's case was final at the time the new rule was announced.

§ 10.13. The first *Teague* exception.

Under the first *Teague* exception, a new rule must be applied retroactively if it "places a class of private conduct beyond the power of the State to proscribe" or prohibits "a certain category of punishment for a class of defendants because of their status or offense." *Graham v. Collins*, 506 U.S. 461, 477, 113 S. Ct. 892, 903, 122 L. Ed. 2d 260 (1993) (internal quotation marks omitted). For example, the claim that the Eighth Amendment prohibits the execution of the mentally retarded falls within this exception. *See Penry v. Lynaugh*, 492 U.S. 302, 329–30, 109 S. Ct. 2934, 2952–53,

106 L. Ed. 2d 256 (1989), *abrogated on other grounds*, *Atkins v. Virginia*, 536 U.S. 304, 122 S. Ct. 2242, 153 L. Ed. 2d 335 (2002).

§ 10.14. The second *Teague* exception.

The second exception applies where the new rule is a "watershed rule of criminal procedure," that is, a rule that is both "implicit in the concept of ordered liberty" *and* crucial to the accuracy of the adjudication. *Graham*, 506 U.S. at 478, 113 S. Ct. at 903 (quoting *Teague*, 489 U.S. at 311, 109 S. Ct. at 1076). Thus, to qualify under this exception, the rule must not only contribute to fact-finding reliability but also "alter our understanding of the *bedrock procedural elements*" essential to the fairness of a proceeding. *Teague*, 489 U.S. at 311, 109 S. Ct. at 1076) (emphasis in original).

Needless to say, this exception is extremely narrow. It applies "only to a small core of rules," most of which have long been recognized as law. *Graham*, 506 U.S. at 478, 113 S. Ct. at 903. Indeed, the Supreme Court has noted that it is "unlikely that any of these watershed rules has yet to emerge." *Tyler v. Cain*, 533 U.S. 656, 666 n.7, 121 S. Ct. 2478, 2484 n.7, 150 L. Ed. 2d 632 (2001) (internal quotation marks omitted).

CHAPTER 11

Fourth Amendment Claims: *Stone v. Powell*

Contents

Introduction

§ 11.01. *Stone* bars habeas corpus relief on most Fourth Amendment claims.

In *Stone v. Powell*, 428 U.S. 465, 96 S. Ct. 3037, 49 L. Ed. 2d 1067 (1976), the Supreme Court greatly restricted the ability of state prisoners to obtain federal habeas corpus relief on Fourth Amendment claims. Under *Stone*, habeas corpus relief is not available to redress the admission at trial of evidence obtained in violation of the Fourth Amendment *unless* the state courts denied the prisoner "an opportunity for full and fair litigation of [the] Fourth Amendment claim" at trial or on direct appeal. *Id.*, 428 U.S. at 482, 96 S. Ct. at 3046. If the prisoner had a full and fair opportunity to litigate the Fourth Amendment claim in state court, *Stone* bars habeas relief, even if the claim is meritorious. *See Siripongs v. Calderon*, 35 F.3d 1308, 1321 (9th Cir. 1994); *Deputy v. Taylor*, 19 F.3d 1485, 1491 (3d Cir. 1994).

Underpinning *Stone* is the concept that the exclusionary rule is a judicially created remedy rather than a personal constitutional right and the belief that if a Fourth Amendment claim was treated seriously in prior judicial proceedings, collateral review is not necessary to retain the exclusionary rule's deterrent effect. *See Stone*, 428 U.S. at 494–95 & n.37, 96 S. Ct. at 3052 & n.37. Consequently, when collateral relief is sought on a Fourth Amendment claim, the federal court must examine the prior proceedings to determine if the prisoner had "an opportunity for full and fair litigation" of the claim. If such an opportunity was had, *Stone* bars relief.

I. Does *Stone v. Powell* Apply to Section 2255 Proceedings?

§ 11.02. There is a circuit split as to whether *Stone* applies to section 2255 cases.

In *Kaufman v. United States*, 394 U.S. 217, 231, 89 S. Ct. 1068, 1076, 22 L. Ed. 2d 227 (1969), the Supreme Court held that "a claim of unconstitutional search and seizure is cognizable in a § 2255 proceeding." In reaching this conclusion, the Court determined that section 2255 relief should parallel the relief afforded state prisoners in habeas corpus proceedings and relied-upon previous decisions wherein habeas corpus relief was granted to state prisoners for Fourth Amendment violations. *Id.*, 394 U.S. at 225, 89 S. Ct. at 1073. Seven years later, however, the Court decided *Stone*.

As a result of this history, there is a split in the circuits as to whether *Stone* applies in section 2255 cases. In the minority, the Eighth Circuit has held that *Stone* does not apply in section 2255 proceedings. *See Baranski v. United States*, 515 F.3d 857, 859–60 (8th Cir. 2008). The Eighth Circuit noted that *Stone* itself "left open the question of whether Fourth Amendment claims may be raised by federal prisoners under § 2255," and that a footnote in *Stone* "suggested a different policy reason might underlie *Kaufman* because of the Court's supervisory role over federal proceedings." *Id.* at 859, 860 (citing *Stone*, 428 U.S. at 481 n.16, 96 S. Ct. at 3046 n.16). Therefore, the Eighth Circuit concluded, *Stone* does not apply to Fourth Amendment claims raised in a section 2255 motion. *Id.* at 860.

Three other circuits, however, have held to the contrary. *See United States v. Ishmael*, 343 F.3d 741, 742 (5th Cir. 2003); *United States v. Cook*, 997 F.2d 1312, 1317 (10th Cir. 1993); *United States v. Hearst*, 638 F.2d 1190, 1196 (9th Cir. 1980). Until the Supreme Court resolves this split, you must be prepared to argue why *Stone* does not apply to any Fourth Amendment claims asserted in your section 2255 motion.

II. The *Stone* Doctrine

§ 11.03. *Stone* applies *only* to Fourth Amendment claims.

The Supreme Court has "repeatedly declined to extend the rule in *Stone* beyond its original bounds" to claims other than those that arise under the Fourth Amendment. *Withrow v. Williams*, 507 U.S. 680, 687, 113 S. Ct. 1745, 1750, 123 L. Ed. 2d 407 (1993). Accordingly, the *Stone* doctrine does not bar collateral relief on separate, distinct, constitutional claims arising out of the same facts that comprise the Fourth Amendment violation.

For example, although *Stone* applies to confessions challenged on Fourth Amendment grounds, it does *not* apply where the voluntariness of a confession under the Fifth Amendment is at issue. *See Cardwell v. Taylor*, 461 U.S. 571, 573, 103 S. Ct. 2015, 2016, 76 L. Ed. 2d 333 (1983). Similarly, although *Stone* bars challenges to the admission of evidence seized in violation of the Fourth Amendment, it does not bar the claim that trial counsel was ineffective in failing to object to the admission of that evidence. *See Kimmelman v. Morrison*, 477 U.S. 365, 382–83, 106 S. Ct 2574, 2587, 91 L. Ed. 2d 305 (1986). You should therefore look closely at the facts that support your Fourth Amendment claim to determine if they support any other claim for relief. If they do, consider pleading the alternative claim in your section 2255 motion in addition to, or instead of, the Fourth Amendment claim.

§ 11.04. Was there a "full and fair opportunity" to litigate the Fourth Amendment claim?

Stone bars collateral relief if a prisoner has had a "full and fair opportunity to litigate the Fourth Amendment claim at trial and present issues on direct appeal." *Cook*, 997 F.2d at 1317; *see Stone*, 428 U.S. at 494 n.37, 96 S. Ct. at 3052 n.37. Thus, *both* the prior trial *and* appellate proceedings must be examined to ensure that the prisoner previously had "an opportunity for full and fair litigation" of the claim. *See id.* at 1317–18 (remanding to determine if prisoner had "full and fair opportunity to raise his Fourth Amendment issues on direct appeal"); *Hearst*, 638 F.2d at 1196. If no such opportunity was had, the prisoner may obtain section 2255 relief on a meritorious claim. *Cook*, 997 F.2d at 1318.

Stone does not specify a test for determining if an opportunity for full and fair litigation of a Fourth Amendment claim has been provided. Instead, in a footnote, it cites *Townsend v. Sain*, 372 U.S. 293, 83 S. Ct. 745, 9 L. Ed. 2d 770 (1963). *See Stone*, 428 U.S. at 494 n.36, 96 S. Ct. at 3052 n.36. *Townsend* lays out certain factors for a federal habeas court to consider in resolving whether a disputed *factual* issue was fully and fairly litigated by a state court. Among these factors are whether the state provided an adequate fact-finding procedure and whether the state court's fact-findings were adequately supported by the record. *See Townsend*, 372 U.S. at 312–13, 83 S. Ct. at 757. In contrast, *Stone* bars relitigation of a Fourth Amendment claim if the prisoner had the "opportunity for full and fair litigation" of both legal *and* factual matters relating to that claim "at trial *and* on direct review." *Stone*, 428 U.S. at 494 n.37, 96 S. Ct. at 3052 n.37 (emphasis added). As a result, the test for what is "full and fair" under *Stone* is not identical to that under *Townsend*, and it is only decisions applying *Stone* that clarify when an opportunity for full and fair litigation of a Fourth Amendment claim has been provided.

§ 11.05. Situations in which there *was* an "opportunity for full and fair litigation."

Certainly, there has been an opportunity for full and fair litigation of a Fourth Amendment claim, and relief is barred under *Stone*, where the claim was raised at trial and on direct appeal, the trial court held a hearing on disputed factual matters, the fact-findings were sufficient for the appellate court to consider the claim, and it did so. *See, e.g., Siripongs*, 35 F.3d at 1321.

Note that *Stone* requires only an "opportunity" for full and fair litigation. If the movant *had* the opportunity to raise a Fourth Amendment claim at trial via a motion to suppress or on appeal, and failed to do so, *Stone* bars relief. *See Huynh v. King*, 95 F.3d 1052, 1058 (11th Cir. 1996) (noting *Stone* bars collateral consideration of a Fourth Amendment claim if the prior proceedings "provided an opportunity for full and fair litigation of the claim 'whether or not the defendant employs those processes'"); *Jennings v. Rees*, 800 F.2d 72, 76–77 (6th Cir. 1986) (*Stone* bars Fourth Amendment issue that was not raised at suppression hearing). This is true even if the provided opportunity was squandered due to the failings of counsel. *See Jennings*, 800 F.2d at 77; *Hearst*, 638 F.2d at 1196; *Hubbard v. Jeffes*, 653 F.2d 99, 103 (3d Cir. 1981).[1]

§ 11.06. Situations in which there was *no* "opportunity for full and fair litigation."

There is no "opportunity for full and fair litigation" of a Fourth Amendment claim, and hence no bar to consideration of that claim in section 2255 proceedings under *Stone*, where:

(1) *No process existed to redress claims of the sort raised by movant. See, e.g., Willett v. Lockhart*, 37 F.3d 1265, 1273 (8th Cir. 1994) *(en banc)* (holding Fourth Amendment claim is not *Stone*-barred if "the state provided no procedure by which the prisoner could raise his Fourth Amendment claim.") For example, if the Fourth Amendment claim is based on a change in the law that occurred after the prior adjudication of the claim at trial or on direct appeal, *Stone* does not bar relief. *See Anderson v. Calderon*, 232 F.3d

1. As discussed earlier, if counsel's failure to present and/or preserve a meritorious Fourth Amendment claim rises to the level of ineffective assistance of counsel, the movant should assert an independent Sixth Amendment violation, which is not barred by *Stone*. *See, e.g., Hearst*, 638 F.2d at 1196 ("If the provided opportunity [for full and fair litigation of the Fourth Amendment claim] has been squandered due to defense counsel's incompetence or misconduct, a convict's only option on collateral review is a Sixth Amendment claim based on inadequate assistance of counsel.")

1053, 1068 (9th Cir. 2000), *overruled on other grounds*, *Osband v. Woodford*, 290 F.3d 1036, 1043 (9th Cir. 2002).[2]

(2) *A process existed, but presentation of the Fourth Amendment claim was frustrated. Stone* does not bar federal court consideration of a Fourth Amendment claim where, although a process existed for adjudicating the claim fully and fairly, the presentation of the claim was frustrated because of the failure of the process itself in the prisoner's case. *See, e.g.*, *Machacek v. Hofbauer*, 213 F.3d 947, 952 (6th Cir. 2000); *Willett*, 37 F.3d at 1273 (holding Fourth Amendment claim is not *Stone*-barred if "the prisoner was foreclosed from using that procedure because of an unconscionable breakdown in the system."). Note that "a breakdown in the mechanism can occur in either the trial court or the . . . appellate court." *Willett*, 37 F.3d at 1272.

(a) *There was a breakdown in the trial mechanism:* Even though the movant may have had a suppression hearing before the trial court, there may have been no full and fair opportunity to litigate the Fourth Amendment claim because, for example:

(i) There was no adequate opportunity to prepare for a suppression hearing. *See Boyd v. Mintz*, 631 F.2d 247, 250–51 (3d Cir. 1980) (counsel had but one day to discover and present Fourth Amendment claim).

(ii) The trial court's actions precluded the movant from presenting defense evidence at the suppression hearing. *See United States ex rel. Bostick v. Peters*, 3 F.3d 1023, 1027–29 (7th Cir. 1993) (trial court's erroneous procedural ruling induced petitioner not to present critical evidence); *Bulger v. McClay*, 575 F.2d 407, 410 (2d Cir. 1978) (trial court failed to conduct full hearing on disputed factual issues and limited cross-examination).

(b) *There was a breakdown in the appellate mechanism:* Even if the Fourth Amendment issue was raised on appeal, the lack of an opportunity for full and fair litigation is shown if:

(i) The appellate court ignored the Fourth Amendment claim in its decision. *See Agee v. White*, 809 F.2d 1487, 1490 (11th Cir. 1987).

(ii) The appellate court applied a procedural rule to deny relief in an unanticipated and unforeseeable way. *See Riley v. Gray*, 674 F.2d 522, 527 (6th Cir. 1982).

---

2. Note, however, that if the change in the law constitutes a new rule of criminal procedure, section 2255 relief is likely barred by the nonretroactivity doctrine of Teague v. Lane, 489 U.S. 288, 109 S. Ct. 1060, 103 L. Ed. 2d 334 (1989). *Teague* is discussed in Chapter 10.

(iii) The movant had no full and fair opportunity to respond to the government's arguments. *See Bailey v. Duckworth*, 699 F.2d 424, 425 (7th Cir. 1983) (appellate court upheld search based on argument first raised in rehearing petition to which defendant had no opportunity to respond).

(iv) The trial court failed to make fact-findings adequate for full and fair consideration of the issue on appeal. *See Tukes v. Dugger*, 911 F.2d 508, 514 & nn. 6, 7 (11th Cir. 1990).

III. Government Waiver and *Sua Sponte* Application by the Courts

§ 11.07. Although *Stone* is not jurisdictional, courts will likely raise it *sua sponte*.

The Supreme Court has stated that the *Stone* doctrine is "not jurisdictional in nature." *Withrow v. Williams*, 507 U.S. 680, 686, 113 S. Ct. 1645, 1750, 123 L. Ed. 2d 407 (1993). Indeed, some courts of appeal have determined that the government has the burden to raise the *Stone* bar in the first instance. *See, e.g., Towne v. Dugger*, 899 F.2d 1104, 1111 n.3 (11th Cir. 1990) (concluding State waived *Stone* defense by failing to assert it in the district court); *Wallace v. Duckworth*, 778 F.2d 1215, 1219 n.1 (7th Cir. 1985) ("[R]espondents never raised any *Stone v. Powell* argument, and since the rule of *Stone v. Powell* is not a jurisdictional rule, we need not raise the issue *sua sponte*.") (internal citation omitted).

The First Circuit, however, has encouraged litigants to make an affirmative showing of the inapplicability of *Stone* even if the government does not assert the defense. *See Tart v. Massachusetts*, 949 F.2d 490, 497 n.6 (1st Cir. 1991). Still other circuits will apply the *Stone* bar *sua sponte*. *See Davis v. Blackburn*, 803 F.2d 1371, 1372 (5th Cir. 1986); *Woolery v. Arave*, 8 F.3d 1325, 1326 (9th Cir. 1993). For these reasons, if your section 2255 motion asserts a Fourth Amendment claim, you should strongly consider making an affirmative showing of the grounds to avoid application of the *Stone* bar. That is, the motion (and/or memorandum in support) should affirmatively allege the facts supporting the contention that the movant was denied a full and fair opportunity to litigate the claim at the trial level, on appeal, or both.

Part V:

Proceedings Before the District Court

The Motion

Contents

Introduction

The motion is the single most important document to be filed in a section 2255 case, and preparation of a complete motion that presents compelling claims for relief has been made more difficult by the changes to section 2255 practice brought about by the statute of limitations and restrictions on second or successive motions enacted by the Antiterrorism and Effective Death Penalty Act of 1996 (AEDPA).[1]

§ 12.01. Be certain of the date the motion is due before preparing it.

As discussed in Chapter 5, if a section 2255 motion is not filed in a timely manner, the results are harsh and complete—the entire case will be dismissed with prejudice by the district court. Accordingly, if you have not already done so, you should at this time become familiar with the workings of section 2255's statute of limitations by reading Chapter 5 and should carefully determine the date the motion is due in order to ensure that it will be timely filed.

1. The AEDPA is discussed in Chapter 2, the statute of limitations governing section 2255 motions is discussed in Chapter 5, and the provisions governing second or successive motions are discussed in Chapter 19.

§ 12.02. The motion must contain *all* available claims at the time it is filed.

As discussed in Chapter 19, the AEDPA has severely restricted the ability to obtain relief on second or successive section 2255 motions. In the vast majority of cases, a prisoner will get *only one* chance to collaterally attack a federal conviction and sentence. Moreover, as discussed in Section VII of this chapter and also in Chapter 5, it is *very* difficult to amend a section 2255 motion to include new claims. For this reason, to the extent possible, the motion must contain *all* available claims at the time it is filed.

Chapter 7 may provide assistance with brainstorming issues to include in a section 2255 motion. It discusses claims that are cognizable in section 2255 proceedings and contains a list of successful section 2255 cases. This chapter discusses how to plead those claims to be presented in the motion.

I. Contents and Format

§ 12.03. The Rules Governing § 2255 Proceedings, the Model Form, and any applicable local rules contain the formal requirements for a motion.

The formal requirements for section 2255 motions are contained in Rules 2 and 3 of the Rules Governing § 2255 Proceedings, and the Model Form for Motions Under 28 U.S.C. § 2255 Proceedings (hereafter, the Model Form), which is appended to the Rules Governing § 2255 Proceedings.[2]

These general requirements may be supplemented by additional requirements set out in the local rules of the district court where the motion is to be filed. Indeed, the district in which the section 2255 motion is to be filed may have developed its own model form that conforms to its local rules. These forms are available at no cost from the district court clerk's office and, in many districts, are also available on the district court's website. Links to all federal court websites can be found at *www.uscourts.gov/courtlinks*. Local rules may *require* that the motion be filed either on the Model Form, or on that district's form.

§ 12.04. Required contents.

Even if the district in which the motion is to be filed does not require the use of a form, the easiest way to ensure that the motion, in both format

2. Both the Rules Governing § 2255 Proceedings and the Model Form are contained in the Appendix.

and content, complies with all legal requirements, is to file it on the Model Form or its local equivalent. If a form is not used, the Rules Governing § 2255 Motions require that the motion substantially conform with the Model Form or the form prescribed by the local district court rules, *see* Rules Governing § 2255 Proceedings, Rule 2(c), and also require that the motion:

1. Specify all available grounds for relief.
2. State the facts supporting each ground for relief.
3. State the relief requested.
4. Be typed or legibly handwritten.
5. Be signed under penalty of perjury by the movant or by a person authorized to sign it for the movant (for example, movant's counsel).

Rules Governing § 2255 Proceedings, Rule 2(b); *id*, Advisory Committee Note. These requirements are discussed in more detail later.

Note that the motion can be directed to only one judgment. If the movant seeks relief from more than one judgment, separate motions must be filed attacking each one. Rules Governing § 2255 Proceedings, Rule 2(d).

§ 12.05. Number of copies, service on the government, and fees.

An original and two copies of the section 2255 motion must be filed with the district court clerk, unless local rules require a different number of copies. *See* Rules Governing § 2255 Proceedings, Rule 3(a).

Once the motion is filed, the clerk of the district court will serve a copy of the motion on the U.S. Attorney in that district, along with a notice of its filing. Rules Governing § 2255 Proceedings, Rule 3(b). Some local rules also require the movant to serve the pleading on the U.S. Attorney.

There is no filing fee. *See* Advisory Committee Note to Rule 3, Rules Governing § 2255 Proceedings. Moreover, the procedures contained in the Prison Litigation Reform Act, Pub. L. No. 104-134, 110 Stat. 1321 (1995), do not apply to section 2255 motions. *See, e.g., Anderson v. Singletary*, 111 F.3d 801, 803–05 (11th Cir. 1997) (collecting cases).

§ 12.06. Time for filing.

The time for filing a motion is governed by 28 U.S.C. § 2255(f), the one-year statute of limitation provision governing section 2255 motions. *See* Rules Governing § 2255 Proceedings, Rule 3(c). The statute of limitations is discussed in detail in Chapter 5.

§ 12.07. Special time considerations for inmate filings.

For inmates filing *pro se* motions, if certain procedures are correctly followed, the motion is considered filed on the date that it was placed in the prison's mail system rather than the later date that it arrived at the courthouse. The easiest way to obtain the benefit of this rule is to include, at the end of the motion, a signed declaration that indicates the date on which the motion was placed in the prison mail. The Model Form suggests the following language:

> I declare (or certify, verify, or state) under penalty of perjury that the foregoing is true and correct and that this Motion under 28 U.S.C. § 2255 was placed in the prison mailing system with first-class postage prepaid on ____________ (month, date, year).
>
> Executed (signed) on ______________(date).
>
> ______________________
>
> Signature of Movant

See Rules Governing § 2255 Proceedings, Rule 3(d); Model Form. If preferred, a notarized statement to the same effect may be included. Rules Governing § 2255 Proceedings, Rule 3(d).

II. Pleading the Legal and Factual Bases for Claims

The core of a section 2255 motion is its allegations regarding the infirmities in the movant's conviction and sentence. A section 2255 motion is a *pleading*, not a legal brief. It should therefore simply list the claims for relief and the facts supporting each claim. It is *critical,* however, that the relevant substantive law is carefully consulted in order to ensure that the motion pleads sufficient facts to state a *prima facie* case for relief as to each claim presented.

§ 12.08. Err on the side of over-inclusion of claims.

The motion must "specify all the grounds for relief available to the moving party." Rules Governing § 2255 Proceedings, Rule 2(b). Accordingly, movants should brainstorm the various legal claims implicated by the underlying facts and err on the side of over-inclusion of claims. The discussion and Appendix contained in Chapter 7 may help in this endeavor.

Moreover, as discussed in Chapter 5 and in Section VII of this chapter, amendment of a section 2255 motion to include a new claim is incredibly difficult, so it is easier to include all potential claims in the original motion, even if they appear only marginally meritorious, than to try to amend the motion later.

§ 12.09. Section 2255 requires the pleading of specific facts that show entitlement to relief.

Unlike the "notice pleading" rules that govern other federal civil actions, a section 2255 motion must "state the facts supporting each ground" for relief. Rules Governing § 2255 Proceedings, Rule 2(b). Although this fact-pleading requirement does not compel a movant to state every relevant fact or list every item of relevant evidence, it does require that the motion contain something more than general, nonspecific, conclusory allegations. As to each claim, sufficient facts must be alleged in order to show an entitlement to relief if those facts are proven.

The facts should be presented in a readable, narrative style, within the confines of the form being used or a numbered paragraph presentation. Be descriptive, but be accurate. Avoid hyperbole; the same effect can often be achieved through a straightforward description of the facts.

§ 12.10. Don't forget to plead prejudice.

Many of the claims typically found in section 2255 motions—ineffective assistance of counsel claims, for example—require a particularized factual showing of prejudice in order to state a *prima facie* case for relief. *See Strickland v. Washington*, 466 U.S. 668, 694, 104 S. Ct. 2052, 2068, 80 L. Ed. 2d 674 (1984). For such claims, take care to specify in detail the facts supporting the "prejudice" element, as well as all other elements of the claim.

III. Special Pleading Considerations

Chapters 8–11 describe the procedural hurdles a movant may have to leap before section 2255 relief may be obtained. These include: the procedural default doctrine, *see* Chapter 9; the nonretroactivity doctrine of *Teague v. Lane*, 489 U.S. 288, 109 S. Ct. 1060, 103 L. Ed. 2d 334 (1989), *see* Chapter 10; and the limitation on Fourth Amendment claims established in *Stone v. Powell*, 428 U.S. 465, 96 S. Ct. 3037, 49 L. Ed. 2d 1067 (1976), *see* Chapter 11. Many of these procedural defenses have pleading implications.

§ 12.11. Procedural default considerations.

As discussed in Chapter 9, section 2255 relief is generally barred on a "procedurally defaulted" claim—that is, a claim that could have been raised on direct appeal, but was not. The motion should, nonetheless, generally include such claims. The government can waive a procedural default either expressly or implicitly, or if the movant can show "cause and prejudice," or that she is actually innocent. *See* §§ 9.05, 9.07–9.17. For example, such claims may be considered on the merits if the failure to raise the claim on direct appeal was the result of ineffective assistance of counsel. *See* § 9.12. In such circumstances, include in the motion both the claim that should have been presented on direct appeal, as well as a claim of ineffective assistance of appellate counsel based on counsel's failure to raise the claim on appeal. And if appellate counsel's failure to raise the claim on appeal was the result of trial counsel's failure to preserve the claim at trial, consider raising trial counsel's ineffectiveness as an issue as well.

§ 12.12. To avoid *Teague*, ground claims in long-standing precedent.

As discussed in Chapter 10, the nonretroactivity doctrine of *Teague v. Lane*, 489 U.S. 288, 109 S. Ct. 1060, 103 L. Ed. 2d 334 (1989), bars section 2255 relief on any claim that seeks to create a new rule of criminal procedure or is based on a new rule of criminal procedure promulgated since the judgment became final on direct review. Accordingly, before filing the motion, determine the date on which the judgment became final,[3] and, to the extent possible, root all claims raised in the motion firmly in precedent that preexisted that date. If possible, avoid asserting that a claim is "novel" or "unique" or controlled by a recent "ground-breaking" decision, and instead try to plead the claim as a simple application of a principle of well-established law.

Importantly, because *Teague* is an affirmative defense that may be waived by the government, it is best not to explicitly mention *Teague* in the motion. *See* § 10.05.

§ 12.13. Pleading Fourth Amendment claims.

As previously discussed in Chapter 11, in most circuits, section 2255 relief is not available for claims premised on the Fourth Amendment unless the movant can show that the district court failed to provide an opportunity for full and fair litigation of the claim. Accordingly, if a Fourth Amendment claim is included in the motion, the motion should affirmatively set forth the reasons the prior court proceedings did not provide an "opportunity for full and fair litigation" of the Fourth Amendment claim. *See* § 11.06. In addition, try to brainstorm alternative constitutional claims that may be premised on the facts underlying the Fourth Amendment claim, such as a claim that trial counsel was ineffective for failing to file a motion to suppress, and include those claims in the motion as well. *See* § 11.03.

3. How to determine this date in discussed in § 10.11.

IV. Documents Accompanying the Motion

§ 12.14. Filing exhibits, a memorandum of law, a discovery request, or a motion for evidentiary hearing along with the motion is not required, but it can be helpful.

Because a section 2255 motion is a pleading, no exhibits demonstrating the *bona fides* of the facts alleged need be attached to it. If, however, such exhibits exist, it makes sense to submit them with the motion so that the district court can better evaluate the strength of the claims, as well as other matters, such as the need for appointment of counsel or whether an evidentiary hearing should be held. For the same reasons, it is often very helpful to file with the motion a memorandum of law in its support. Note, too, that although neither the Rules Governing § 2255 Proceedings nor the Model Form require that a memorandum of law accompany the motion, local rules may.

Formal motions for discovery, an evidentiary hearing, or other like requests generally should not be filed until *after* the motion has been filed. Of course, the strategies for filing such documents differ in every case, and you may well wish to take the offensive when litigating the motion. Indeed, the early filing of a compelling discovery request or motion for evidentiary hearing may thwart the court's summary resolution of the motion's claims.

§ 12.15. Application for leave to proceed *in forma pauperis*.

There is no filing fee for a section 2255 motion. It is, however, wise for indigent movants to file an application to proceed *in forma pauperis* along with the motion. Once a court grants *in forma pauperis* status, it can appoint counsel, and pay other costs that may arise in the course of litigation, such as for the preparation of transcripts. Applications to proceed *in forma pauperis* can be found on most district court websites. Links to district court websites can be found at *www.uscourts.gov/courtlinks*.

If the motion is filed on the Model Form, there is no need to file a separate *in forma pauperis* application. Instead, the movant need only fill out the last page of the Model Form and submit with the form "a certificate signed by an officer at the institution where you are confined showing the amount of money that the institution is holding for you." Model Form, Instruction #6. Local district "form" section 2255 motions may also eliminate the need for a separate *in forma pauperis* application.

§ 12.16. Motion for appointment of counsel.

There is no right to appointment of counsel in a section 2255 proceeding, unless the court determines that counsel is necessary for effective discovery or has ordered an evidentiary hearing. *See* Rules Governing § 2255 Proceedings, Rules 6(a) & 8(c); *United States v. Angelone*, 894 F.2d 1129, 1130 (9th Cir. 1990). In all other circumstances, the district court may appoint counsel upon a finding that the movant is indigent and appointment is required in "the interests of justice." *See* 18 U.S.C. § 3006A(a)(2)(B). Generally, counsel will not be appointed to assist with the preparation of a section 2255 motion; rather, courts will consider the claims presented in a *pro se* motion to determine whether appointment of counsel is required.

V. Venue, Docketing, and Assignment to Judges

§ 12.17. File the motion in the district court in which the movant was convicted and sentenced.

A section 2255 motion must be filed in the district court "which imposed the sentence" being challenged. 28 U.S.C. § 2255(a).

§ 12.18. Docketing.

Once a section 2255 motion is filed, the district court clerk must docket it as an entry in the original criminal proceeding that resulted in the judgment being challenged. Rules Governing § 2255 Proceedings, Rule 3(b). In some districts, however, the clerk will also simultaneously open a new civil case in which the section 2255 motion is the first docket entry, and any proceedings thereafter on the section 2255 motion will be docketed under the civil case number.

§ 12.19. The judge who conducted the proceedings being challenged will hear the motion.

Once the motion is filed, the clerk must "promptly" forward it to "the judge who conducted the trial and imposed sentence." Rules Governing § 2255 Proceedings, Rule 4(a). If, however, the sentence was imposed by a judge different from the one who presided over the guilty plea or trial, the motion will be forwarded "to the judge who conducted the proceedings being challenged." *Id.* If the appropriate judge is not available, the case will be assigned according to the court's random assignment procedure. *Id.*

Section 2255 motions are assigned to the trial judge so that the motion will "be passed on by the judge who is familiar with the facts and circumstances surrounding the trial." *See* Advisory Committee Note to Rule 4, Rules Governing § 2255 Proceedings. Nonetheless, the assignment of a section 2255 motion to the same judge whose rulings are under attack raises the possibility of bias. If the bias of the trial judge is an issue, the Advisory Committee Note to Rule 4 of the Rules Governing § 2255 Proceedings states that a movant is "not without remedy" and suggests that the movant "file an affidavit of bias," stating the facts supporting the claim of bias and asking to disqualify the trial judge. *Id.*

VI. Bail

§ 12.20. Bail will be granted rarely in section 2255 cases.

Federal courts have inherent authority to admit section 2255 movants to bail pending the decision of their cases, but that power is "to be exercised very sparingly." *Cherek v. United States*, 767 F.2d 335, 337 (7th Cir. 1985) (collecting cases). This "parsimonious exercise" of power derives from fact that a section 2255 movant's conviction has already become final, and "the interest in the finality of criminal proceedings is poorly served by deferring execution of sentence till long after the defendant has been convicted." *Id.*

Accordingly, before a section 2255 movant may be released on bail, she must be able to show a substantial claim of law upon which there is a high probability of success, or some exceptional circumstance that makes the grant of bail necessary in the interests of justice. *See United States v. Mett*, 41 F.3d 1281, 1282 (9th Cir. 1994); *Ostrer v. United States*, 584 F.2d 594, 596 n.1 (2d Cir. 1978); *Aronson v. May*, 85 S. Ct. 3, 5, 13 L. Ed. 2d 6 (1964) (Douglas, J., on application for bail).

VII. Amending or Supplementing the Motion

The near impossibility of obtaining relief on a second or successive section 2255 motion makes it imperative to attempt to litigate all claims in the context of the first motion.[4] Accordingly, the movant should consider amending or supplementing the motion if, after filing the motion, new claims or new facts are uncovered, or different or additional relief is desired.

4. Second and successive motions are discussed in Chapter 19.

§ 12.21. Federal Rule of Civil Procedure 15 governs amendments to a section 2255 motion.

A section 2255 motion may be amended in the same manner as any other civil action, and that process is governed by Federal Rule of Civil Procedure 15. *See* Rules Governing § 2255 Proceedings, Rule 12; *United States v. Saenz*, 282 F.3d 354, 355–56 (5th Cir. 2002); *Mederos v. United States*, 218 F.3d 1252, 1254 (11th Cir. 2000); 28 U.S.C. § 2242. Generally, an amended pleading completely supersedes the original pleading, and once a pleading is "amended," the only issues before the court are those raised in the text of the amended pleading, unless the amended pleading refers to or adopts the prior pleading. *See, e.g., Newell v. Hanks*, 283 F.3d 827, 834 (7th Cir. 2002); 6 C. Wright, A. Miller & M. Kane, Federal Practice and Procedure § 1476, at 556–57 (1990 & 2007 Supp.).

§ 12.22. A motion may be amended once as of right.

Federal Rule of Civil Procedure 15(a) allows amendment "once *as a matter of course*" without leave of court at any time before the movant is served with the government's responsive pleading. Fed. R. Civ. P. 15(a)(1)(A) & (B) (emphasis added). Only an answer is considered a responsive pleading for purposes of Rule 15(a); a motion to dismiss does not qualify. *See Rogers v. United States*, 180 F.3d 349, 352 & n.4 (1st Cir. 1999). Therefore, neither the filing *nor the granting* of a motion to dismiss before the answer is filed terminates the right to amend.

§ 12.23. After the government answers, amendment is only with leave of court or consent.

After the government files its answer, a motion may be amended only with leave of court or written consent of the government. Fed. R. Civ. P. 15(a)(2). "The court should freely give leave when justice so requires." *Id.* That is,

> [i]n the absence of any apparent or declared reason—such as undue delay, bad faith or dilatory motive on the part of the movant, repeated failure to cure deficiencies by amendments previously allowed, undue prejudice to the opposing party by virtue of allowance of the amendment, futility of amendment, etc.—the leave sought should, as the rules require, be "freely given."

Foman v. Davis, 371 U.S. 178, 182, 83 S. Ct. 227, 230, 9 L. Ed. 2d 222 (1962).

§ 12.24. Amendments and supplements differ in important ways.

While Rule 15(a) governs "amendments" to pleadings, Rule 15(d) allows for "supplemental" pleadings. Fed. R. Civ. P. 15(d). The distinction is of little moment in most circumstances, but there are at least two ways in which the nomenclature matters. First, although a party may amend a motion as of right before a responsive pleading is filed under Rule 15(a), a supplement under Rule 15(d) *always* requires leave of court. *See* Fed. R. Civ. P. 15(d); *United States v. Hicks*, 283 F.3d 380, 385 (D.C. Cir. 2002).

Second, the distinguishing feature of a supplement is that it must set forth a "transaction, occurrence, or event that happened after the date of the pleading to be supplemented." Fed. R. Civ. P. 15(d). Accordingly, supplements generally relate to events that have transpired *since* the filing of the original pleading, whereas amendments typically involve matters in place *prior* to the filing of the original pleading. *See Hicks*, 283 F.3d at 284.

§ 12.25. The statute of limitations complicates the amendment/supplementation process.

Unfortunately, section 2255's one-year statute of limitations complicates the process of amending or supplementing a section 2255 motion. Any amendment or supplement to a motion will not be timely unless the claims contained therein are independently timely under § 2255(f), or the court determines that the amendment or supplement "relates back" to the date of the original motion under Federal Rule of Civil Procedure 15(c). Chapter 5 discusses the "relation-back" doctrine, and other complications caused by the statute of limitations when one attempts to amend or supplement a motion. *See* §§ 5.36–5.38.

VIII. Appendix

A. Federal Rule of Civil Procedure 15 (2008)

Rule 15. Amended and Supplemental Pleadings

(a) Amendments Before Trial.

- **(1)** ***Amending as a Matter of Course.*** A party may amend its pleading once as a matter of course:
  - **(A)** before being served with a responsive pleading; or
  - **(B)** within 20 days after serving the pleading if a responsive pleading is not allowed and the action is not yet on the trial calendar.
- **(2)** ***Other Amendments.*** In all other cases, a party may amend its pleading only with the opposing party's written consent or the court's leave. The court should freely give leave when justice so requires.
- **(3)** ***Time to Respond.*** Unless the court orders otherwise, any required response to an amended pleading must be made within the time remaining to respond to the original pleading

or within 10 days after service of the amended pleading, whichever is later.

(b) Amendments During and After Trial.

(1) ***Based on an Objection at Trial.*** If, at trial, a party objects that evidence is not within the issues raised in the pleadings, the court may permit the pleadings to be amended. The court should freely permit an amendment when doing so will aid in presenting the merits and the objecting party fails to satisfy the court that the evidence would prejudice that party's action or defense on the merits. The court may grant a continuance to enable the objecting party to meet the evidence.

(2) ***For Issues Tried by Consent.*** When an issue not raised by the pleadings is tried by the parties' express or implied consent, it must be treated in all respects as if raised in the pleadings. A party may move—at any time, even after judgment—to amend the pleadings to conform them to the evidence and to raise an unpleaded issue. But failure to amend does not affect the result of the trial of that issue.

(c) Relation Back of Amendments.

(1) ***When an Amendment Relates Back.*** An amendment to a pleading relates back to the date of the original pleading when:

(A) the law that provides the applicable statute of limitations allows relation back;

(B) the amendment asserts a claim or defense that arose out of the conduct, transaction, or occurrence set out—or attempted to be set out—in the original pleading; or

(C) the amendment changes the party or the naming of the party against whom a claim is asserted, if Rule 15(c)(1)(B) is satisfied and if, within the period provided by Rule 4(m) for serving the summons and complaint, the party to be brought in by amendment:

(i) received such notice of the action that it will not be prejudiced in defending on the merits; and

(ii) knew or should have known that the action would have been brought against it, but for a mistake concerning the proper party's identity.

(2) ***Notice to the United States.*** When the United States or a United States officer or agency is added as a defendant by amendment, the notice requirements of Rule 15(c)(1)(C)(i) and (ii) are satisfied if, during the stated period, process was delivered or mailed to the United States attorney or the

United States attorney's designee, to the Attorney General of the United States, or to the officer or agency.

(d) Supplemental Pleadings. On motion and reasonable notice, the court may, on just terms, permit a party to serve a supplemental pleading setting out any transaction, occurrence, or event that happened after the date of the pleading to be supplemented. The court may permit supplementation even though the original pleading is defective in stating a claim or defense. The court may order that the opposing party plead to the supplemental pleading within a specified time.

Chapter 13

Summary Proceedings, the Government's Response, and the Movant's Reply

Contents

Introduction

Once the movant has filed a section 2255 motion, Rule 4 of the Rules Governing § 2255 Proceedings requires the district court to consider whether the motion is frivolous and therefore subject to summary dismissal. If the court does not summarily dismiss the motion under Rule 4, it must order a response from the government. Thereafter, the movant may file a reply or otherwise respond to the government's actions.

I. Summary Dismissal

§ 13.01. Rule 4(b) allows for summary dismissal.

The Rules Governing § 2255 Proceedings give district courts the authority to dismiss facially nonmeritorious motions summarily without first calling for an answer. Once the motion is filed and assigned to a judge, Rule 4(b) of the Rules Governing § 2255 Proceedings requires the assigned judge to "promptly examine it" to determine "[i]f it plainly appears from the motion, any attached exhibits, and the record of prior proceedings that the [movant] is not entitled to relief." Rules Governing § 2255 Proceedings, Rule 4(b).

If it does not "plainly appear[]" that the movant "is not entitled to relief," and the motion is *not* dismissed summarily, then "the judge must order the United States attorney to file an answer, motion, or other response within a fixed time, or to take other action the judge may order." *Id.* If it *does* "plainly appear[]" that the movant "is not entitled to relief," then the court "must dismiss the motion" without service on the government, and "direct the clerk to notify the moving party." *Id.*

§ 13.02. Summary dismissal of "palpably incredible" or "patently false" allegations.

Summary dismissal by the court under Rule 4(b) is justified only if the "allegations, when viewed against the record [available to the court are] so palpably incredible, so patently frivolous or false, as to warrant summary dismissal." *Blackledge v. Allison*, 431 U.S. 63, 76, 97 S. Ct. 1621, 1630, 52 L. Ed. 2d 136 (1977) (internal quotation marks and citation omitted). To meet this standard, the record before the court must (1) demonstrate conclusively that the motion's allegations fail to state a claim for relief, *see, e.g., Baumann v. United States*, 692 F.2d 565, 572 (9th Cir. 1982), or (2) wholly preclude the court from finding any facts to support the claims asserted, *see United States v. Cermark*, 622 F.2d 1049, 1051–52 (1st Cir. 1980) (movant's factual allegations were "palpably false"). The judge's own recollection of the prior proceedings may be relied on to determine whether summary dismissal is appropriate. *See, e.g., Blackledge*, 431 U.S. at 74 n.4, 97 S. Ct. at 1629 n.4.

Importantly, Rule 4(b) also allows summary dismissal where the claims are vague or conclusory, and therefore fail to comply with the "fact-pleading" requirement applicable to section 2255 motions. *See Blackledge*, 431 U.S. at 75 & n.7, 97 S. Ct. at 1630 & n.7.[1] In such circumstances, however, the court may take actions short of outright dismissal, such as allowing the movant to amend the motion to provide clarifying factual support. *See, e.g., Sanders v. United States*, 373 U.S. 1, 19, 83 S. Ct. 1068, 1079, 10 L. Ed. 2d 148 (1963) (noting that although district court had the power to dismiss section 2255 motion "because it stated only bald legal conclusions with no supporting factual allegations, . . . the better course might have been to direct petitioner to amend his motion"); *United States v. Thomas*, 221 F.3d 430, 437–38 (3d Cir. 2000).

1. This fact-pleading requirement, which is stated in Rule 2(b), Rules Governing § 2255 Proceedings, is discussed in Chapter 12. *See* § 12.09.

§ 13.03. *Pro se* pleadings must be liberally construed.

The vast majority of section 2255 motions are brought by prisoners proceeding without legal representation. Generally, the allegations of a *pro se* applicant, "however inartfully pleaded," are subject to "less stringent standards than formal pleadings drafted by lawyers." *Haines v. Kerner*, 404 U.S. 519, 520, 92 S. Ct. 594, 596, 30 L. Ed. 2d 652 (1972) *(per curiam)*. As such, courts will "liberally construe" *pro se* pleadings in deciding whether or not to dismiss them summarily. *See, e.g., United States v. Howard*, 381 F.3d 873, 883 (9th Cir. 2004); *Green v. United States*, 260 F.3d 78, 83 (2d Cir. 2001).

II. The Government's Response

§ 13.04. For nonfrivolous motions, the court must order an answer or other response.

If a motion is not dismissed summarily, then "the judge must order the United States attorney to file an answer, motion, or other response . . . , or to take other action the judge may order." Rules Governing § 2255 Proceedings, Rule 4(b). However, the government is "not required to answer the motion unless a judge so orders." Rules Governing § 2255 Proceedings, Rule 5(a). If the court allows the government to file a "response" rather than an "answer," the government may file a nonsubstantive response, such as a motion to dismiss on timeliness grounds. It is the judge who determines the date on which the answer or response is due. Rules Governing § 2255 Proceedings, Rule 4(b).

§ 13.05. The government's answer must respond to the motion's allegations.

If the court orders the government to answer the motion, Rule 5 of the Rules Governing § 2255 Proceedings controls its contents. The purpose of the answer is to frame the issues in dispute, as well as to ferret out unmeritorious motions. *See* Advisory Committee Note to Rule 5, Rules Governing § 2254 Cases (incorporated by reference in Advisory Committee Note to Rule 5, Rules Governing § 2255 Proceedings). To this end, Rule 5 requires that the answer "address the allegations in the motion." Rules Governing § 2255 Proceedings, Rule 5(b). In addition, the answer must also state whether the movant "has used any other federal remedies, including any prior post-conviction motions," and whether the movant "received an evidentiary hearing." *Id.* Neither Rule 5, nor the Advisory Committee Notes, set out any further requirements for the answer's contents.

§ 13.06. The government must attach relevant briefing and transcripts to the answer.

If the answer refers to "briefs or transcripts of the prior proceedings that are not available in the court's records," the court "must order" the government "to furnish them within a reasonable time that will not unduly delay the proceedings." Rules Governing § 2255 Proceedings, Rule 5(c).

III. The Movant's Reply

§ 13.07. Although not required, a reply should be filed in most cases.

A section 2255 movant "may," but need not, "submit a reply to the respondent's answer or other pleading." Rules Governing § 2255 Proceedings, Rule 5(d). The rules do not specify a time to reply. Instead, any reply must be filed "within a time fixed by the judge." *Id.*

Although a reply (sometimes called a "traverse") is not required, in most cases one should be filed to respond to the government's answer. Certainly, a reply should be filed if the answer contains misleading or inaccurate information, or raises legal defenses that might bar full consideration of the merits. Such defenses include procedural default, *see* Chapter 9; the *Teague v. Lane* non retroactivity bar, *see* Chapter 10; or the *Stone v. Powell* doctrine, *see* Chapter 11. The failure to file a reply in such circumstances may invite denial of the claim by the court.

IV. Motions for Summary Judgment

§ 13.08. Either party may move for summary judgment as to any of the claims in the motion.

Either the movant or the government may file a motion for summary judgment or judgment on the pleadings as to any or all claims in the motion. *See* Rule 12, Rules Governing § 2255 Proceedings (incorporating the appropriate sections of the Federal Rules of Civil and Criminal Procedure); *Blackledge*, 431 U.S. at 80, 97 S. Ct. at 1632 ("As in civil cases generally, there exists a procedure [in habeas corpus cases] whose purpose is to test whether facially adequate allegations have sufficient basis in fact to warrant plenary presentation of evidence. That procedure is, of course, the motion for summary judgment.")

Summary judgment is particularly appropriate for cases in which the section 2255 motion contains multiple claims, some of which require evidentiary findings to resolve and some of which do not. Or a movant may wish to move for summary judgment where, for example, the answer admits the movant's version of the controlling facts, or a recent decision of a higher court controls and mandates relief. Summary judgment motions may also be premised on facts developed through discovery or expansion of the record,[2] or on affidavits that are the result of additional investigation conducted by the parties.

Summary judgment motions should be filed using the procedures found in Rule 56 of the Federal Rules of Civil Procedure, which is set out in the Appendix to this chapter.

V. Appendix

A. Federal Rule of Civil Procedure 56 (2008)

Rule 56. Summary Judgment

(a) By a Claiming Party. A party claiming relief may move, with or without supporting affidavits, for summary judgment on all or part of the claim. The motion may be filed at any time after:

(1) 20 days have passed from commencement of the action; or

(2) the opposing party serves a motion for summary judgment.

(b) By a Defending Party. A party against whom relief is sought may move at any time, with or without supporting affidavits, for summary judgment on all or part of the claim.

(c) Serving the Motion; Proceedings. The motion must be served at least 10 days before the day set for the hearing. An opposing party may serve opposing affidavits before the hearing day. The judgment sought should be rendered if the pleadings, the discovery and disclosure materials on file, and any affidavits show that there is no genuine issue as to any material fact and that the movant is entitled to judgment as a matter of law.

(d) Case Not Fully Adjudicated on the Motion.

(1) ***Establishing Facts***. If summary judgment is not rendered on the whole action, the court should, to the extent practicable, determine what material facts are not genuinely at issue. The court should so determine by examining the pleadings and evidence before it and by interrogating the attorneys. It should then issue an order specifying what facts—including items of damages or other relief—are not genuinely at issue. The facts so specified must be treated as established in the action.

2. Discovery and expansion of the record are discussed in Chapter 15.

(2) ***Establishing Liability***. An interlocutory summary judgment may be rendered on liability alone, even if there is a genuine issue on the amount of damages.

(e) **Affidavits; Further Testimony**.

(1) ***In General***. A supporting or opposing affidavit must be made on personal knowledge, set out facts that would be admissible in evidence, and show that the affiant is competent to testify on the matters stated. If a paper or part of a paper is referred to in an affidavit, a sworn or certified copy must be attached to or served with the affidavit. The court may permit an affidavit to be supplemented or opposed by depositions, answers to interrogatories, or additional affidavits.

(2) ***Opposing Party's Obligation to Respond***. When a motion for summary judgment is properly made and supported, an opposing party may not rely merely on allegations or denials in its own pleading; rather, its response must—by affidavits or as otherwise provided in this rule—set out specific facts showing a genuine issue for trial. If the opposing party does not so respond, summary judgment should, if appropriate, be entered against that party.

(f) **When Affidavits Are Unavailable**. If a party opposing the motion shows by affidavit that, for specified reasons, it cannot present facts essential to justify its opposition, the court may:

(1) deny the motion;

(2) order a continuance to enable affidavits to be obtained, depositions to be taken, or other discovery to be undertaken; or

(3) issue any other just order.

(g) **Affidavit Submitted in Bad Faith**. If satisfied that an affidavit under this rule is submitted in bad faith or solely for delay, the court must order the submitting party to pay the other party the reasonable expenses, including attorney's fees, it incurred as a result. An offending party or attorney may also be held in contempt.

CHAPTER 14

Magistrate Judge Practice

Contents

Introduction

§ 14.01. In many jurisdictions, section 2255 motions are first considered by magistrate judges.

In many jurisdictions, section 2255 motions are referred to U.S. Magistrate Judges for initial consideration either of some preliminary matter relating to litigation of the motion or the motion in its entirety. When considered together, the Magistrates Act, 28 U.S.C. § 631 *et. seq.*, the Rules Governing § 2255 Proceedings, and the Federal Rules of Civil Procedure empower district courts to designate magistrate judges to consider both nondispositive and dispositive matters in section 2255 proceedings. *See* 28 U.S.C. § 636(b); Rules 8(b) & 10, Rules Governing § 2255 Proceedings; Fed. R. Civ. P. 72(a).[1]

I. Nondispositive Matters

§ 14.02. Magistrate judges may hear nondispositive matters in all cases.

In all federal cases, including section 2255 proceedings, the Magistrates Act allows a district judge to designate a magistrate judge to adjudicate and resolve almost any "nondispositive" matter. *See* 28 U.S.C. § 636(b)(1)(A) (district judge "may designate a magistrate judge to hear and determine

1. The text of both 28 U.S.C. § 636(b) and FED. R. CIV. P. 72(a) can be found in the Appendix to this chapter.

any pretrial matter pending before the court, except a motion for injunctive relief, for judgment on the pleadings, for summary judgment, . . . to dismiss or to permit maintenance of a class action, to dismiss for failure to state a claim upon which relief can be granted, and to involuntarily dismiss an action"). A matter is considered "nondispositive" if its grant or denial would *not* result in a final, appealable judgment that would dispose of the entire case. In section 2255 proceedings, nondispositive matters generally include such things as discovery motions, motions to proceed *in forma pauperis,* motions for appointment of counsel, and continuance motions.

§ 14.03. You have ten days from the date of service of the magistrate's order to file objections.

Once designated to hear a nondispositive matter, magistrate judges must "promptly" conduct the required proceedings and, thereafter, issue a written order setting forth the decision on the matter. Fed. R. Civ. P. 72(a). The parties have ten days after being served with the magistrate judge's order to file objections to it. *Id.* That is, the ten days run from the date of *service*, not the date that the order was filed. The ten-day period is counted using the method prescribed in Federal Rule of Civil Procedure 6. Under Rule 6(a), weekends and federal holidays do not count toward the ten-day period. *See* Fed. R. Civ. P. 6(a)(2).[2]

If objections are timely filed, the district judge "must" consider them, and "modify or set aside" any part of the order that "is clearly erroneous or contrary to law." Fed. R. Civ. P. 72(a).

§ 14.04. Failure to object may preclude review by the district court and court of appeals.

Movants must proceed with caution when it comes to the filing of objections on nondispositive matters. A party cannot "assign as error a defect" in the magistrate judge's order to which no timely objection was made. *Id.* Accordingly, the failure to timely file objections to the magistrate judge's order will waive review of that order by the district judge and the court of appeals. *See id.*, Advisory Committee Notes ("objections to magistrate's orders that are not timely shall not be considered"). Because of the importance of filing objections to the magistrate judge's order in a timely man-

2. The text of Fed. R. Civ. P. 6 can be found in the Appendix to Chapter 5. Some circuits have held that the "mailbox" rule for pleadings filed by *pro se* prisoners—which deems a document filed upon delivery to prison officials for mailing—applies to a *pro se* prisoner's written objections to a magistrate judge's report. *See* Thompson v. Raspberry, 993 F.2d 513, 515 (5th Cir. 1993) (*per curiam*); Dunn v. White, 880 F.2d 1188, 1190 (10th Cir. 1989).

ner, if you are uncertain whether you will be able to file within the ten days allotted, ask the district judge for an extension of time before the ten-day period has run.

II. Dispositive Matters

§ 14.05. Magistrate judges may hear dispositive matters in section 2255 cases without the consent of the parties.

In most federal civil proceedings, the Magistrates Act requires the consent of the parties before a district judge may refer dispositive matters to a magistrate judge. *See* 28 U.S.C. § 636(c). That is not true, however, in section 2255 proceedings. A district court may, in its discretion, refer a section 2255 case *as a whole* to a magistrate judge with instructions to conduct whatever proceedings and propose whatever dispositions are appropriate, whether or not the parties consent. § 636(b)(1)(B); Rules Governing § 2255 Proceedings, Rules 8(b) & 10. *See McCarthy v. Bronson*, 500 U.S. 136, 140, 111 S. Ct. 1737, 1740, 114 L. Ed. 2d 194 (1991).

§ 14.06. Local practice controls whether a case is referred to a magistrate judge for disposition.

Neither the Magistrates Act nor the Rules Governing § 2255 Proceedings specify exactly how district judges are to decide whether to refer a section 2255 case to a magistrate judge for disposition. Rather, it is local court rules and practices—or the caseloads and personal preferences of specific district judges—that generally control whether it is a magistrate judge or a district judge who will hear a section 2255 motion. For example, in some districts, all noncapital section 2255 matters are automatically referred to a magistrate judge. In others, only *pro se* noncapital section 2255 motions are referred. In still others, the decision to order a referral lies with the district judge to whom the motion is assigned. Accordingly, to determine whether your section 2255 motion will be considered initially by a magistrate judge, you should check the local rules, and, if possible, consult someone with experience litigating section 2255 cases in your district.

§ 14.07. Once a case is referred, the magistrate judge conducts all proceedings and issues a report with a recommended disposition.

When the district judge refers an entire case to the magistrate judge, the magistrate judge makes all the preliminary procedural decisions about the case and may conduct hearings, including evidentiary hearings. 28 U.S.C. § 636(b)(1)(B); Rules Governing § 2255 Proceedings, Rules 8(b) & 10. The magistrate judge also makes a preliminary determination of the merits of the claims in a report to the district judge. After the magistrate judge files the report's "proposed findings of fact and recommendations for disposition," the court clerk must serve the parties with a copy. Rule 8(b), Rules Governing § 2255 Proceedings; *accord* § 636(b)(1)(C).

It is the district judge who has the final say as to whether relief is granted or denied; only the district judge has the power to enter final judgment. Importantly, however, the level of scrutiny that the district judge (and the court of appeals) will give to the findings in the magistrate judge's report and its recommended disposition depends largely on whether a party has timely filed objections to that report.

§ 14.08. Failure to timely object to the magistrate's report may preclude further review.

Simply by objecting in a timely manner, a party may obtain a *de novo* determination by the district judge of any aspect of the magistrate judge's report on a dispositive matter. § 636(b)(1); Rules Governing § 2255 Proceedings, Rule 8(b). The failure to file timely objections, however, has serious repercussions. As discussed later in § 14.10, the failure to timely object may preclude the district court from conducting *de novo* review of unfavorable portions of the magistrate judge's report *and* entirely preclude appellate review by the court of appeals. Thus, if review by the district judge or court of appeals of any aspect of the magistrate judge's report is desired, it is critical that comprehensive objections be filed in a timely manner.

§ 14.09. File objections to the report within ten days from the date of service.

The district judge is required to consider a party's objections to a magistrate judge's report *only* if those objections are filed in a timely manner. Unless the magistrate judge's report expressly states otherwise, any party who wishes to file objections to any aspect of the report must do so within ten days after being *served* with the report. Rules Governing § 2255 Proceedings, Rule 8(b); § 636(b)(1). That is, the ten-day period runs from the date of service of the magistrate judge's report, *not* the date the report was filed.

The ten-day period is counted using the method prescribed in Federal Rule of Civil Procedure 6.[3] Because of the importance of filing objections to the magistrate judge's report in a timely manner, if you are uncertain whether you will be able to file within the ten days allotted, move the district judge for an extension of time before the ten-day period has run.

§ 14.10. Unless timely objections are filed, the district court need not conduct *de novo* review.

Once a timely objection is filed to a magistrate judge's report on dispositive matters, the district judge is required to "make a *de novo* determination of those portions of the report or specified proposed findings or recommendations to which objection is made." § 636(b)(1); *accord* Rule 8(b), Rules Governing § 2255 Proceedings.[4] That is, if a party timely objects to some aspect of the magistrate judge's report, the district judge:

(1) *must* review that aspect of the report *de novo*—whether it is a legal conclusion or a factual finding. *See Thomas v. Arn*, 474 U.S. 140, 150 & n.8, 106 S. Ct. 466, 472 & n.8, 88 L. Ed. 2d 435 (1985). Where the magistrate judge held an evidentiary hearing, this *de novo* review requires the district judge to review the record of the hearing. Mere review of the magistrate judge's report and recommendations will not suffice: "In conducting [*de novo*] review, the district court must, at a minimum, listen to a tape recording or read a transcript of the evidentiary hearing." *Jones v. Pillow*, 47 F.3d 251, 252 (8th Cir. 1995) (internal quotation marks omitted). *Accord Coolspring Stone Supply, Inc. v. American States Life Ins. Co.*, 10 F.3d 144, 147 (3d Cir. 1993); *United States v. Remsing*, 874 F.2d 614, 618 (9th Cir. 1989) (collecting cases).

(2) may "reject, or modify, in whole or in part" any finding, reasoning, or conclusion with which the district judge disagrees; that is,

---

3. The text of FED. R. CIV. P. 6 can be found in the Appendix to Chapter 5. Some circuits have held that the "mailbox" rule for pleadings filed by *pro se* prisoners—which deems a document filed upon delivery to prison officials for mailing—applies to a *pro se* prisoner's written objections to a magistrate judge's report. *See* Thompson v. Raspberry, 993 F.2d 513, 515 (5th Cir. 1993) (*per curiam*); Dunn v. White, 880 F.2d 1188, 1190 (10th Cir. 1989).

4. As discussed earlier, the district court need only review the magistrate judge's ruling on *non*dispositive matters to determine whether they are "clearly erroneous or contrary to law." *See* § 14.03.

the district judge may substitute her judgment for that of the magistrate judge on the matter. § 636(b)(1); *accord* Rules Governing § 2255 Proceedings, Rule 8(b).

(3) may determine whether it is necessary to "receive further evidence or recommit the matter to the magistrate with instructions." § 636(b)(1).

In sharp contrast, if no timely objection is filed, a district judge may adopt the magistrate judge's recommendation as a final judgment without so much as having read it. *See Thomas*, 474 U.S. at 152, 106 S. Ct. at 473. But the district judge is not *required* to adopt the magistrate judge's recommendation, despite the lack of an objection. Even if no objection is made, the district judge retains the discretion to undertake further review of the magistrate judge's report, "under a *de novo* or any other standard." *Id.*, 474 U.S. at 154, 106 S. Ct. at 474.

§ 14.11. Unless you object, you may forfeit review in the court of appeals.

It is also critical to file objections to the magistrate judge's report on dispositive matters if you want the court of appeals to review some aspect of that report. In the vast majority of circuits, the failure to file objections to a magistrate judge's report will *entirely preclude* appellate review of the factual determinations and legal conclusions contained therein. *See, e.g., Moore v. United States*, 950 F.2d 656, 659 (10th Cir. 1999) ("Our waiver rule provides that the failure to make timely objection to the magistrate's findings or recommendations waives appellate review of both factual and legal questions."); *Thomas*, 474 U.S. at 146 n.4, 106 S. Ct. at 470 n.4 (noting that the First, Second, Fourth, Fifth, and Sixth Circuits have adopted such a rule). In other circuits, the failure to file objections also precludes appellate review, but only of the factual findings contained in the report. *See id.*, 474 U.S. at 146 n.4, 106 S. Ct. at 470 n.4 (noting that Ninth and Eleventh Circuits "have concluded that the failure to file objections waives only factual issues on the appeal").

Although these waiver rules need not be applied when the "interests of justice" so dictate, *Thomas*, 474 U.S. at 155, 106 S. Ct. at 475, the safest course to ensure that the court of appeals will review any objection you may have to the legal conclusions and factual determinations contained in the magistrate judge's report is to file comprehensive objections in a timely manner. The failure to do so may result in the inability to obtain appellate review of the denial of section 2255 relief.

III. Appendix

A. 28 U.S.C. § 636(b) (2008)

§ 636. Jurisdiction, powers, and temporary assignment

* * *

(b) **(1)** Notwithstanding any provision of law to the contrary—

(A) a judge may designate a magistrate judge to hear and determine any pretrial matter pending before the court, except a motion for injunctive relief, for judgment on the pleadings, for summary judgment, to dismiss or quash an indictment or information made by the defendant, to suppress evidence in a criminal case, to dismiss or to permit maintenance of a class action, to dismiss for failure to state a claim upon which relief can be granted, and to involuntarily dismiss an action. A judge of the court may reconsider any pretrial matter under this subparagraph (A) where it has been shown that the magistrate judge's order is clearly erroneous or contrary to law.

(B) a judge may also designate a magistrate judge to conduct hearings, including evidentiary hearings, and to submit to a judge of the court proposed findings of fact and recommendations for the disposition, by a judge of the court, of any motion excepted in subparagraph (A), of applications for posttrial relief made by individuals convicted of criminal offenses and of prisoner petitions challenging conditions of confinement.

(C) the magistrate judge shall file his proposed findings and recommendations under subparagraph (B) with the court and a copy shall forthwith be mailed to all parties.

Within ten days after being served with a copy, any party may serve and file written objections to such proposed findings and recommendations as provided by rules of court. A judge of the court shall make a de novo determination of those portions of the report or specified proposed findings or recommendations to which objection is made. A judge of the court may accept, reject, or modify, in whole or in part, the findings or recommendations made by the magistrate judge. The judge may also receive further evidence or recommit the matter to the magistrate judge with instructions.

(2) A judge may designate a magistrate judge to serve as a special master pursuant to the applicable provisions of this title and the Federal Rules of Civil Procedure for the United States district courts. A judge may designate a magistrate judge to serve as a special master in any civil case, upon consent of the parties, without regard to the provisions of rule 53(b) of the Federal Rules of Civil Procedure for the United States district courts.

(3) A magistrate judge may be assigned such additional duties as are not inconsistent with the Constitution and laws of the United States.

(4) Each district court shall establish rules pursuant to which the magistrate judges shall discharge their duties.

* * *

B. Federal Rule of Civil Procedure 72(a) (2008)

Rule 72. Magistrate Judges: Pretrial Order

(a) **Nondispositive Matters**. When a pretrial matter not dispositive of a party's claim or defense is referred to a magistrate judge to hear and decide, the magistrate judge must promptly conduct the required proceedings and, when appropriate, issue a written order stating the decision. A party may serve and file objections to the order within 10 days after being served with a copy. A party may not assign as error a defect in the order not timely objected to. The district judge in the case must consider timely objections and modify or set aside any part of the order that is clearly erroneous or is contrary to law.

* * *

CHAPTER 15

Expanding the Record, Discovery, and Evidentiary Hearings

Contents

Introduction

§ 15.01. Use fact-development procedures to ensure a complete record.

The proceedings before the district court will usually be the last and best opportunity to develop facts and present evidence in support of the claims raised in a section 2255 motion. Consequently, care should be taken to ensure that all favorable evidence is presented to the district court prior to its decision on the merits of the claims. This is especially true given that it is extremely difficult to obtain relief on a second or successive section 2255 motion.[1]

§ 15.02. You cannot rely upon an evidentiary hearing to develop the facts.

The most typical vehicle for presentation of the facts in support of claims in a section 2255 motion is an evidentiary hearing before the district court. An evidentiary hearing, however, is not a place for fact *development.* The best evidentiary hearings, like the best trials, are those where there are no surprises; where, because of extensive investigation and preparation, and the prior use of the tools available for fact development, the hearing is an organized presentation of the facts in a light most favorable to the movant.

1. Second and successive section 2255 motions are discussed in Chapter 19.

Moreover, "[c]ourts are busy places. Not surprisingly, then, evidentiary hearings on [section 2255] motions are the exception, not the rule." *United States v. McGill*, 11 F.3d 223, 225 (1st Cir. 1993). Because the overburdened federal district courts are often reluctant to hold evidentiary hearings, if you are granted a hearing, it will likely be limited in scope. For these reasons, as early in the process as possible, you should endeavor to develop the facts to support all of your claims using as many of the available fact-development tools as possible, and to present those facts to the district court in a timely manner. To this end, you should consider whether a motion to expand the record or a discovery motion would assist with full development of the factual record supporting your claims.

I. Expanding the Record

§ 15.03. Rule 7 governs expansion of the record.

The record before the district court need not be limited to the record of the prior criminal proceeding. Rule 7 of the Rules Governing § 2255 Proceedings explicitly allows the district court to "expand the record" to include additional materials submitted by the parties. Expanding the record is a relatively uncomplicated way to place favorable evidence before the court, given that it allows the record to be expanded with many kinds of documentary evidence that would constitute inadmissible hearsay in other federal proceedings. Moreover, even if the district court denies the motion to expand the record, the materials presented therewith "are part of the record on appeal." *See Schlup v. Delo*, 513 U.S. 298, 308 n.18, 115 S. Ct. 851, 858 n.18, 130 L. Ed. 2d 808 (1995).

§ 15.04. The record can be expanded with virtually any relevant materials.

Under Rule 7, either on a party's motion or *sua sponte,* "the judge may direct the parties to expand the record by submitting additional materials relating to the motion."[2] Rules Governing § 2255 Proceedings, Rule 7(a). Rule 7 further provides that the record can be expanded to "include letters predating the filing of the motion, documents, exhibits, and answers under oath to written interrogatories propounded by the judge. Affidavits also may be submitted and considered as part of the record." Rules Governing § 2255 Proceedings, Rule 7(b).

2. The district court may deny a motion to expand the record if it has summarily dismissed the motion under Rule 4 of the Rules Governing § 2255 Proceedings. *See* Rules Governing § 2255 Proceedings, Rule 7(a). Summary dismissals are discussed in Chapter 13.

Under Rule 7, virtually *any* materials relating to the motion can be added to the record "to clarify the relevant facts." *Vasquez v. Hillery*, 474 U.S. 254, 258, 106 S. Ct. 617, 620, 88 L. Ed. 2d 598 (1986) (statistical analysis sought by district court). *See, e.g., Ruiz v. United States*, 339 F.3d 39, 41 (1st Cir. 2003) (police report movant obtained via public records request); *United States v. Chacon-Palomares*, 208 F.3d 1157, 1160 (9th Cir. 2000) (affidavits from both parties); *United States v. Nieuwsma*, 779 F.2d 1359, 1360 n.3 (8th Cir. 1985) (pre-sentence investigation report). Moreover, the materials submitted under Rule 7 need not relate only to the *merits* of the claims in the motion; the record may also be expanded with materials that relate to other issues involving the motion, such as whether it is timely filed. *See* Advisory Committee Note to Rule 7, Rules Governing § 2255 Proceedings (referencing Advisory Committee Note to Rule 7, Rules Governing § 2254 Cases, which states that "a court may wish to expand the record in order to assist it in deciding an issue other than the merits of the petition").

§ 15.05. The record can be expanded at any time in the proceedings.

Rule 7 can be used to expand the record at any time. The timing of a motion to expand the record under Rule 7 depends on your purpose. You may seek to expand the record under Rule 7 early in the proceedings to demonstrate that the claims in the motion either can or cannot be resolved without a hearing. A Rule 7 motion filed with a request for an evidentiary hearing, or filed after the court has granted a hearing, may be used to narrow the issues to be addressed at a hearing or to limit the number of witnesses to be presented via live testimony on a particular issue. *See* Advisory Committee Note to Rule 7, Rules Governing § 2255 Proceedings (referencing Advisory Committee Note to Rule 7, Rules Governing § 2254 Cases, which states that "[a]n expanded record may . . . be helpful when an evidentiary hearing is ordered.") You may also want to expand the record in conjunction with a motion for reconsideration following the district court's denial of certain claims or the entire motion.[3]

§ 15.06. Procedure under Rule 7.

When filing a motion to expand the record, the materials you seek to include in the record should accompany the motion, as should a brief memorandum of law that discusses how the proffered materials relate to the claims in the motion, and reasons why the court should exercise its discretion to expand the record. The court *may*, but need not, require the

3. Reconsideration motions are discussed in Chapter 16.

authentication of any materials proffered for inclusion in the record. *See* Rules Governing § 2255 Proceedings, Rule 7(a).

§ 15.07. Opposing a Rule 7 motion.

Rule 7(c) requires the court to afford the party against whom the additional materials are offered "an opportunity to admit or deny their correctness." Rules Governing § 2255 Proceedings, Rule 7(c). In addition, if affidavits are admitted by the district court, any party has "the right to propound written interrogatories to the affiants, or to file answering affidavits." 28 U.S.C. § 2246.[4] If the parties submit contradictory affidavits or other evidence to the court under Rule 7, and the court must determine the credibility of the proffered evidence, an evidentiary hearing is generally required. *See* Advisory Committee Note to Rule 7, Rules Governing § 2255 Proceedings (referencing Advisory Committee Note to Rule 7, Rules Governing § 2254 Cases, which states that "[w]hen the issue is one of credibility, resolution on the basis of affidavits can rarely be conclusive").

II. Discovery

§ 15.08. Discovery in section 2255 proceedings requires a showing of "good cause."

A section 2255 movant, unlike the usual civil litigant, is not entitled to discovery as a matter of course. Rather, discovery in section 2255 proceedings requires leave of the court, and is controlled by Rule 6 of the Rules Governing § 2255 Proceedings. Rule 6(a) allows a section 2255 movant to use, in the court's discretion and "for good cause," all of the discovery procedures available under the Federal Rules of Criminal Procedure *and* the Federal Rules of Civil Procedure. Rules Governing § 2255 Proceedings, Rule 6(a). Such rules include Federal Rules of Criminal Procedure 16 and 26.2, and Federal Rules of Civil Procedure 26–37.[5]

---

4. Section 2246 states:

> On application for a writ of habeas corpus, evidence may be taken orally or by deposition, or, in the discretion of the judge, by affidavit. If affidavits are admitted any party shall have the right to propound written interrogatories to the affiants, or to file answering affidavits.

28 U.S.C. § 2246. Section 2246 applies in section 2255 proceedings. *See* Reed v. United States, 438 F.2d 1154, 1156 (10th Cir. 1971).

5. The text of Federal Rule of Criminal Procedure 26.2 can be found in the Appendix to this chapter. Note that several of the Federal Rules of Civil Procedure governing discovery specifically *exclude* section 2255 cases from some of their requirements. *See, e.g.*, Fed. R. Civ. P. 26(a)(1)(B)(iii) & 26(f)(1).

Discovery can be an extremely useful tool for development of the facts to support a claim raised in a section 2255 motion. Deposing witnesses, making requests for admissions, obtaining production of documents, and propounding interrogatories are appropriate mechanisms in a broad range of situations where the facts were not adequately developed in the prior proceedings. A discussion of the federal criminal and civil rules governing discovery is, however, beyond the scope of this book.[6] This chapter will instead focus on discovery procedures and concerns specific to section 2255 proceedings.

§ 15.09. The "good cause" standard explained.

In *Bracy v. Gramley*, the Supreme Court concluded that "good cause" for discovery under Rule 6(a) has been shown "'where specific allegations before the court show reason to believe that the petitioner may, if the facts are fully developed, be able to demonstrate that he is . . . entitled to relief.'" 520 U.S. 899, 908–09, 117 S. Ct. 1793, 1799, 138 L. Ed. 2d 97 (1997) (quoting *Harris v. Nelson*, 394 U.S. 286, 300, 89 S. Ct. 1082, 1091, 22 L. Ed. 2d 281 (1969)).[7] Once "good cause" has been shown under Rule 6, "'it is the *duty* of the court to provide the necessary facilities and procedures for an adequate inquiry.'" *Id.*, 520 U.S. at 909, 117 S. Ct. at 1799 (quoting *Harris*, 394 U.S. at 300, 89 S. Ct. at 1091) (emphasis added here).

Movants need not state a *prima facie* case for relief prior to seeking discovery. Rather, Rule 6(a)'s good cause standard permits the use of discovery to *establish* a *prima facie* case for relief. That is, good cause is shown even if the movant's allegations support "only a theory . . . [that] is not supported by any solid evidence" at the time of the discovery request. *Bracy*, 520 U.S. at 908, 117 S. Ct. at 1799. Indeed, "[i]t may well be . . . that [the movant] will be unable to obtain evidence sufficient to" establish the claim, but if specific allegations are made that suggest the movant *may* be able to demonstrate a right to relief, good cause is established, and the district court has a "duty" to allow discovery. *Id.*, 520 U.S. at 909, 117 S. Ct. at 1799.

Rule 6 "does not, however, authorize fishing expeditions." *Harris v. Johnson*, 81 F.3d 535, 540 (5th Cir. 1996); *accord Charles v. Artuz*, 21

6. On criminal discovery generally, *see, e.g.*, 2 C. Wright, Federal Practice and Procedure: Criminal 3d §§ 246–261, at 48–211 (2000) (discussing Fed. R. Crim. P. 16); 2A *id.*, §§ 436–439, at 190–249 (discussing Fed. R. Crim. P. 26.2). On civil discovery generally, *see, e.g.*, 8 C. Wright, A. Miller, & R. Marcus, Federal Practice and Procedure §§ 2001–2100 (2d ed. 1994 & 2007 Supp.) (discussing Civil Rules 26–30); 8A id., §§ 2101–2300 (discussing Civil Rules 30–37).

7. Although *Bracy* involved discovery in habeas corpus proceedings pursuant to Rule 6 of the Rules Governing § 2254 Cases, its discussion of the "good cause" standard is fully applicable to Rule 6 of the Rules Governing § 2255 Proceedings. *See* United States v. Roane, 378 F.3d 382, 402–03 (4th Cir. 2004).

F. Supp. 2d 168, 169 (E.D.N.Y. 1998). Generalized statements about the possible existence of discovery material are insufficient to constitute good cause. *See Harris*, 81 F.3d at 540 ("conclusory allegations will not suffice to mandate . . . discovery"); *Green v. Artuz,* 990 F. Supp. 267, 271 (E.D.N.Y. 1998). Rather, the movant must make a particularized showing that the requested materials will support a claim in the motion. *See Harris*, 81 F.3d at 540.

Once a movant has demonstrated good cause for discovery, "the scope and extent of such discovery is a matter confided to the discretion of the District Court." *Bracy*, 520 U.S. at 909, 117 S. Ct. at 1799.

§ 15.10. Discovery and evidentiary hearings.

Discovery is available for good cause shown, "regardless of whether there is to be an evidentiary hearing." *Jones v. Wood*, 114 F.3d 1002, 1009 (9th Cir. 1997). However, discovery under Rule 6, in conjunction with the ability to expand the record under Rule 7 of the Rules Governing § 2255 Proceedings, is not only a means for establishing or narrowing the issues for presentation at an evidentiary hearing. It is also considered, in appropriate cases, a substitute for such hearings. *See Blackledge v. Allison*, 431 U.S. 63, 82, 97 S. Ct. 1621, 1633, 52 L. Ed. 2d 136 (1977). If a hearing is desired, be prepared to demonstrate that certain discovery procedures—especially depositions—are inadequate substitutes for an evidentiary hearing. If an evidentiary hearing is granted, and prior requests for discovery were denied or granted on a limited basis, consider renewing or expanding upon these requests, arguing that the grant of a hearing demonstrates "good cause" for pre-hearing discovery under Rule 6.

§ 15.11. The mechanics of a discovery request.

Rule 6(b) requires a party requesting discovery to "provide reasons for the request." Rules Governing § 2255 Proceedings, Rule 6(b). Moreover, before it may address whether a movant is entitled to discovery to develop facts related to a particular claim, a district court "must first identify the 'essential elements' of that claim." *Bracy*, 520 U.S. at 904, 117 S. Ct at 1797. Given that one cannot demonstrate "good cause" for discovery without first "provid[ing] reasons" related to the "essential elements" of the claim, the discovery motion (and memorandum in support) should specifically explain how the requested discovery items are directly relevant to at least one of the elements of one of the legal claims contained in the motion.

Rule 6(b) also requires that the discovery request "include any proposed interrogatories and requests for admission, and . . . specify any requested documents." Rules Governing § 2255 Proceedings, Rule 6(b). Therefore, a movant must submit those specific items *with the discovery motion,* or the request will be denied. Similarly, a deposition request should include a list of documents the applicant will ask the deponent to produce and should also indicate those matters on which the movant seeks to question the deponent.

§ 15.12. Appointment of counsel.

Rule 6(a) mandates appointment of counsel for indigent movants "[i]f necessary for effective discovery." Rules Governing § 2255 Proceedings, Rule 6(a). As the Advisory Committee Notes recognize, it ordinarily is true that counsel is necessary when discovery is granted, in order to "assist the petitioner who seeks to utilize discovery to stave off dismissal of his petition, . . . or to demonstrate that an evidentiary hearing is necessary." Advisory Committee Note to Rule 6, Rules Governing § 2254 Cases (incorporated by reference into Advisory Committee Note to Rule 6, Rules Governing § 2255 Proceedings). Accordingly, "if the judge grants petitioner's request for discovery prior to making a decision as to the necessity for an evidentiary hearing, he should determine whether counsel is necessary for the effective utilization of such discovery and, if so, appoint counsel for the petitioner if the petitioner qualifies for such appointment." *Id.*

§ 15.13. The government must also meet the good cause standard.

If the government seeks discovery, it must also meet the good cause standard articulated in Rule 6(a). *See* Rules Governing § 2255 Proceedings, Rule 6(a) (requiring leave of court before a "party" may conduct discovery). Therefore, a movant may oppose a discovery motion filed by the government by showing that the government has failed to establish good cause for its request, or is simply on a "fishing expedition." In addition, objections should be lodged if the discovery serves no purpose, is harassing, or violates the attorney-client, work-product, Fifth Amendment, or some other privilege. If the government is allowed to rely on affidavits in lieu of a hearing or otherwise makes affidavits part of the record, the movant has a right to propound written interrogatories to the affiants, or to file answering affidavits. 28 U.S.C. § 2246.[8]

Note, however, that if the motion includes a claim of ineffective assistance of counsel, the movant implicitly waives the attorney-client and

8. The text of section 2246 is contained in note 4, *supra*.

work-product privileges to the extent necessary to resolve the claim. *See In re Lott*, 424 F.3d 446, 453–54 (6th Cir. 2005) (collecting cases), *cert. denied*, 547 U.S. 1092, 126 S. Ct. 1772, 164 L. Ed. 2d 557 (2006).

III. Evidentiary Hearings

§ 15.14. Statutory standards governing evidentiary hearings.

Subsection (b) of section 2255 states:

> Unless the motion and the files and records of the case conclusively show that the prisoner is entitled to no relief, the court shall cause notice thereof to be served upon the United States attorney, grant a prompt hearing thereon, determine the issues and make findings of fact and conclusions of law with respect thereto.

28 U.S.C. § 2255(b). This language is intended to incorporate the standards governing evidentiary hearings in habeas corpus cases that were articulated by the Supreme Court in *Townsend v. Sain*, 372 U.S. 293, 312, 83 S. Ct. 745, 756, 9 L. Ed. 2d 770 (1963). *See* Advisory Committee Note to Rule 8, Rules Governing § 2254 Cases (incorporated by reference into Advisory Committee Note to Rule 8, Rules Governing § 2255 Proceedings).[9]

§ 15.15. Under *Townsend v. Sain*, a hearing is required where the facts alleged, if true, would entitle the movant to relief, and the facts have not yet been reliably found.

In *Townsend*, the Supreme Court held that the district court *must* hold an evidentiary hearing (1) if the prisoner alleges facts that, if true, would entitle him to relief; and (2) the relevant facts have not yet been reliably found after a full and fair hearing. *Id.*, 372 U.S. at 312–13, 83 S. Ct. at 757.[10] Actual proof of those facts alleged in the motion is not required in order to demonstrate entitlement to a hearing. "The law is clear that, in order to be entitled to an evidentiary hearing, a petitioner need only *allege*—not

9. The Advisory Committee Note to Rule 8 of the Rules Governing § 2255 Proceedings states, "The standards for § 2255 hearings are essentially the same as for evidentiary hearings under a habeas petition, except that the previous federal fact-finding proceeding is in issue [in determining whether a hearing is necessary] rather than the state's."

10. Once the movant has alleged facts that, if true, would entitled him to relief, a hearing is *required* under *Townsend* in the following six circumstances: (1) the district court previously did not resolve the merits of the factual dispute in a full and fair hearing; (2) the district court previously determined the facts, but that determination is not fairly supported by the record as a whole; (3) the district court previously determined the facts, but the fact-finding procedure was not adequate to afford a full and fair hearing; (4) there is a substantial allegation of newly discov-

prove—reasonably specific, nonconclusory facts that, if true, would entitle him to relief." *Aron v. United States*, 291 F.3d 708, 715 n.6 (11th Cir. 2002) (emphasis in original).

Thus, if the record of the case does not "'conclusively show' that under no circumstances could the [movant] establish facts warranting relief under § 2255," the movant must be afforded a hearing in the district court. *Fontaine v. United States*, 411 U.S. 213, 215, 93 S. Ct. 1461, 1463, 36 L. Ed. 2d 169 (1973). *See Aron*, 219 F.3d at 715 n.6 ("If the [movant's] allegations are not affirmatively contradicted by the record and the claims are not patently frivolous, the district court is required to hold an evidentiary hearing. It is in such a hearing that the [movant] must offer proof"); *Arredondo v. United States*, 178 F.3d 778, 782, 788–89 (6th Cir. 1999) (denying a hearing on claim that counsel was ineffective for failing to convey plea offer where evidence offered by movant was incredible, inadmissible hearsay; but, concluding a hearing was required on claim that counsel was ineffective in failing to challenge at sentencing the drug quantity attributed to movant because these allegations were not "'contradicted by the record, inherently incredible, or conclusions rather than statements of fact'").

As a result, a hearing is generally required if the motion presents a colorable claim that arises from matters outside the record. *See United States v. Magini*, 973 F.2d 261, 264 (4th Cir. 1992) ("When a colorable . . . claim is presented, and where material facts are in dispute involving inconsistencies beyond the record, a hearing is necessary."); *Shah v. United States*, 878 F.2d 1156, 1158 (9th Cir. 1989) ("Where section 2255 motions have been based on alleged occurrences outside the record, we have often held that an evidentiary hearing was required."). Thus, evidentiary hearings are more likely to be granted to resolve those claims—such as the ineffectiveness of counsel or the prosecutor's failure to disclose exculpatory evidence—that generally involve factual disputes regarding matters outside the record.

§ 15.16. The federal court always has discretion to grant an evidentiary hearing.

Under *Townsend*, once a movant alleges material facts that entitle him to relief, a federal evidentiary hearing is *permitted*, even if the circumstances

---

ered evidence; (5) the material facts were not adequately developed in the prior federal proceedings; and (6) if, for any other reason, the district court did not provide the movant with a full and fair hearing on the merits of the factual dispute. *See Townsend*, 372 U.S. at 313. In Keeney v. Tomayo-Reyes, 504 U.S. 1, 112 S. Ct. 1715, 118 L. Ed. 2d 318 (1992), the Supreme Court modified the fifth *Townsend* circumstance to hold that if the failure to develop the material facts in the prior proceeding was the fault of the movant (or movant's counsel), this constitutes a "procedural default," and an evidentiary hearing is required only if there is "cause" and "prejudice" for the failure to present the evidence previously or the movant can demonstrate "actual innocence." Procedural default, cause and prejudice, and actual innocence are discussed in Chapter 9.

are such that a hearing is not required. The federal court *always* has the discretion to grant an evidentiary hearing. *See Townsend*, 372 U.S. at 318, 83 S. Ct. at 760 ("In all . . . cases where the material facts are in dispute, the holding of such a hearing is in the discretion of the district judge.").

§ 15.17. If a hearing is ordered, appointment of counsel is required.

If the court grants an evidentiary hearing, and the movant is indigent, appointment of counsel is *mandatory*. Rule 8(c) of the Rules Governing § 2255 Proceedings provides that "if an evidentiary hearing is warranted, the judge *must appoint* an attorney" for an indigent movant. *Id.* (emphasis added). Rules Governing § 2255 Proceedings, Rule 8(c). If the statutory right to counsel under Rule 8(c) is abridged, the error is presumed prejudicial and not amenable to harmless error analysis. *See, e.g., Shepherd v. United States*, 253 F.3d 585, 588 (11th Cir. 2001) *(per curiam)* (collecting cases).

§ 15.18. The hearing must be conducted "as soon as practicable."

An evidentiary hearing is to be conducted "as soon as practicable after giving the attorneys adequate time to investigate and prepare." Rules Governing § 2255 Proceedings, Rule 8(c). In setting a hearing date, the court should consider "the complexity of the case, the availability of important materials, the workload of [counsel for the government], and the time required by appointed counsel to prepare." Advisory Committee Notes to Rule 8, Rules Governing § 2254 Cases (incorporated by reference into Advisory Committee Notes to Rule 8, Rules Governing § 2255 Proceedings).

§ 15.19. Hearings in section 2255 cases are different.

The right to relief in section 2255 cases can be difficult to prove. Given that many claims are based on events that occurred at or before trial, the passage of time makes it likely that memories have faded and relevant documents are difficult to find. Key witnesses may be hard to locate or reluctant to cooperate. Because the hearing is conducted before a judge or magistrate, as opposed to a jury, allocation of the burdens of production and persuasion can be critical.

Most importantly, claims requiring a showing of "prejudice" as an element of proof place especially complex demands on section 2255 counsel. For example, to establish that trial counsel was constitutionally ineffective, the movant must demonstrate not only that trial counsel's actions fell below an objective standard of reasonableness, but also that but for trial counsel's actions, the result of the proceedings would have been different.

See Strickland v. Washington, 466 U.S. 668, 104 S. Ct. 2052, 80 L. Ed. 2d 674 (1984). This requires movant's counsel to

> conduct for the federal judge what amounts to two criminal trials: (1) a reprise of the [prior] trial as it *did* occur, including a description of its pretrial investigatory phase, in order to reveal—perhaps with the assistance of an expert witness—that prior counsel's representation was not reasonably competent; and (2) the trial as it *would* have occurred but for prior counsel's unreasonable conduct, in order to show that a reasonably competent defense could have led to a more favorable outcome than did the actual trial.

1 R. Hertz & J. Liebman, *Federal Habeas Corpus Practice and Procedure*, § 21.1a at 1010 (5th ed. 2005) (emphases in original).

§ 15.20. The Federal Rules of Evidence govern the presentation of evidence.

The hearing will be governed by the Federal Rules of Evidence. *See* Fed. R. Evid. 1101(e). Although evidentiary hearings in section 2255 cases proceed much like bench trials and are generally more informal than jury trial proceedings, thorough knowledge of these rules is still a necessity. If an evidentiary ruling will affect the planning for and conduct of the hearing, consider seeking a pre-hearing ruling on the issue by filing a motion *in limine,* or asking the court to hold a pre-hearing conference. *See* Advisory Committee Note to Rule 8, Rules Governing § 2255 Proceedings (incorporating Advisory Committee Note to Rule 8, Rules Governing § 2254 Cases, which states that a pre-hearing conference is an appropriate way "to explore evidentiary problems that may be expected to arise"). You may also seek stipulations from the government regarding the evidence to be presented at the hearing. If the court limits the claims or the scope of the evidence to be presented live at the hearing in a manner detrimental to the movant, consider filing a motion to expand the record to include affidavits, depositions, or other materials in lieu of live testimony. *See* §§ 15.03–15.07.

§ 15.21. Right to production of prior witness statements.

Rule 8(d) explicitly authorizes the court to order the production of prior statements of any witness who testifies at an evidentiary hearing by extending the scope of Federal Rule of Criminal Procedure 26.2(a)–(d) and (f)[11]

11. The text of Federal Rule of Criminal Procedure 26.2 can be found in the Appendix to this chapter.

to apply to section 2255 proceedings. Rules Governing § 2255 Proceedings, Rule 8(d). If the court orders production of a prior witness statement and a party refuses to comply, "the court must not consider that witness's testimony." *Id.*

§ 15.22. If the movant is a fact witness, her presence at the hearing is required.

Section 2255 provides that "[a] court may entertain and determine [a section 2255] motion without requiring the production of the prisoner at the hearing." § 2255(c). However, the United States Supreme Court has interpreted this provision to require the movant's presence if "there are substantial issues of fact as to events in which the prisoner participated." *United States v. Hayman*, 342 U.S. 205, 223, 72 S. Ct. 263, 274, 96 L. Ed. 232 (1952). Thus, for many claims typically presented in section 2255 motions, such as claims of ineffective assistance of counsel, the movant's presence will be required at the hearing. *See id.*, 342 U.S. at 219, 72 S. Ct. at 272 (movant's presence was required at evidentiary hearing where critical issue in case was whether movant waived trial counsel's conflict of interest). Indeed, many district courts *always* require the presence of the movant when a hearing is ordered. If the district court desires the movant's presence at a hearing, it has the power to compel the government to produce the movant, no matter where the movant is confined. *Id.*, 342 U.S. at 222–23, 72 S. Ct. at 274. This is usually accomplished by the issuance of a writ of habeas corpus ad testificandum upon the movant's custodian.

IV. Appendix

A. Federal Rule of Criminal Procedure 26.2 (2008)

Rule 26.2. Producing a Witness's Statement

(a) **Motion to Produce**. After a witness other than the defendant has testified on direct examination, the court, on motion of a party who did not call the witness, must order an attorney for the government or the defendant and the defendant's attorney to produce, for the examination and use of the moving party, any statement of the witness that is in their possession and that relates to the subject matter of the witness's testimony.

(b) **Producing the Entire Statement**. If the entire statement relates to the subject matter of the witness's testimony, the court must order that the statement be delivered to the moving party.

(c) **Producing a Redacted Statement**. If the party who called the witness claims that the statement contains information that is privileged or does not relate to the subject matter of the witness's testimony, the court must inspect the statement in camera. After excising any privileged or unrelated portions, the court must order delivery of the redacted statement to the moving party. If the defendant objects to an excision, the court must preserve the entire statement with the excised portion indicated, under seal, as part of the record.

(d) Recess to Examine a Statement. The court may recess the proceedings to allow time for a party to examine the statement and prepare for its use.

(e) Sanction for Failure to Produce or Deliver a Statement. If the party who called the witness disobeys an order to produce or deliver a statement, the court must strike the witness's testimony from the record. If an attorney for the government disobeys the order, the court must declare a mistrial if justice so requires.

(f) "Statement" Defined. As used in this rule, a witness's "statement" means:

- **(1)** a written statement that the witness makes and signs, or otherwise adopts or approves;
- **(2)** a substantially verbatim, contemporaneously recorded recital of the witness's oral statement that is contained in any recording or any transcription of a recording; or
- **(3)** the witness's statement to a grand jury, however taken or recorded, or a transcription of such a statement.

(g) Scope. This rule applies at trial, at a suppression hearing under Rule 12, and to the extent specified in the following rules:

- **(1)** Rule 5.1(h) (preliminary hearing);
- **(2)** Rule 32(i)(2) (sentencing);
- **(3)** Rule 32.1(e) (hearing to revoke or modify probation or supervised release);
- **(4)** Rule 46(j) (detention hearing); and
- **(5)** Rule 8 of the Rules Governing Proceedings under 28 U.S.C. § 2255.

Relief

Contents

Introduction

§ 16.01. Section 2255 is a broad and flexible remedy.

The section 2255 remedy is "broad and flexible, and entrusts to the courts the power to fashion an appropriate remedy." *United States v. Hadden*, 475 F.3d 652, 661 (4th Cir. 2007) (internal quotation marks omitted).

I. Two-Step Process for Resolving a Section 2255 Motion

§ 16.02. If relief is warranted, the district court must vacate and set aside the judgment.

Section 2255(b) provides, in pertinent part,

> If the court finds that the judgment was [unlawful for various specified reasons], the court shall vacate and set the judgment aside and shall discharge the prisoner or resentence him or grant a new trial or correct the sentence as may appear appropriate.

28 U.S.C. § 2255(b).[1]

Accordingly, a district court's resolution of a section 2255 motion proceeds in two steps. First, the district court must determine whether the

1. Section 2255(b) provides that a judgment is unlawful, and relief is available, where "the judgment was rendered without jurisdiction," where the conviction or sentence is unconstitutional or violates other federal law, or where the conviction or sentence is otherwise "vulnerable to collateral attack." § 2255(b). Chapter 7 discusses the various claims that are cognizable in section 2255 proceedings.

prisoner's judgment is unlawful for one of the reasons specified. *Id.* If the district court concludes that the judgment is lawful, then it must deny the motion. If, however, the district court concludes that the judgment is unlawful, the court "shall vacate and set . . . aside" the judgment. *Id.*

Second, if the judgment is set aside, the district court "shall" grant the movant an "appropriate" remedy. *Id.*

II. Four Appropriate Remedies

§ 16.03. If the judgment is set aside, there are four appropriate remedies.

If the judgment is set aside, section 2255(b) lists four appropriate remedies: (1) "discharge the prisoner," (2) "grant [the prisoner] a new trial," (3) "resentence [the prisoner]," or (4) "correct the [prisoner's] sentence." *Id.* The end result of a successful section 2255 proceeding must therefore be "the vacatur of the prisoner's unlawful sentence (and perhaps one or more of his convictions) and one of the following: (1) the prisoner's release, (2) the grant of a future new trial to the prisoner, (3) or a new sentence, be it imposed by (a) a resentencing or (b) a corrected sentence." *Hadden*, 475 F.3d at 661 (internal footnote omitted).

§ 16.04. A new sentence need not be substantially different from the original sentence.

Although one of the possible outcomes of a successful section 2255 motion is a "new" sentence, that does not mean that the "new" sentence must be different from the original one. *See id.* at 661 n.9.

III. Remedy for Counsel's Failure to File a Timely Notice of Appeal

§ 16.05. Reentry of original sentence is remedy for counsel's failure to timely appeal.

A common claim for section 2255 relief is that defense counsel failed to file a timely notice of appeal from the movant's judgment of conviction and sentence. If the district court determines that relief is warranted on such a claim due to ineffective assistance of counsel, the common remedy is to vacate and then reenter the original sentence, so as to allow the movant a new ten-day period within which to timely notice an appeal from the original judgment. *See id.*; *United States v. Phillips*, 225 F.3d 1198, 1200–01 (11th Cir. 2000).

CHAPTER 17

Postjudgment Motions and Release Pending Appeal

Contents

Introduction

§ 17.01. A movant may, but need not, seek reconsideration of an adverse district court decision, or release pending appeal if victorious.

Either party may seek reconsideration of a district court's decision to grant or deny section 2255 relief. If the district court rules adversely as to some or all of the claims in a section 2255 motion, strategic considerations govern whether a movant should do so. In some cases, it may be beneficial to file a reconsideration motion to allow the district court the opportunity to correct, modify, or add to the record before litigating the appeal. In other cases, such as where the district court is hostile and appears to have made a serious mistake of fact or law in its ruling, the better course may be not to file a such a motion.

Although section 2255 motions are, in some ways, the continuation of a criminal proceeding, it is to the Federal Rules of *Civil* Procedure that one must look to find the rules governing motions seeking reconsideration of the district court's decision granting or denying section 2255 relief. *See Browder v. Director*, 434 U.S. 257, 270, 98 S. Ct. 556, 564, 54 L. Ed. 2d 521 (1978); *United States v. Fiorelli*, 337 F.3d 282, 286 (3d Cir. 2003) (collecting cases); Rules Governing § 2255 Proceedings, Rule 12.

The primary postjudgment motions in section 2255 proceedings are (1) a motion to alter or amend judgment under Federal Rule of Civil Procedure 59(e), and (2) a motion for relief from judgment under Federal Rule of Civil Procedure 60(b). The text of these rules can be found in the Appendix to this chapter.

A movant who is victorious in the district court may seek release pending appeal under Federal Rule of Appellate Procedure 23. The text of Rule 23 can also be found in the Appendix to this chapter.

I. Motions to Alter or Amend Judgment under Fed. R. Civ. P. 59(e)

§ 17.02. A Rule 59(e) motion must be filed within ten days of entry of judgment.

A motion to alter or amend the judgment pursuant to Rule 59(e) is timely if *filed* within ten days of the entry of the district court's judgment either granting, denying, or dismissing the motion. Fed. R. Civ. P. 59(e). Federal Rule of Civil Procedure 6[1] governs the procedure for counting days to determine when the strict ten-day period has run. Under Rule 6, weekends and federal holidays do not count toward the ten-day period. *See* Fed. R. Civ. P. 6(a)(2). Importantly, this ten-day period *cannot* be enlarged by the court. Fed. R. Civ. P. 6(b)(2); *Fiorelli*, 337 F.3d at 288. Most courts, however, have held that the "mailbox rule" applies to *pro se* motions filed pursuant to Rule 59(e). *See Fiorelli*, 337 F.3d at 289–90; *Edwards v. United States*, 266 F.3d 756, 758 (7th Cir. 2001) (collecting cases).[2]

§ 17.03. A timely Rule 59(e) motion tolls the time for appeal.

If timely made within the allotted ten-day period, a Rule 59(e) motion tolls the time for appeal. *See* Fed. R. App. P. 4(a)(4)(A)(iv).[3] The time for filing an appeal begins to run anew from the date the district court rules on the motion. *Id.*; *Browder*, 434 U.S. at 264, 98 S. Ct. at 561. Moreover, an appeal from the denial of a motion under Rule 59(e) brings up the entire underly-

1. The text of Federal Rule of Civil Procedure 6 can be found in the Appendix to Chapter 14.

2. The Supreme Court established the "mailbox rule" in Houston v. Lack, 487 U.S. 266, 108 S. Ct. 2379, 101 L. Ed. 2d 245 (1988). There, the Court decided that a notice of appeal filed by a *pro se* prisoner would be considered "filed" at the moment of delivery to prison authorities, rather than at the later point in time when the notice was received by the court. The "mailbox rule" has since been extended to cover numerous other court filings by *pro se* prisoners.

3. The text of Federal Rule of Appellate Procedure 4 can be found in the Appendix to Chapter 18.

ing judgment for review. *See Foman v. Davis*, 371 U.S. 178, 181–82, 83 S. Ct. 227, 229–30, 9 L. Ed. 2d 222 (1962).

If, however, the party files a Rule 59(e) motion that is *untimely* because it was filed outside the ten-day period, the time to appeal is *not* tolled. How to timely file an appeal in a section 2255 proceeding is discussed in Chapter 18.

§ 17.04. Almost any reason justifying reconsideration can be asserted in a Rule 59(e) motion.

A motion under Rule 59(e) is a "device to relitigate the original issue decided by the district court, and used to allege legal error." *Fiorelli*, 337 F.3d at 288 (internal quotation marks omitted). Almost any substantive reason justifying reconsideration of the district court's decision may be asserted in a motion premised on Rule 59(e). A Rule 59(e) motion may also seek reconsideration of procedural rulings by the district court, such as the erroneous denial of an evidentiary hearing. *See Browder*, 434 U.S. at 265–67, 98 S. Ct. at 561–62.

II. Fed. R. Civ. P. 60(b) Motions for Relief from Judgment

§ 17.05. Rule 60(b) motions allow reopening of the judgment after ten days have passed.

Federal Rule of Civil Procedure 60(b) allows the district court to reopen its judgment in a section 2255 proceeding *after* the ten-day period for filing a Rule 59(e) motion has passed. Under Rule 60(b), the district court may consider a motion for "Relief from a Judgment or Order" if that motion is filed within a year of the judgment *and* is based on (1) "mistake, inadvertence, surprise, or excusable neglect"; (2) "newly discovered evidence that, with reasonable diligence could not have been discovered in time to move for a new trial"; or (3) "fraud . . . , misrepresentation, or misconduct" by the opposing party. Fed. R. Civ. P. 60(b)(1), (b)(2), (b)(3), & (c)(1). Rule 60(b) also allows a motion to be brought within a "reasonable time" if the motion asserts (4) "the judgment is void"; (5) the judgment has been satisfied or is based on an earlier judgment that has been reversed or vacated, or applying it prospectively is "no longer equitable"; or (6) "any other reason" justifying relief. Fed. R. Civ. P. 60(b)(4), (b)(5), (b)(6), & (c)(1).

"Rule 60(b) has an unquestionably valid role to play in habeas cases." *See Gonzalez v. Crosby*, 545 U.S. 524, 534, 125 S. Ct. 2641, 2649, 162 L. Ed. 2d 480 (2005). Indeed, Rule 60(b) allows the district court to grant relief from its prior judgment in a wide variety of circumstances. However, a Rule 60(b) motion that argues only that the district court committed "legal error, without more" does not warrant relief under that provision. *Fiorelli*, 337 F.3d at 288 (internal quotation marks omitted).

§ 17.06. Filing a timely Rule 59(e) motion is generally preferable to a Rule 60(b) motion.

Although Rule 59(e) and Rule 60(b) motions both allow the district court to reopen its judgment, there are a number of reasons the timely filing of a motion under Rule 59(e), if possible, is preferable.

1. Unlike timely motions for reconsideration under Rule 59(e), a Rule 60(b) motion does *not* toll the time for appeal or affect the finality of the district court's judgment unless it is filed within ten days of the original judgment. *See* Fed. R. App. P. 4(a)(4)(A)(vi); Fed. R. Civ. P. 60(c)(2); *Stone v. I.N.S.*, 514 U.S. 386, 401, 115 S. Ct. 1537, 1547, 131 L. Ed. 2d 465 (1995); *Browder*, 434 U.S. at 263 n.7, 98 S. Ct. at 560 n.7.
2. Although the district court's denial of a Rule 60(b) motion is appealable, the appeal brings up for review only the denial of the motion, *not* the merits of the underlying judgment. *See Browder*, 434 U.S. at 263 & n.7, 98 S. Ct. at 560 & n.7; *Stone*, 514 U.S. at 401, 115 S. Ct. at 1547; *United States v. Vargas*, 393 F.3d 172, 174 (D.C. Cir. 2004), *cert. denied*, 546 U.S. 1011, 126 S. Ct. 644, 163 L. Ed. 2d 521 (2005).
3. The district court loses jurisdiction to *grant* a Rule 60(b) motion once a notice of appeal has been filed. Therefore, if a Rule 60(b) motion is pending before the district court and a notice of appeal has also been filed, steps must be taken to revest the district court with jurisdiction before it can grant Rule 60(b) relief. In most circuits this requires the district court to indicate if it is inclined to grant the Rule 60(b) motion, and, if so, the movant must then request a limited remand from the court of appeals so that the district court has jurisdiction to consider the Rule 60(b) motion. *See, e.g., Fobian v. Storage Technology Corp.*, 164 F.3d 887, 891 (4th Cir. 1999); *Boyko v. Anderson*, 185 F.3d 672, 674 (7th Cir. 1999); *Carriger v. Lewis*, 971 F.2d 329, 332 (9th Cir. 1992) *(en banc)*.

§ 17.07. The most compelling reason to avoid filing a Rule 60(b) motion is that it may be considered a second or successive section 2255 motion.

The most important reason to avoid filing a Rule 60(b) motion is that a Rule 60(b) motion that "attacks . . . the substance of the federal court's resolution of the claim on the merits, [rather than] some defect in the integrity of the federal habeas proceedings" must be treated as a second or successive section 2255 motion. *See Gonzalez*, 545 U.S. at 532, 125 S. Ct. at 2648. That is not the case with a "true" Rule 59(e) motion—one that seeks to alter, amend, reconsider, or revise the district court's judgment. *See Curry v. United States*, 307 F.3d 664, 665 (7th Cir. 2002) (collecting cases). Given the near impossibility of obtaining relief on a second or successive section 2255 motion,[4] you should consider carefully the decision to seek relief from the judgment by means of a Rule 60(b) motion rather than by timely filing a Rule 59(e) motion.

III. Release Pending Appeal

§ 17.08. The grant of section 2255 relief creates a presumption in favor of release pending appeal.

If a section 2255 motion is granted and the district court either orders a new trial or a new sentencing that will likely result in the movant's immediate release, and the government appeals the district court's decision, the movant may seek release from custody pending appeal. A court's decision whether to release or detain a section 2255 movant pending the outcome of an appeal is guided by Federal Rule of Appellate Procedure 23(c).[5] *Hilton v. Braunskill*, 481 U.S. 770, 772, 107 S. Ct. 2113, 2116–17, 95 L. Ed. 2d 724 (1987); *United States v. Mett*, 41 F.3d 1281, 1282 (9th Cir. 1995). Movants should apply first to the district court for release pending appeal.

Rule 23(c) creates a "preference for release" of a victorious section 2255 movant while appellate proceedings are ongoing. *Hilton*, 481 U.S. at 778, 107 S. Ct. at 2120. It states:

> While a decision ordering the release of a prisoner is under review, the prisoner *must*—unless the court or judge rendering the decision, or the court of appeals, or the Supreme Court, or a judge or justice of either court orders otherwise—*be released on personal recognizance, with or without surety.*

Fed. R. App. P. 23(c) (emphasis added). Moreover, under Rule 23(d), a district court order granting release is presumed correct, and this presumption may be overcome in the appellate court only "for special reasons shown." Fed. R. App. P. 23(d).

4. Second or successive motions are discussed in Chapter 19.

5. The text of Federal Rule of Appellate Procedure 23 is contained in the Appendix to this chapter.

Rule 23(c) also alters the manner in which a court must balance the factors governing the government's motion for a stay pending appeal of an order granting the movant's release. The court must still weigh the traditional stay factors, that is, "(1) whether the stay applicant has made a strong showing that he is likely to succeed on the merits; (2) whether the applicant will be irreparably injured absent a stay; (3) whether issuance of the stay will substantially injure the other parties interested in the proceeding; and (4) where the public interest lies." *Hilton*, 481 U.S. at 776, 107 S. Ct. at 2119. In balancing these factors, however, the court may also consider whether "there is a risk that the prisoner will pose a danger to the public if released." *Id.*, 481 U.S. at 777, 107 S. Ct. at 2120. It may also consider "[t]he [government]'s interest in continuing custody and rehabilitation pending a final determination of the case on appeal." *Id.*, 481 U.S. at 777, 107 S. Ct. at 2119. This interest will be strongest where the remaining portion of the sentence to be served is long, and weakest where there is little of the sentence remaining to be served." *Id.*, 481 U.S. at 777, 107 S. Ct. at 2120.

Importantly, Rule 23(c)'s "preference for release should control" if the government cannot establish either "that it has a strong likelihood of success on appeal, or . . . a substantial case on the merits." *Id.*, 481 U.S. at 778, 107 S. Ct. at 2120. Thus, under Rule 23(c), the government's failure to show a *strong* likelihood of success on the merits, standing alone, is sufficient to deny a stay of a district court order requiring the movant's immediate release.

IV. Appendix

A. Federal Rule of Civil Procedure 59 (2008)

Rule 59. New Trial; Altering or Amending a Judgment

(a) In General.

(1) ***Grounds for New Trial.*** The court may, on motion, grant a new trial on all or some of the issues—and to any party—as follows:

(A) after a jury trial, for any reason for which a new trial has heretofore been granted in an action at law in federal court; or

(B) after a nonjury trial, for any reason for which a rehearing has heretofore been granted in a suit in equity in federal court.

(2) ***Further Action After a Nonjury Trial.*** After a nonjury trial, the court may, on motion for a new trial, open the judgment if one has been entered, take additional testimony, amend findings of fact and conclusions of law or make new ones, and direct the entry of a new judgment.

(b) Time to File a Motion for a New Trial. A motion for a new trial must be filed no later than 10 days after the entry of judgment.

(c) Time to Serve Affidavits. When a motion for a new trial is based on affidavits, they must be filed with the motion. The opposing party has 10 days after being served to file opposing affidavits; but that period may be extended for up to 20 days, either by the court for good cause or by the parties' stipulation. The court may permit reply affidavits.

(d) New Trial on the Court's Initiative or for Reasons Not in the Motion. No later than 10 days after the entry of judgment, the court, on its own, may order a new trial for any reason that would justify granting one on a party's motion. After giving the parties notice and an opportunity to be heard, the court may grant a timely motion for a new trial for a reason not stated in the motion. In either event, the court must specify the reasons in its order.

(e) Motion to Alter or Amend a Judgment. A motion to alter or amend a judgment must be filed no later than 10 days after the entry of the judgment.

B. Federal Rule of Civil Procedure 60 (2008)

Rule 60. Relief from a Judgment or Order

(a) Corrections Based on Clerical Mistakes; Oversights and Omissions. The court may correct a clerical mistake or a mistake arising from oversight or omission whenever one is found in a judgment, order, or other part of the record. The court may do so on motion or on its own, with or without notice. But after an appeal has been docketed in the appellate court and while it is pending, such a mistake may be corrected only with the appellate court's leave.

(b) Grounds for Relief from a Final Judgment, Order, or Proceeding. On motion and just terms, the court may relieve a party or its legal representative from a final judgment, order, or proceeding for the following reasons:

(1) mistake, inadvertence, surprise, or excusable neglect;

(2) newly discovered evidence that, with reasonable diligence, could not have been discovered in time to move for a new trial under Rule 59(b);

(3) fraud (whether previously called intrinsic or extrinsic), misrepresentation, or misconduct by an opposing party;

(4) the judgment is void;
(5) the judgment has been satisfied, released or discharged; it is based on an earlier judgment that has been reversed or vacated; or applying it prospectively is no longer equitable; or
(6) any other reason that justifies relief.

(c) Timing and Effect of the Motion.

(1) ***Timing.*** A motion under Rule 60(b) must be made within a reasonable time—and for reasons (1), (2), and (3) no more than a year after the entry of the judgment or order or the date of the proceeding.
(2) ***Effect on Finality.*** The motion does not affect the judgment's finality or suspend its operation.

(d) Other Powers to Grant Relief. This rule does not limit a court's power to:

(1) entertain an independent action to relieve a party from a judgment, order, or proceeding;
(2) grant relief under 28 U.S.C. § 1655 to a defendant who was not personally notified of the action; or
(3) set aside a judgment for fraud on the court.

(e) Bills and Writs Abolished. The following are abolished: bills of review, bills in the nature of bills of review, and writs of coram nobis, coram vobis, and audita querela.

C. Federal Rule of Appellate Procedure 23 (2008)

Rule 23. Custody or Release of a Prisoner in a Habeas Corpus Proceeding

(a) Transfer of Custody Pending Review. Pending review of a decision in a habeas corpus proceeding commenced before a court, justice, or judge of the United States for the release of a prisoner, the person having custody of the prisoner must not transfer custody to another unless a transfer is directed in accordance with this rule. When, upon application, a custodian shows the need for a transfer, the court, justice, or judge rendering the decision under review may authorize the transfer and substitute the successor custodian as a party.

(b) Detention or Release Pending Review of Decision Not to Release. While a decision not to release a prisoner is under review, the court or judge rendering the decision, or the court of appeals, or the Supreme Court, or a judge or justice of either court, may order that the prisoner be:

(1) detained in the custody from which release is sought;
(2) detained in other appropriate custody; or
(3) released on personal recognizance, with or without surety.

(c) Release Pending Review of Decision Ordering Release. While a decision ordering the release of a prisoner is under review, the prisoner must—unless the court or judge rendering the decision, or the court of appeals, or the Supreme Court, or a judge or justice of either court orders otherwise—be released on personal recognizance, with or without surety.

(d) Modification of the Initial Order on Custody. An initial order governing the prisoner's custody or release, including any recognizance or surety, continues in effect pending review unless for special reasons shown to the court of appeals or the Supreme Court, or to a judge or justice of either court, the order is modified or an independent order regarding custody, release, or surety is issued.

Part VI:

The Appeal and Subsequent Motions

Perfecting the Appeal

Contents

Introduction

§ 18.01. There is no appeal as of right from the denial of a section 2255 motion.

The Antiterrorism and Effective Death Penalty Act of 1996 (AEPDA) changed the process for appealing the denial of section 2255 relief.[1] Pre-AEDPA, a prisoner's appeal from a district court order denying section 2255 relief was perfected simply by timely filing a notice of appeal. That is no longer true. Now, a section 2255 movant seeking to perfect an appeal must both timely file a notice of appeal *and* secure a "certificate of appealability."

This chapter discusses only the procedures required to *perfect* an appeal in a section 2255 proceeding. Once an appeal is perfected, section 2255 appeals proceed in the same manner as other appeals.

I. The Notice of Appeal

§ 18.02. The time to appeal is 60 days from entry of a final order.

For purposes of calculating the time to appeal, a section 2255 case is considered "civil" in nature and therefore governed by Federal Rule of Appellate

1. The AEDPA is discussed in Chapter 2.

Procedure 4(a).[2] *United States v. Hayman*, 342 U.S. 205, 209 n.4, 72 S. Ct. 263, 267 n. 4, 96 L.Ed. 232 (1952); Rules Governing § 2255 Proceedings, Rule 11 ("Federal Rule of Appellate Procedure 4(a) governs the time to appeal an order entered" on a section 2255 motion). Because the United States is a party in a section 2255 proceeding, the time allowed to appeal is 60 days. Fed. R. App. P. 4(a)(1)(B); 28 U.S.C. § 2107(b). That is, to be timely, a notice of appeal must be filed within 60 days of entry of the judgment or order from which appeal is taken. Fed. R. App. P. 4(a)(1)(B); 28 U.S.C. § 2107(b).

This 60-day limit is *mandatory and jurisdictional. Bowles v. Russell*, ___ U.S. ___, 127 S. Ct. 2360, 2363, 168 L. Ed. 2d 96 (2007); *Hohn v. United States*, 524 U.S. 236, 247, 118 S. Ct. 1969, 1975, 141 L. Ed. 2d 242 (1998); *United States v. Feuver*, 236 F.3d 725, 727 (D.C. Cir. 2001). It cannot be extended, either by the district court or the court of appeals, except in the limited circumstances permitted by Federal Rules of Appellate Procedure 4(a)(5) (allowing a "motion for extension of time" to appeal) and 4(a)(6) (allowing for "reopening of the time to file an appeal"). *See* Fed. R. App. P. 26(b)(1) ("the court may not extend the time to file . . . a notice of appeal (except as authorized in Rule 4)"); *Bowles*, ___ U.S. at ___, 127 S. Ct. at 2366.

§ 18.03. If the district court *grants* section 2255 relief and the movant is resentenced, that order is not considered "final" for purposes of appeal.

The 60-day time period for filing an appeal starts to run when the district court issues a "final" order. *See Andrews v. United States*, 373 U.S. 334, 338, 83 S. Ct. 1236, 1239, 10 L. Ed. 2d 383 (1963); 28 U.S.C. §§ 1291, 2253. If the district court has *granted* section 2255 relief as to the movant's sentence and its order requires only the *resentencing* of the movant, that order is not considered to be a "final" order, and a government appeal will not be permitted until after the movant has been resentenced. *See Andrews*, 373 U.S. at 340, 83 S. Ct. at 1240; *United States v. Hayes*, 532 F.3d 349 (5th Cir. 2008); *United States v. Futch*, 518 F.3d 887, 894 (11th Cir. 2008). Where, however, the district court vacates the movant's *conviction* and orders a new trial, that is a final order, and the government may immediately appeal. *See United States v. Gordon*, 156 F.3d 376, 379 (2d Cir. 1998); *United States v. Allen*, 613 F.2d 1248, 1250 (3d Cir. 1980).

2. The text of Fed. R. App. P. 4 can be found in the Appendix to this chapter.

§ 18.04. The time to appeal begins to run when the district court enters a separate judgment.

The separate document requirement of Federal Rule of Civil Procedure 58[3] applies in appeals from final orders in section 2255 cases. *See United States v. Fiorelli*, 337 F.3d 282, 287 (3d Cir. 2003); *United States v. Johnson*, 254 F.3d 279, 284 & n.3 (D.C. Cir. 2001) (collecting cases). *But see Williams v. United States*, 984 F.2d 28, 30 (2d Cir. 1993) (declining to apply Rule 58 to section 2255 proceedings). The 60-day time period to appeal does not begin to run until a qualifying Rule 58 judgment is entered on the docket. *Fiorelli*, 337 F.3d at 287.

§ 18.05. To be timely, the notice of appeal must be *filed* within the 60-day time period.

To be timely, the notice of appeal must be *filed* with the district court clerk within 60 days. Fed. R. App. P. 3(a)(1) ("An appeal . . . may be taken only by filing a notice of appeal with the district court clerk within the time allowed by Rule 4.").

There is one important exception to this rule. In *Houston v. Lack*, 487 U.S. 266, 108 S. Ct. 2379, 101 L. Ed. 2d 245 (1988), the Supreme Court established a "mailbox rule," whereby a notice of appeal filed by a *pro se* prisoner is considered "filed" at the moment of delivery to prison authorities for mailing, rather than at the later point in time when the notice arrived at the court. Following *Houston*, an incarcerated *pro se* inmate's notice of appeal is "timely" if the inmate deposited it "in the institution's internal mail system on or before the last day for filing." Fed. R. App. P. 4(c)(1). "Timely filing may be shown by a declaration in compliance with 28 U.S.C. § 1746 or by a notarized statement, either of which must set forth the date of deposit [in the prison's system for legal mail] and state that first-class postage has been prepaid." *Id.*[4]

---

3. The current text of Fed. R. Civ. P. 58 can be found in the Appendix to this chapter.
4. The following language complies with 28 U.S.C. § 1746:

   I declare (or certify, verify, or state) under penalty of perjury that the foregoing is true and correct and that this Notice of Appeal was placed in the prison mailing system with first-class postage prepaid on ____________ (month, date, year).
   Executed (signed) on ______________(date).

   ____
   Signature

§ 18.06. Motions under Fed. R. Civ. P. 59(e) and Fed. R. Civ. P. 60(b) toll the time to appeal only if filed within ten days of entry of judgment.

A timely motion to alter or amend judgment under Federal Rule of Civil Procedure 59(e) that is *filed by any party* will toll the running of the time for filing a notice of appeal *for all parties*. Fed. R. App. P. 4(a)(4)(A)(iv). To toll the time for appeal, however, the Rule 59(e) motion *must be timely*—that is, filed within ten days of entry of judgment. *See* Fed. R. Civ. P. 59(e); *see also* Fed. R. Civ. P. 6(b)(2) (precluding enlargement of time for filing a motion under Rule 59(e)).[5] A motion for relief from judgment under Federal Rule of Civil Procedure 60(b), which in most cases may be filed up to a year after entry of judgment, *does not* toll the time for appeal, unless "filed no later than 10 days after entry of judgment." Fed. R. Civ. P. 4(a)(4)(A)(vi). If a Rule 59(e) or 60(b) motion is filed within ten days of entry of judgment, a new 60-day period for filing a notice of appeal begins to run from the date of entry of the order granting or denying the postjudgment motion. Fed. R. App. P. 4(a)(4)(A).[6]

If a Rule 59(e) or Rule 60(b) motion is filed within ten days of entry of judgment, and a notice of appeal is filed before the district court rules on the motion, the notice of appeal does not become "effective" until the entry of the order disposing of the motion. Fed. R. App. P. 4(a)(4)(B)(i). Note, however, that if you file a notice of appeal while a postjudgment motion is pending and then later wish to challenge the district court's disposition of the motion in addition to the underlying judgment, you must file either a new notice of appeal or an amended notice of appeal within 60 days of the entry of the order disposing of the postjudgment motion. Fed. R. App. P. 4(a)(4)(B)(ii).

Postjudgment motions are discussed in greater detail in Chapter 17.

II. Certificates of Appealability

§ 18.07. A timely notice of appeal *and* certificate of appealability are required to appeal the denial of a section 2255 motion.

Under pre-AEDPA law, federal prisoners in section 2255 proceedings could perfect an appeal simply by timely filing a notice of appeal. *See* 28 U.S.C. § 2253 (1995); Fed. R. App. P. 22(b) (1995). Following enactment of

5. The text of FED. R. CIV. P. 6 can be found in the Appendix to Chapter 5.

6. The separate document requirement does not apply to orders disposing of motions under Federal Rules of Civil Procedure 59(e) and 60(b). FED. R. CIV. P. 58(a).

the AEDPA, however, in addition to a timely notice of appeal, a prisoner seeking to appeal in a section 2255 proceeding must also obtain a "certificate of appealability" (COA) either from the district court or the court of appeals. 28 U.S.C. § 2253(c)(1)(B); Fed. R. App. P. 22(b)(1).[7]

In contrast, the government need not obtain a COA to appeal. Fed. R. App. P. 22(b)(3). Importantly, if the district court has *granted* the movant section 2255 relief as to one or more claims, and the government appeals, the movant cannot cross-appeal the district court's denial of relief as to any additional claims without first obtaining a COA as to those claims. *See Rios v. Garcia*, 390 F.3d 1082, 1087 (9th Cir. 2004)(collecting cases), *cert. denied*, 546 U.S. 827, 126 S. Ct. 37, 163 L. Ed. 2d 74 (2005).

§ 18.08. The certificate of appealability requirement is jurisdictional.

The requirement that a section 2255 movant obtain a COA to appeal is jurisdictional in nature; that is, the absence of a COA will preclude a prisoner's appeal. *See Miller-El v. Cockrell*, 537 U.S. 322, 336, 123 S. Ct. 1029, 1039, 154 L. Ed. 2d 931 (2003); *United States v. Hadden*, 475, 652, 659 & 660 n.4 (4th Cir. 2007).

§ 18.09. A COA is required to appeal a "final order" in a section 2255 proceeding.

A COA is required to appeal "the final order in a proceeding under section 2255." § 2253(c)(1)(B). "Final" orders include orders other than those denying the motion. For example, a prisoner is required to obtain a COA to appeal a final *collateral* order, such as the district court's denial of bond pending the resolution of the motion. *See Pagan v. United States*, 353 F.3d 1343, 1346 (11th Cir. 2003). A COA is also required to appeal the district court's order denying a motion under Federal Rule of Civil Procedure 60(b) that was filed more than ten days after entry of judgment, *United States v. Vargas*, 393 F.3d 172, 174–75 (D.C. Cir. 2004) (collecting cases), *cert. denied*, 546 U.S. 1011, 126 S. Ct. 644, 163 L. Ed. 2d 521 (2005), and to appeal the district court's order denying a motion to reopen the time to file an appeal under Federal Rule of Appellate Procedure 4(a)(6), *see United States v. Rinaldi*, 447 F.3d 192, 195 (3d Cir. 2006), *cert. denied*, ___ U.S. ___, 127 S. Ct. 300, 166 L. Ed. 2d 227 (2006); *Eltayib v. United States*, 294 F.3d 397, 399 (2d Cir. 2002).

---

7. The current text of 28 U.S.C. § 2253(c) and Fed. R. App. P. 22(b) can be found in the Appendix to this chapter.

No COA, however, is required to appeal the denial of a recusal motion in a section 2255 proceeding. *See Trevino v. Johnson*, 168 F.3d 173, 177 (5th Cir. 1999).

§ 18.10. A COA is required upon a "substantial showing of the denial of a constitutional right."

A COA may issue "only if the [movant] has made a substantial showing of the denial of a constitutional right." § 2253(c)(2). To obtain a COA under this standard, the applicant must show "that reasonable jurists could debate whether (or, for that matter, agree that) the petition should have been resolved in a different manner or that the issues presented were adequate to deserve encouragement to proceed further." *Slack v. McDaniel*, 529 U.S. 473, 484, 120 S. Ct. 1595, 1603–04, 146 L. Ed. 2d 542 (2000) (internal quotation marks omitted).

Accordingly, a movant need not establish that he will win on the merits in order to make the "substantial showing" required to obtain a COA; he need only demonstrate that the questions he raises are debatable among reasonable jurists. The Supreme Court has emphasized that a court "should not decline the application for a COA merely because it believes that the applicant will not demonstrate entitlement to relief." *Miller-El*, 537 U.S. at 337, 123 S. Ct. at 1039. Noting that a COA is necessarily sought in the context in which the movant has lost on the merits, the Supreme Court explained, "We do not require petitioner to prove, before the issuance of a COA, that some jurists would grant the petition. . . . Indeed, a claim can be debatable even though every jurist of reason might agree, after the COA has been granted and the case has received full consideration, that petitioner will not prevail." *Id.*, 537 U.S. at 338, 123 S. Ct at 1040.

Under this "debatable among reasonable jurists" standard, a question of first impression likely warrants issuance of a COA. *See United States v. Espinoza-Saenz*, 235 F.3d 501, 502 (10th Cir. 2000). The fact that there is a split in the courts of appeal on the question also satisfies the standard for obtaining a COA. *See Lambright v. Stewart*, 220 F.3d 1022, 1028–29 (9th Cir. 2000).

§ 18.11. No COA will be granted to review a nonconstitutional question.

A COA "may issue . . . only if the applicant has made a substantial showing of the denial of a *constitutional* right." § 2253(c)(2) (emphasis added). Accordingly, a court cannot grant a COA to review a nonconstitutional question. For this reason, federal courts have declined to issue a COA:

(1) *to address errors in the implementation of the Sentencing Guidelines. See United States v. Cepero*, 224 F.3d 256, 267–68 (3d Cir. 2000); *Buggs v. United States*, 153 F.3d 439, 443 (7th Cir. 1998).
(2) *to consider a claim alleging the denial of a federal statutory right. See United States v. Christensen*, 456 F.3d 1205, 1206 (10th Cir. 2006) (denying COA on matter of statutory interpretation); *United States v. Taylor*, 454 F.3d 1075, 1078–79 (11th Cir. 2006) (court cannot grant COA on Speedy Trial Act claim).
(3) *to address a claim based on a violation of the Federal Rules of Criminal Procedure. See United States v. Brooks*, 230 F.3d 643, 646 (3d Cir. 2000) (denying COA on claim that district court violated Fed. R. Crim. P. 32 by failing to advise defendant of his right to appeal).
(4) *to allow the appeal of a claim asserting a violation of treaty rights. See Murphy v. Netherland*, 116 F.3d 97, 100 (4th Cir. 1997).
(5) *to consider challenges to restitution. See United States v. Mikels*, 236 F.3d 550, 551 (9th Cir. 2001).

Thus, for these and other nonconstitutional issues, the district court's denial of relief is final and not appealable.

§ 18.12. There is a two-part test for a COA on a procedural matter.

Because a COA may issue only for the denial of a constitutional right, what happens when the district court denies section 2255 relief on the basis of a preliminary procedural question, such as that the motion is time-barred or contains procedurally defaulted claims? These questions were answered by the Supreme Court in *Slack v. McDaniel*. There, the Court announced the inquiry federal courts should undertake in such circumstances:

> When the district court denies a habeas petition on procedural grounds without reaching the prisoner's underlying constitutional claim, a COA should issue when the prisoner shows, at least, that jurists of reason would find it debatable whether the petition states a valid claim of the denial of a constitutional right and that jurists of reason would find it debatable whether the district court was correct in its procedural ruling.

Slack, 529 U.S. at 484, 120 S. Ct. at 1604.

Accordingly, under *Slack* there are "two components" involved in whether a COA should issue when the district court has dismissed the motion on procedural grounds: "one directed at the underlying constitutional claims and one directed at the district court's procedural holding." *Id.*, 529 U.S. at 484–85, 120 S. Ct. at 1604. Each is part of a "threshold inquiry" the court must undertake in determining whether a COA should issue. *Id.*, 529 U.S. at 485, 120 S. Ct. at 1604. Where the movant has made a substantial showing with respect to the preliminary procedural issue, however, this inquiry into the merits of the underlying claims is not searching. Before granting a COA, the court need only take a "quick look" at the application to determine whether it contains at least *one* claim that, on its face, alleges the denial of a constitutional right. *See Mateo v. United States*, 310 F.3d 39, 41 (1st Cir. 2002) (collecting cases); *Slack*, 529 U.S. at 484, 120 S. Ct. at 1604 ("a COA should issue when the prisoner shows, at least, that jurists of reason would find it debatable whether the petition states *a* valid claim of the denial of a constitutional right") (emphasis added).

§ 18.13. What if the district court's COA is silent as to a preliminary procedural matter?

What happens if the district court issues a COA that is silent as to a preliminary procedural matter that must be resolved in order to address the merits? For example, what if the district court concludes that section 2255 relief should be denied on a claim because it was procedurally defaulted, but nonetheless issues a COA only as to the merits of the claim? Most courts have held that in such circumstances, the court of appeals does not lack jurisdiction to consider the district court's procedural determination. Rather, the appellate court will assume that the COA also encompasses any procedural issues that must be addressed on appeal. *See McCoy v. United States*, 266 F.3d 1245, 1248 n.2 (11th Cir. 2001); *United States v. Howard*, 381 F.3d 873, 877 n.3 (9th Cir. 2004). *But see Rhagi v. Artuz*, 309 F.3d 103, 105–06 (2d Cir. 2002) *(per curiam)* (holding that in such circumstances, the COA is "incomplete," and court of appeals will consider in the first instance whether a COA should have issued on the procedural question).

§ 18.14. Apply first to the district court for a COA, then the court of appeals.

Any application for a COA must be first considered by the district court. *See* Fed. R. App. 22(b)(1); *United States v. Mitchell*, 216 F.3d 1126, 1129–30 (D.C. Cir. 2000) (collecting cases). If the district court grants a certificate on all issues on which the movant wishes to appeal, the appeal may proceed and the movant need not seek a second certificate from the court of appeals. If, however, the district court denies a COA as to some or all issues, the movant may seek a COA on those issues from the court of appeals.

§ 18.15. You need not file a formal COA request in the district court, but you should do so.

According to Federal Rule of Appellate Procedure 22(b)(1), "[i]f the applicant files a notice of appeal, the district judge who rendered the judgment must either issue a certificate of appealability or state why a certificate should not issue." Fed. R. App. P. 22(b)(1). Pursuant to this rule, a notice of appeal will be construed as an application for a COA, and if a notice of appeal has been filed, the district court must determine whether a COA is warranted, even though no formal COA request was made. *See id.*; *Castro v. United States*, 310 F.3d 900, 902 (6th Cir. 2002); *Mitchell*, 216 F.3d at 1130. Better practice, however, is to move for a COA. A COA application should make a "substantial showing of the denial of a constitutional right" as to each issue for which a COA is requested. Without guidance from counsel, the district court may overlook issues on which an appeal is warranted.

Neither 28 U.S.C. § 2253 nor Fed. R. App. P. 22 specify a time period for filing a COA request in the district court. Check your local district court rules to see if any time limits govern the filing of a COA application in your jurisdiction. If no local rules apply, file a COA application in the district court at the same time as the notice of appeal.

§ 18.16. If the district court denies a COA, you may obtain one from the court of appeals.

If the district court denies a COA as to *all issues,* the court of appeals will automatically consider whether it should grant a COA as to any issue. Fed. R. App. P. 22(b)(1); *Futch*, 518 F.3d at 894. Under the plain language of Rule 22(b)(1), "an applicant . . . gets two bites at the appeal certificate apple: one before the district judge, and if that one is unsuccessful, he gets a second one before a circuit judge." *Jones v. United States*, 224 F.3d 1251, 1255 (11th Cir. 2000) (internal quotation marks omitted). The court of appeals must therefore revisit a district court's complete refusal to issue a COA, even if no express request was made to the appellate court. *Jones*, 224 F.3d at 1256. Although no formal request to the court of appeals is required if the district court denies certification on *all* issues, you should strongly consider filing one. A formal COA request in the court of appeals allows you to craft the issues for appeal and to respond fully to the district court's reasons, if any, for denying a certificate.

The timing and procedures governing a COA application in the courts of appeal vary by circuit, so you should consult your local rules and local practitioners. *See Hohn v. United States*, 524 U.S. 236, 242–43, 118 S. Ct. 1969, 1973, 141 L. Ed. 2d 242 (1998) (listing local rules and internal operating procedures for handling of COAs in the courts of appeal). Depending on the circuit, a COA request may first be considered by a single judge, a two-judge panel, or a three-judge panel. *See Salgado v. Garcia*, 384 F.3d 769, 774–75 (9th Cir. 2004) (collecting authority), *cert. denied*, 544 U.S. 931, 125 S. Ct. 1670, 161 L. Ed. 2d 496 (2005). In some circuits, the denial of a COA may be reconsidered by the court of appeals *en banc*. *See id.*, 384 F.3d at 775; *Thomas v. United States*, 328 F.3d 305, 308–09 (7th Cir. 2003).

§ 18.17. A COA must specify the issues on which an appeal is allowed.

A COA must "indicate which specific issue or issues satisfy the showing required. . . ." § 2253(c)(3). Consequently, a court must review any COA application issue by issue and, if it grants a COA, specify only those claims as to which the movant has made a substantial showing of the denial of a constitutional right. Issues not specified in a COA cannot be addressed on appeal. *See, e.g., United States v. Magallanes*, 301 F.3d 1267, 1269 (10th Cir. 2002) ("a COA is an issue-by-issue jurisdictional prerequisite to a merits determination on appeal"); *Johnson v. United States*, 246 F.3d 655, 660–61 (6th Cir. 2001); *Pruitt v. United States*, 233 F.3d 570, 572–73 (8th Cir. 2000).

§ 18.18. The circuits are divided on whether a formal motion to expand the COA must be filed.

If a district court grants a COA as to some, but not all, of the issues on which certification is sought, the court of appeals has jurisdiction to consider the remaining issues only if it expands the COA to include them. The circuits are divided as to whether an appellant must expressly ask the court of appeals to expand a COA. In some circuits, the court of appeals will construe the inclusion of an issue denied certification by the district court in the briefing on appeal to be an implicit request to expand the COA; in others, an express request to expand the COA, separate from any briefing, must be filed in the court of appeals. *See Jones*, 224 F.3d at 1255–56 & nn.8 & 9 (discussing split). To be safe, if the district court grants only a partial COA and the movant desires to appeal on additional grounds, the best course is to file with the court of appeals a formal motion to expand the COA to include all issues on which review is sought.

§ 18.19. A petition for writ of *certiorari* may be filed to review the denial of a COA.

If both the district court and the court of appeals deny a COA as to all issues, a petition for writ of *certiorari* may be filed in the United States

Supreme Court seeking review of that denial. *Hohn v. United States*, 524 U.S. 236, 118 S. Ct. 1969, 141 L. Ed. 2d 242 (1998).

III. APPENDIX

A. Federal Rule of Appellate Procedure 4 (2008).

Rule 4. Appeal as of Right—When Taken

(a) Appeal in a Civil Case.

(1) Time for Filing a Notice of Appeal.

(A) In a civil case, except as provided in Rules 4(a)(1)(B), 4(a)(4), and 4(c), the notice of appeal required by Rule 3 must be filed with the district clerk within 30 days after the judgment or order appealed from is entered.

(B) When the United States or its officer or agency is a party, the notice of appeal may be filed by any party within 60 days after the judgment or order appealed from is entered.

(C) An appeal from an order granting or denying an application for a writ of error coram nobis is an appeal in a civil case for purposes of Rule 4(a).

(2) Filing Before Entry of Judgment. A notice of appeal filed after the court announces a decision or order—but before the entry of the judgment or order—is treated as filed on the date of and after the entry.

(3) Multiple Appeals. If one party timely files a notice of appeal, any other party may file a notice of appeal within 14 days after the date when the first notice was filed, or within the time otherwise prescribed by this Rule 4(a), whichever period ends later.

(4) Effect of a Motion on a Notice of Appeal.

(A) If a party timely files in the district court any of the following motions under the Federal Rules of Civil Procedure, the time to file an appeal runs for all parties from the entry of the order disposing of the last such remaining motion:

(i) for judgment under Rule 50(b);

(ii) to amend or make additional factual findings under Rule 52(b), whether or not granting the motion would alter the judgment;

(iii) for attorney's fees under Rule 54 if the district court extends the time to appeal under Rule 58;

(iv) to alter or amend the judgment under Rule 59;

(v) for a new trial under Rule 59; or

(vi) for relief under Rule 60 if the motion is filed no later than 10 days after the judgment is entered.

(B) (i) If a party files a notice of appeal after the court announces or enters a judgment—but before it disposes of any motion listed in Rule 4(a)(4)(A)—the notice becomes effective to appeal a judgment or order, in whole or in part, when the order disposing of the last such remaining motion is entered.

(ii) A party intending to challenge an order disposing of any motion listed in Rule 4(a)(4)(A), or a judgment altered or amended upon such a motion, must file a notice of appeal, or an amended notice of appeal—in compliance with Rule 3(c)—within the time prescribed by this Rule measured from the entry of the order disposing of the last such remaining motion.

(iii) No additional fee is required to file an amended notice.

(5) Motion for Extension of Time.

(A) The district court may extend the time to file a notice of appeal if:

(i) a party so moves no later than 30 days after the time prescribed by this Rule 4(a) expires; and

(ii) regardless of whether its motion is filed before or during the 30 days after the time prescribed by this Rule 4(a) expires, that party shows excusable neglect or good cause.

(B) A motion filed before the expiration of the time prescribed in Rule 4(a)(1) or (3) may be ex parte unless the court requires otherwise. If the motion is filed after the expiration of the prescribed time, notice must be given to the other parties in accordance with local rules.

(C) No extension under this Rule 4(a)(5) may exceed 30 days after the prescribed time or 10 days after the date when the order granting the motion is entered, whichever is later.

(6) Reopening the Time to File an Appeal. The district court may reopen the time to file an appeal for a period of 14 days after the date when its order to reopen is entered, but only if all the following conditions are satisfied:

(A) the court finds that the moving party did not receive notice under Federal Rule of Civil Procedure 77(d) of the entry of the judgment or order sought to be appealed within 21 days after entry;

(B) the motion is filed within 180 days after the judgment or order is entered or within 7 days after the moving party receives notice under Federal Rule of Civil Procedure 77(d) of the entry, whichever is earlier; and

(C) the court finds that no party would be prejudiced.

(7) Entry Defined.

(A) A judgment or order is entered for purposes of this Rule 4(a):

(i) if Federal Rule of Civil Procedure 58(a)(1) does not require a separate document, when the judgment or order is entered in the civil docket under Federal Rule of Civil Procedure 79(a); or

(ii) if Federal Rule of Civil Procedure 58(a)(1) requires a separate document, when the judgment or order is entered in the civil docket under Federal Rule of Civil Procedure 79(a) and when the earlier of these events occurs:

- the judgment or order is set forth on a separate document, or
- 150 days have run from entry of the judgment or order in the civil docket under Federal Rule of Civil Procedure 79(a).

(B) A failure to set forth a judgment or order on a separate document when required by Federal Rule of Civil Procedure 58(a)(1) does not affect the validity of an appeal from that judgment or order.

* * *

(c) Appeal by an Inmate Confined in an Institution.

(1) If an inmate confined in an institution files a notice of appeal in either a civil or a criminal case, the notice is timely if it is deposited in the institution's internal mail system on or before the last day for filing. If an institution has a system designed for legal mail, the inmate must use that system to receive the benefit of this rule. Timely filing may be shown by a declaration in compliance with 28 U.S.C. § 1746 or by a notarized statement, either of which must set forth the date of deposit and state that first-class postage has been prepaid.

(2) If an inmate files the first notice of appeal in a civil case under this Rule 4(c), the 14-day period provided in Rule 4(a)(3) for another party to file a notice of appeal runs from the date when the district court dockets the first notice.

(3) When a defendant in a criminal case files a notice of appeal under this Rule 4(c), the 30-day period for the government to file its notice of appeal runs from the entry of the judgment or order appealed from or from the district court's docketing of the defendant's notice of appeal, whichever is later.

(d) **Mistaken Filing in the Court of Appeals.** If a notice of appeal in either a civil or a criminal case is mistakenly filed in the court of appeals, the clerk of that court must note on the notice the date when it was received and send it to the district clerk. The notice is then considered filed in the district court on the date so noted.

B. Federal Rule of Civil Procedure 58 (2008).

Rule 58. Entering Judgment

(a) **Separate Document.** Every judgment and amended judgment must be set out in a separate document, but a separate document is not required for an order disposing of a motion:

- **(1)** for judgment under Rule 50(b);
- **(2)** to amend or make additional findings under Rule 52(b);
- **(3)** for attorney's fees under Rule 54;
- **(4)** for a new trial, or to alter or amend the judgment, under Rule 59; or
- **(5)** for relief under Rule 60.

(b) **Entering Judgment.**

- **(1)** ***Without the Court's Direction.*** Subject to Rule 54(b) and unless the court orders otherwise, the clerk must, without awaiting the court's direction, promptly prepare, sign, and enter the judgment when:
  - **(A)** the jury returns a general verdict;
  - **(B)** the court awards only costs or a sum certain; or
  - **(C)** the court denies all relief.
- **(2)** ***Court's Approval Required.*** Subject to Rule 54(b), the court must promptly approve the form of the judgment, which the clerk must promptly enter, when:
  - **(A)** the jury returns a special verdict or a general verdict with answers to written questions; or
  - **(B)** the court grants other relief not described in this subdivision (b).

(c) **Time of Entry.** For purposes of these rules, judgment is entered at the following times:

- **(1)** if a separate document is not required, when the judgment is entered in the civil docket under Rule 79(a); or

(2) if a separate document is required, when the judgment is entered in the civil docket under Rule 79(a) and the earlier of these events occurs:

(A) it is set out in a separate document; or

(B) 150 days have run from the entry in the civil docket.

(d) **Request for Entry**. A party may request that judgment be set out in a separate document as required by Rule 58(a).

(e) **Cost or Fee Awards**. Ordinarily, the entry of judgment may not be delayed, nor the time for appeal extended, in order to tax costs or award fees. But if a timely motion for attorney's fees is made under Rule 54(d)(2), the court may act before a notice of appeal has been filed and become effective to order that the motion have the same effect under Federal Rule of Appellate Procedure 4(a)(4) as a timely motion under Rule 59.

C. 28 U.S.C. § 2253 (2008).

§ 2253. Appeal

(a) In a habeas corpus proceeding or a proceeding under section 2255 before a district judge, the final order shall be subject to review, on appeal, by the court of appeals for the circuit in which the proceeding is held.

(b) There shall be no right of appeal from a final order in a proceeding to test the validity of a warrant to remove to another district or place for commitment or trial a person charged with a criminal offense against the United States, or to test the validity of such person's detention pending removal proceedings.

(c) **(1)** Unless a circuit justice or judge issues a certificate of appealability, an appeal may not be taken to the court of appeals from—

(A) the final order in a habeas corpus proceeding in which the detention complained of arises out of process issued by a State court; or

(B) the final order in a proceeding under section 2255.

(2) A certificate of appealability may issue under paragraph (1) only if the applicant has made a substantial showing of the denial of a constitutional right.

(3) The certificate of appealability under paragraph (1) shall indicate which specific issue or issues satisfy the showing required by paragraph (2).

D. Federal Rule of Appellate Procedure 22(b) (2008).

Rule 22. Habeas Corpus and Section 2255 Proceedings

* * *

(b) Certificate of Appealability.

(1) In a habeas corpus proceeding in which the detention complained of arises from process issued by a state court, or in a 28 U.S.C. § 2255 proceeding, the applicant cannot take an appeal unless a circuit justice or a circuit or district judge issues a certificate of appealability under 28 U.S.C. § 2253(c). If an applicant files a notice of appeal, the district judge who rendered the judgment must either issue a certificate of appealability or state why a certificate should not issue. The district clerk must send the certificate or statement to the court of appeals with the notice of appeal and the file of the district-court proceedings. If the district judge has denied the certificate, the applicant may request a circuit judge to issue the certificate.

(2) A request addressed to the court of appeals may be considered by a circuit judge or judges, as the court prescribes. If no express request for a certificate is filed, the notice of appeal constitutes a request addressed to the judges of the court of appeals.

(3) A certificate of appealability is not required when a state or its representative or the United States or its representative appeals.

CHAPTER 19

Second or Successive Motions

Contents

Introduction

§ 19.01. Post-AEDPA, it is nearly impossible to win relief on a second or successive motion.

Before enactment of the Antiterrorism and Effective Death Penalty Act of 1996 (AEDPA),[1] a federal prisoner who wished to obtain relief on a second or successive section 2255 motion first had to demonstrate either "cause and prejudice," or "actual innocence" before her claims could be considered.[2] *See* Rules Governing § 2255 Proceedings, Rule 9(b) (1995); *McCleskey v. Zant*, 499 U.S. 467, 494–95, 111 S. Ct. 1454, 1470, 113 L. Ed. 2d 517 (1991); *In re Hanserd*, 123 F.3d 922, 928 (6th Cir. 1997). It was *very* difficult to obtain relief on a subsequent motion under this pre-AEDPA standard. The substantive provisions enacted by AEDPA, and codified in subsection (h) of section 2255, now make it nearly impossible. *See* 28 U.S.C. § 2255(h)(1) & (h)(2). Given the difficulty of obtaining relief on a second or successive section 2255 motion: "it is essential that [movants] include in their first [motion] *all* potential claims for which they might desire to seek review and relief." *Mason v. Meyers*, 208 F.3d 414, 417 (3d Cir. 2000) (emphasis in original).

1. The AEDPA is discussed in Chapter 2.
2. "Cause and prejudice" and "actual innocence" are discussed in Chapter 9.

§ 19.02. The AEDPA complicated the procedures governing second or successive motions.

The AEDPA changed not only the substantive standards governing second or successive motions, but also the procedures governing such motions. A pre-AEDPA second or successive motion was simply filed in the district court. Now, the movant must obtain authorization from the court of appeals *before* she may file a second or successive motion in the district court. *See* Rules Governing § 2255 Proceedings, Rule 9. The AEDPA also made myriad other changes to the processing of second or successive motions.

I. Is the Motion Truly "Second or Successive"?

The AEDPA's restrictions on relief and procedural complications come into play *only* if a subsequent pleading is truly "second or successive." *See Panetti v. Quarterman*, ___ U.S. ___, 127 S. Ct. 2842, 2855, 168 L. Ed. 2d 662 (2007); *Stewart v. Martinez-Villareal*, 523 U.S. 637, 642, 118 S. Ct. 1618, 1621, 140 L. Ed. 2d 849 (1998). Accordingly, as a threshold inquiry, it is critical to determine whether the subsequent pleading at issue actually *is* a second or successive section 2255 motion.

§ 19.03. Not all subsequent motions are second or successive.

Neither section 2255 nor the AEDPA define "second or successive." Rather, the phrase "takes its full meaning from [the Supreme Court's] case law, including decisions predating the enactment of the [AEDPA]." *Panetti*, 127 S. Ct. at 2853. Review of this case law demonstrates that the Supreme Court has "declined to interpret 'second or successive' as referring to all . . . applications filed second or successively in time, even when the later filings address a . . . judgment already challenged in a prior . . . application." *Id.* As such, you must not assume that every motion filed *after* an initial section 2255 motion is a "second or successive" motion.

§ 19.04. Situations where a subsequent section 2255 motion is *not* second or successive.

A subsequent section 2255 motion is *not* second or successive where:

(1) *The prior motion was not determined on the merits.* If the prior motion was not adjudicated and decided on the merits, any

subsequent motion is not second or successive. *See, e.g., Slack v. McDaniel*, 529 U.S. 473, 485–86, 120 S. Ct. 1595, 1604–05, 146 L. Ed. 2d 542 (2000); *Muniz v. United States*, 236 F.3d 122, 123 (2d Cir. 2001); *Sustache-Rivera v. United States*, 221 F.3d 8, 13 (1st Cir. 2000).

Of course, this also means that a subsequent motion *is* second or successive where the prior motion was adjudicated on the merits. *See, e.g., United States v. Barrett*, 178 F.3d 34, 45 (1st Cir. 1999). Note that a prior motion has been adjudicated "on the merits" if it was (a) dismissed as "time-barred," *see Bottone v. United States*, 350 F.3d 59, 63 (2d Cir. 2003); (b) denied because all the claims were procedurally defaulted, *see Thai v. United States*, 391 F.3d 491, 495 (2d Cir. 2004); *Villanueva v. United States*, 346 F.3d 55, 60 (2d Cir. 2003); or (c) denied because relief is barred by *Stone v. Powell*, 428 U.S. 465, 96 S. Ct. 3037, 49 L. Ed. 2d 1067 (1976), *see Villanueva*, 346 F.3d at 60.[3]

(2) *The prior motion was dismissed without prejudice or voluntarily dismissed.* Generally, any motion filed after a prior motion was dismissed without prejudice by the court is not second or successive. *See Haro-Arteaga v. United States*, 199 F.3d 1195, 1196–97 (10th Cir. 1999). The same is true where the movant voluntarily dismisses the prior motion. *See id.*; *Garrett v. United States*, 178 F.3d 940, 942–43 (7th Cir. 1999). In the latter circumstance, however, courts will focus on the substance of the prior proceedings: "[I]f a petitioner clearly concedes upon withdrawal of a § 2255 petition that the petition lacks merit, the withdrawal is akin to a dismissal on the merits and subsequent petitions will count as successive." *Thai*, 391 F.3d at 495 (collecting cases).

(3) *The subsequent motion is a motion to amend under Federal Rule of Civil Procedure 15.* A motion to amend filed before the district court rules on the merits of a section 2255 motion is not a second or successive motion under § 2255(h). *Johnson v. United States*, 196 F.3d 802, 805 (7th Cir. 1999); *Littlejohn v. Artuz*, 271 F.3d 360, 362 (2d Cir. 2001). This is because "the AEDPA allows every prisoner one full opportunity to seek collateral review. Part of that opportunity—part of every civil case—is an entitlement to add or drop issues while the litigation proceeds." *Johnson*, 196 F.3d at 805. Be warned, however, that amending a section 2255 motion can be tricky; amendment is discussed in detail in Chapter 12.

3. Section 2255's statute of limitations is discussed in Chapter 5; the procedural default doctrine is discussed in Chapter 9; *Stone v. Powell* is discussed in Chapter 11.

(4) *The subsequent motion was filed while the initial motion was still pending.* "[I]n general, when a second § 2255 motion is filed before adjudication of an initial § 2255 motion is complete, the district court should construe the second § 2255 motion as a motion to amend the pending § 2255 motion" rather than a second or successive motion. *Ching v. United States*, 298 F.3d 174, 177 (2d Cir. 2002). *Accord Woods v. Carey*, 525 F.3d 886, 890 (9th Cir. 2008); *Whab v. United States*, 408 F.3d 116, 119 (2d Cir. 2005) (motion not second or successive because filed while appellate proceedings remained pending). *But see Ochoa v. Sirmons*, 485 F.3d 538, 540 (10th Cir. 2007) (expressly disagreeing with *Whab*).

(5) *The subsequent motion presents a claim that was not ripe at the time of the first motion. See Panetti*, 127 S. Ct. at 2855; *Martinez-Villareal*, 523 U.S. at 644–45, 118 S. Ct. at 1622; *United States v. Grant*, 493 F.3d 464, 468 n.3 (5th Cir. 2007) ("the instant motion is not second or successive because the facts underlying this motion arose only after his prior § 2255 motion was disposed of by the district court"); *Hernandez v. United States*, 226 F.3d 839, 841 (7th Cir. 2000).

(6) *The prior motion was dismissed due to some technical deficiency unrelated to the substantive claims for relief. See Benton v. Washington*, 106 F.3d 162, 164–65 (7th Cir. 1996) (failure to pay the filing fee); *Phillips v. Seiter*, 173 F.3d 609, 610 (7th Cir. 1999) (failure to file in the proper district).

(7) *The court limited the presentation of substantive claims in the prior proceeding. See Reeves v. Little*, 120 F.3d 1136, 1139–40 (10th Cir. 1997).

(8) *The prisoner obtained relief on a prior motion and the subsequent motion raised only claims that originated from the retrial or resentencing. See Hawkins v. United States*, 415 F.3d 738, 740 (7th Cir. 2005); *Sustache-Rivera*, 221 F.3d at 13; *In re Green*, 215 F.3d 1195, 1195 (11th Cir. 2000); *Esposito v. United States*, 135 F.3d 111, 111 (2d Cir. 1997). Note, however, that if the successful first motion results only in relief as to sentence, any later challenge to the underlying conviction may be considered second or successive. *See Hawkins*, 415 F.3d at 740; *Galtieri v. United States*, 128 F.3d 33, 35 (2d Cir. 1997).

(9) *The prior motion was incorrectly dismissed as untimely or as second or successive. See Muniz*, 236 F.3d at 128 (prior motion incorrectly dismissed as untimely) *(per curiam); In re Moore*, 196 F.3d 252, 255 (D.C. Cir. 1999) (prior motion incorrectly dismissed

as successive). Note, however, that the *correct* dismissal of a prior motion as time-barred *is* considered a decision "on the merits" that renders any subsequent motion second or successive. *See Bottone*, 350 F.3d at 63.

(10) *The movant used his first motion solely to reinstate his right to direct appeal. See In re Olabode*, 325 F.3d 166, 171–73 (3d Cir. 2003); *McIver v. United States*, 307 F.3d 1327, 1330 (11th Cir. 2002) (collecting cases). *But see Pratt v. United States*, 129 F.3d 54, 61–63 (1st Cir. 1997) (requiring prisoner to join all attacks on his judgment, including his appeal reinstatement claim, in his first section 2255 motion); *United States v. Orozco-Ramirez*, 211 F.3d 862, 869–70 (5th Cir. 2000) (same).

§ 19.05. A subsequent motion is not second or successive where the prior or subsequent motion was not a section 2255 motion.

Section 2255's restrictions on relief and complicated procedures apply only to "[a] second or successive *motion*" under section 2255. *See* § 2255(h) (emphasis added). Accordingly, they do not apply if the prior or subsequent filing was not a section 2255 motion. *See Gonzalez v. Crosby*, 545 U.S. 524, 532, 125 S. Ct. 2641, 2648, 162 L. Ed. 2d 480 (2005) (Rule 60(b) motion which "attacks . . . some defect in the integrity" of the section 2255 proceeding is not a second or successive section 2255 motion); *United States v. Esogbue*, 357 F.3d 532, 534 (5th Cir. 2004) (subsequent filing was a true writ of error *coram nobis*); *Jacobs v. McCaughtry*, 251 F.3d 596, 597 (7th Cir. 2001) (subsequent application sought relief available only via petition for writ of habeas corpus under 28 U.S.C. § 2241); *United States v. Campbell*, 294 F.3d 824, 826–27 (7th Cir. 2002) (subsequent application was a *bona fide* motion under Federal Rule of Criminal Procedure 6(e)(3)(C)(i)(I) seeking disclosure of matters occurring before the grand jury).

This does not mean that simply relabeling a subsequent filing will suffice. Courts will "look beyond the formal title affixed to a motion if the motion is the functional equivalent of a motion under section 2255." *United States v. Rich*, 141 F.3d 550, 551 (5th Cir. 1998). *See Evans*, 224 F.3d at 672 ("we hold that any post-judgment motion in a criminal proceeding that fits the description of [§ 2255(a)] is a motion under § 2255, and that the second (and all subsequent) of these requires appellate approval"). If the court determines a later filing is indeed a second or successive section 2255 motion, it will *sua sponte* apply the restrictions on such motions to a mislabeled filing, no matter whether it is called: a section 2241 habeas corpus petition, *see Tolliver v. Dobre*, 211 F.3d 876,

877–78 (5th Cir. 2000); a writ of error *coram nobis*, *see United States v. Torres*, 282 F.3d 1241, 1246 (10th Cir. 2002); a motion under Federal Rule of Criminal Procedure 33, *see United States v. Evans*, 224 F.3d 670, 672 (7th Cir. 2000); a motion under Federal Rule of Civil Procedure 60(b), *see, e.g., Gonzalez*, 545 U.S. at 532, 125 S. Ct. at 2648; *United States v. Nelson*, 465 F.3d 1145, 1148–49 (10th Cir. 2006); a motion to reopen, *see Jackson v. United States*, 463 F.3d 635, 637, 639 (7th Cir. 2006), *cert. denied*, ___ U.S. ___, 127 S. Ct. 2246, 167 L. Ed. 2d 1095 (2007); a motion for reduction of sentence under 18 U.S.C. § 3582, *see United States v. Lloyd*, 398 F.3d 978, 979–80 (7th Cir. 2005); or a motion to recall the mandate in the court of appeals, *see Calderon v. Thompson*, 523 U.S. 538, 118 S. Ct. 1489, 140 L. Ed. 2d 720 (1998); *United States v. Ford*, 383 F.3d 567, 568 (7th Cir. 2004), *cert. denied*, 543 U.S. 1074, 125 S. Ct. 927, 160 L. Ed. 2d 813 (2005).

§ 19.06. A subsequent motion is not second or successive where the court recharacterized a pleading as an initial section 2255 motion but failed to warn a *pro se* movant.

In *Castro v. United States*, 540 U.S. 375, 124 S. Ct. 786, 157 L. Ed. 2d 778 (2003), the Supreme Court held that if a court recharacterizes a *pro se* litigant's pleading as a first section 2255 motion but does not provide the litigant with certain specific warnings, that motion does not count as a first motion in determining whether a subsequent pleading is a second or successive motion. The Court stated:

> when a court recharacterizes a *pro se* litigant's motion as a first § 2255 motion . . . the district court must notify the *pro se* litigant that it intends to recharacterize the pleading, warn the litigant that this recharacterization means that any subsequent § 2255 motion will be subject to the restrictions on "second or successive" motions, and provide the litigant an opportunity to withdraw the motion or to amend it so that it contains all the § 2255 claims he believes he has.

Id., 540 U.S. at 383, 124 S. Ct at 792. If the district court fails to give the required notice, "the motion cannot be considered to have become a § 2255 motion for purposes of applying to later motions the law's 'second or successive' restrictions." *Id.*, 540 U.S. at 383, 124 S. Ct at 792.

The recharacterization of postjudgment motions as section 2255 motions raises a number of important issues, which are discussed in detail in Chapter 3.

§ 19.07. If your subsequent motion is not second or successive, file it in the district court.

If section 2255's second or successive provisions do not apply to a subsequent filing, the movant should file the pleading in the first instance in the district court. *See In re Moore*, 196 F.3d at 254. If the subsequent motion is truly a "first" motion, permission to file need not be obtained from the court of appeals. *See id.*

§ 19.08. The district court's dismissal of a motion as second or successive is appealable.

If the district court dismisses a section 2255 motion because it believes that motion is second or successive, that dismissal is an appealable final order. *See Pratt v. United States*, 129 F.3d 54, 57–58 (1st Cir. 1997). In some circuits, the court of appeals has decided that "in the interests of justice," the district court may, in its discretion, transfer to the court of appeals under 28 U.S.C. § 1631 an unauthorized second or successive motion, rather than dismissing it. *See id.* at 57 & n.3; *Boyd v. United States*, 304 F.3d 813, 814 (8th Cir. 2002). In addition, a court of appeals may construe a notice of appeal from a district court's dismissal order as an application seeking leave to file a second or successive motion in the court of appeals. *See United States v. Gallegos*, 142 F.3d 1211, 1212 (10th Cir. 1998); *Pratt*, 129 F.3d at 58.

II. Substantive Prerequisites for Second or Successive Motions

§ 19.09. A second or successive motion will be authorized only in rare, specific circumstances.

Under section 2255(h), a court of appeals can authorize the filing of a second or successive motion only if the motion contains either:

(1) newly discovered evidence that, if proven and viewed in light of the evidence as a whole, would be sufficient to establish by clear and convincing evidence that no reasonable fact-finder would have found the movant guilty of the offense; or

(2) a new rule of constitutional law, made retroactive to cases on collateral review by the Supreme Court, that was previously unavailable.

28 U.S.C. § 2255(h)(1) & (h)(2). These requirements are extremely stringent.

§ 19.10. Section 2255(h)(1): Newly discovered evidence of actual innocence.

Under section 2255(h)(1), the movant must show "newly discovered evidence that, if proven and viewed in light of the evidence as a whole, would be sufficient to establish by clear and convincing evidence that no reasonable factfinder would have found the movant guilty of the offense." § 2255(h)(1). To satisfy this standard, the movant must make a two-part showing:

§ 19.11. "newly discovered evidence. . . ."

First, the movant must demonstrate that the evidence supporting the claim is "newly discovered." *Id.* Evidence is not "newly discovered" under section 2255(h)(1) if the movant could have discovered the facts before filing the first motion, *In re Nailor,* 487 F.3d 1018, 1023 (6th Cir. 2007); *Villanueva*, 346 F.3d at 64 (alibi affidavits offered by movant "do not constitute newly discovered evidence because they could have been obtained . . . prior to his first § 2255 petition"); *In re Boshears*, 110 F.3d 1538, 1540–41 (11th Cir. 1997), or at least by the time the district court denied relief on the first motion, *In re McGinn*, 213 F.3d 884, 885 (5th Cir. 2000) (denying request to file successive petition seeking leave to conduct exculpatory DNA testing that was not available to time of trial, where applicant presented no evidence that the new DNA testing was not available for presentation to district court before first petition was denied).

§ 19.12. " . . . establish[ing] by clear and convincing evidence that no reasonable factfinder would have found the movant guilty of the offense."

In addition to being "newly discovered," the evidence must, "if proven and viewed in light of the evidence as a whole, . . . be sufficient to establish by clear and convincing evidence that no reasonable factfinder would have found the movant guilty of the offense." § 2255(h)(1). The "clear and convincing" standard is stringent. *See Kutzner v. Cockrell*, 303 F.3d 333, 337 (5th Cir. 2002) (noting that even if DNA tests of evidence collected at scene were negative, it would be insufficient to establish by clear and convincing evidence that the outcome of the trial would have been different because other evidence presented at trial, although circumstantial, was not weak).

Moreover, the language "no reasonable factfinder would have found the movant guilty of the offense" in section 2255(h)(1) forecloses all claims unrelated to guilt or innocence, including claims asserting:

(1) *sentencing error, including claims of "actual innocence" of the sentence. See In re Dean*, 341 F.3d 1247, 1248 (11th Cir. 2003); *Hope v. United States*, 108 F.3d 119, 120 (7th Cir. 1997); *In re Vial*, 115 F.3d 1192, 1198 (4th Cir. 1997) *(en banc).*

(2) *the bias or misconduct of a judge or juror. See Villafuerte v. Stewart*, 142 F.3d 1124, 1126 (9th Cir. 1998) (biased judge); *In re Buenoano*, 137 F.3d 1445, 1447 (11th Cir. 1998) *(per curiam)* (juror misconduct); *In re Magwood*, 113 F.3d 1544, 1552 (11th Cir. 1997) (biased juror).

(3) *prior counsel has been disbarred or was ineffective in matters unrelated to guilt or innocence. See United States v. Winestock*, 340 F.3d 200, 208 (4th Cir. 2003) (appellate counsel was recently disbarred); *In re Siggers*, 132 F.3d 333, 338 (6th Cir. 1997) (trial counsel gave petitioner erroneous advice regarding the government's plea offer).

(4) *an arraignment was unconstitutionally delayed. See Siggers*, 132 F.3d at 338 ("Siggers has failed to demonstrate that the timing of his arraignment has any bearing on the question of his guilt or innocence.").

§ 19.13. Section 2255(h)(2): A new, retroactive, previously unavailable rule of constitutional law.

If a section 2255 movant cannot demonstrate that her second or successive motion is based on newly discovered evidence of innocence, then she may obtain relief only if she can demonstrate that the motion relies on "a new rule of constitutional law, made retroactive to cases on collateral review by the Supreme Court, that was previously unavailable." § 2255(h)(2). To satisfy this standard, the movant must make a four-pronged showing.

§ 19.14. ". . . a new rule . . ."

First, the rule of law upon which movant relies must be "new." § 2255(h)(2). Even a recent Supreme Court decision is not new if that decision simply "applied a long-established principle . . . to a particular claim," *Outlaw v. Sternes*, 233 F.3d 453, 455 (7th Cir. 2000), or clarified the application of an earlier decision, *see In re Garza*, 253 F.3d 201, 202-03 (5th Cir. 2001). In determining when a rule of law is new for purposes of section 2255(h)(2), the analysis employed in *Teague v. Lane*, 489 U.S. 288, 109 S.

Ct. 1060, 103 L. Ed. 2d 334 (1989),[4] may be looked to for guidance. *See Bannister v. Bowersox*, 128 F.3d 621, 622–23 (8th Cir. 1997).

§ 19.15. "... of constitutional law ..."

Second, the new rule must be one of "constitutional" law. § 2255(h)(2). For example, where a recent Supreme Court decision involves only a matter of statutory interpretation, it is not a new rule of "constitutional" law, and therefore no successive motion may be filed. *See, e.g., United States v. Reyes*, 358 F.3d 1095, 1097 (9th Cir. 2004) (claim under *Richardson v. United States*, 526 U.S. 813, 119 S. Ct. 1707, 143 L. Ed. 2d 985 (1999), cannot form basis for second or successive motion because it involved a matter of statutory interpretation, not constitutional law); *United States v. Prevatte*, 300 F.3d 792, 798 (7th Cir. 2002) (same as to claim under *Jones v. United States*, 529 U.S. 848, 120 S. Ct. 1904, 146 L. Ed. 2d 902 (2000)); *Gray-Bey v. United States*, 209 F.3d 986, 988–89 (7th Cir. 2000) *(per curiam)* (same as to claim under *Bailey v. United States*, 516 U.S. 137, 116 S. Ct. 501, 133 L. Ed. 2d 472 (1995)).

§ 19.16. "... made retroactive to cases on collateral review by the Supreme Court ..."

Third, to come within section 2255(h)(2), the new rule of constitutional law must have been "made retroactive to cases on collateral review by the Supreme Court." § 2255(h)(2). A new rule may be "made retroactive" to collateral cases if a holding of the Supreme Court has applied the rule retroactively or stated that the rule so applies. *See Tyler v. Cain*, 533 U.S. 656, 662, 121 S. Ct. 2478, 2482, 150 L. Ed. 2d 632 (2001). A new rule may also be "made retroactive" "if Supreme Court holdings *dictate* the conclusion that the new rule ... has been made retroactive to cases on collateral review." *In re Turner*, 267 F.3d 225, 229 (3d Cir. 2001) (emphasis in original).

Importantly, however, the new rule must be made retroactive to cases on collateral review *by the Supreme Court*, or relief is unavailable. *See* § 2255(h)(2); *Tyler*, 533 U.S. at 662–63, 121 S. Ct. at 2482 (noting that the "Supreme Court is the only entity that can 'ma[k]e' a new rule retroactive" such that a second or successive pleading is allowed); *Villanueva*, 346 F.3d at 64 (*Apprendi v. New Jersey*, 530 U.S. 466, 120 S. Ct. 2348, 147 L. Ed. 2d 435 (2000), has not yet been "made retroactive" by the Supreme Court as required for second or successive motion); *Leonard v. United States*, 383 F.3d 1146, 1148 (10th Cir. 2004) *(per curiam)* (same as to *Blakely v.*

4. *Teague* is discussed in Chapter 10.

Washington, 542 U.S. 296, 124 S. Ct. 2531, 159 L. Ed. 2d 403 (2004)); *In re Olopade*, 403 F.3d 159, 162–63 (3d Cir. 2005) (same as to *United States v. Booker*, 543 U.S. 220, 125 S. Ct. 738, 160 L. Ed. 2d 621 (2005)).

§ 19.17. "... that was previously unavailable."

Fourth and finally, even if a new rule of constitutional law has been made retroactive by the Supreme Court, no relief may be granted under section 2255(h)(2) unless that rule was also "previously unavailable;" that is, not available to the movant until *after* proceedings on the first motion were completed.[5] *See In re Hill*, 113 F.3d 181, 182–83 (11th Cir. 1997); *In re Smith*, 142 F.3d 832, 834 (5th Cir. 1998); *Villafuerte*, 142 F.3d at 1125 (holding Vienna Convention claim not "previously unavailable" given that Convention has been in effect since 1969).

III. Procedures Governing Second or Successive Motions

§ 19.18. There is now a "gatekeeping" mechanism for second or successive motions.

In addition to its stringent substantive requirements for second or successive section 2255 motions, the AEDPA also created an elaborate pre-filing procedure—a so-called gatekeeping mechanism—requiring a movant to receive permission from the court of appeals to file a second or successive motion before being able to proceed in the district court. *See Felker v. Turpin*, 518 U.S. 651, 657, 116 S. Ct. 2333, 2337, 135 L. Ed. 2d 827 (1996). This mechanism can be found in 28 U.S.C. § 2244(b), which states, in pertinent part:

> (b) (3) (A) Before a second or successive application permitted by this section is filed in the district court, the applicant shall move in the appropriate court of appeals for an order authorizing the district court to consider the application.
>
> (B) A motion in the court of appeals for an order authorizing the district court to consider a second or successive application shall be determined by a three-judge panel of the court of appeals.

5. For this reason, if the Supreme Court announces a "new rule" while a first section 2255 motion is still pending, the best course is to attempt to amend that motion to include a claim based on the new rule. Amendments are discussed in Chapter 12.

(C) The court of appeals may authorize the filing of a second or successive application only if it determines that the application makes a prima facie showing that the application satisfies the requirements of this subsection.

(D) The court of appeals shall grant or deny the authorization to file a second or successive application not later than 30 days after the filing of the motion.

(E) The grant or denial of an authorization by a court of appeals to file a second or successive application shall not be appealable and shall not be the subject of a petition for rehearing or for a writ of certiorari.

(4) A district court shall dismiss any claim presented in a second or successive application that the court of appeals has authorized to be filed unless the applicant shows that the claim satisfies the requirements of this section.

28 U.S.C. § 2244(b)(3) & (4).

Pursuant to this mechanism, before a movant may file a second or successive section 2255 motion in the district court, he must first "obtain an order from the appropriate court of appeals authorizing the district court to consider the motion." Rules Governing § 2255 Proceedings, Rule 9. Without preauthorization from the court of appeals, a district court has no jurisdiction to address the merits of a second or successive motion. *See Potts v. United States*, 210 F.3d 770, 771 (7th Cir. 2000); *United States v. Key*, 205 F.3d 773, 774 (5th Cir. 2000); *United States v. Gallegos*, 142 F.3d 1211, 1212 (10th Cir. 1998).

§ 19.19. A "*prima facie* showing" to the court of appeals must be made.

A court of appeals will not grant leave to file a second or successive motion in the district court unless the movant has made a "*prima facie* showing" that the motion satisfies the stringent substantive requirements contained in section 2255(h)(1) or (h)(2). § 2244(b)(3)(C). A *prima facie* showing is "simply a sufficient showing of possible merit to warrant a fuller exploration by the district court. . . . If in light of the documents submitted with the application it appears reasonably likely that the application satisfies the stringent requirements for the filing of a second or successive petition, we shall grant the application." *Bennett v. United States*, 119 F.3d 468, 469–70 (7th Cir. 1997).

Section 2244(b)(3)(C)'s requirement of a *prima facie* showing "*does not* direct the appellate court to engage in a preliminary merits assessment." *Ochoa*, 485 F.3d at 541 (emphasis added). Rather, it focuses the inquiry by the court of appeals solely on the conditions specified in § 2255(h)(1) & (h)(2). *Id.* As such, merits review is simply not part of the court of appeals' gatekeeping role. *Id.* at 543 (discussing cases). Nor is it appropriate for the court of appeals to consider whether the motion is timely. *See In re McDonald*, 514 F.3d 539, 543–44 (6th Cir. 2008).

§ 19.20. Check for local rules and local forms governing applications for leave to file a second or successive motion.

Many circuits have local rules governing applications for leave to file second or successive section 2255 motions. *See, e.g.*, 1st Cir. R. 22.2; 3d Cir. 22.5; 4th Cir. R 22(d); 6th Cir. R. 22(b); 7th Cir. R. 22.2, 8th Cir. R. 22B; 9th Cir. R. 22-3; 11th Cir. R. 22-3. Check these local rules to be sure that an application complies with all the procedural requirements imposed in the circuit in which it is to be filed. In addition, many circuits have form applications for leave to file a second or successive section 2255 motion. In some circuits, such as the First and the Eleventh, the use of these forms is *required* in noncapital cases. In those circuits where they are used, these form applications can be obtained from the clerk of the court of appeals, and may also be found on the courts' websites. The websites for the federal courts of appeal can be found at *http://www.ca*.uscourts.gov,* where "*" is the number for the circuit. For example, *http://www.ca8.uscourts.gov* is the website for the United States Court of Appeals for the Eighth Circuit.

§ 19.21. The court of appeals has at least 30 days to grant or deny authorization.

A court of appeals must "grant or deny the authorization to file a second or successive application not later than 30 days after the filing of the motion." § 2244(b)(3)(D). However, the courts of appeal have construed this time limit very flexibly and routinely extend it in complex cases. *See, e.g., Browning v. United States*, 241 F.3d 1262, 1263–64 (10th Cir. 2001) *(en banc); Gray-Bey v. United States*, 201 F.3d 866, 867 (7th Cir. 2000).

§ 19.22. Procedure if authorization is granted.

If the court of appeals determines that the application makes a *prima facie* showing that a claim meets the requirements of section 2255(h)(1) or (h)(2), it should "authorize the prisoner to file the *entire* application in district court, even if some of the claims in the application do not satisfy the applicable standards." *United States v. Winestock*, 340 F.3d 200, 205 (4th Cir. 2003) (emphasis added). The district court must thereafter review the motion claim by claim to determine if the requirements of section 2255(h)

(1) or (h)(2) are met. *Id.* If the district court finds that the movant has not satisfied these requirements, the district court must dismiss any motion the court of appeals has allowed to be filed, without reaching its merits. *See Reyes-Requena v. United States*, 243 F.3d 893, 899 (5th Cir. 2001); *Bennett*, 119 F.3d at 470. In other words, "the movant must get through two gates before the merits of the motion can be considered." *Bennett*, 119 F.3d at 470. Thereafter, the district court may consider whether the motion is timely. *See McDonald*, 514 F.3d at 543–44.

IV. Review of the Court of Appeals' Gatekeeping Decision

§ 19.23. The "gatekeeping" decision by the court of appeals is not appealable, nor subject to rehearing or *certiorari* review.

The decision of a court of appeals exercising its "gatekeeping" function "shall not be appealable and shall not be the subject of a petition for rehearing nor a writ of *certiorari*." § 2244(b)(3)(E). *See Felker*, 518 U.S. at 658–59, 116 S. Ct. at 2337. Any such appeal or petition will be dismissed as unauthorized, or not ruled upon at all. *See United States v. Lorentsen*, 106 F.3d 278, 279 (9th Cir. 1997); *In re Sonshine*, 132 F.3d 1133, 1134 (6th Cir. 1997). Section 2244(b)(3)(E) does not, however, prohibit the court of appeals from ordering rehearing *sua sponte*. *See In re Byrd*, 269 F.3d 585, 585 (6th Cir. 2001); *Triestman v. United States*, 124 F.3d 361, 367 (2d Cir. 1997).

§ 19.24. Review may be had by an original habeas petition filed in the Supreme Court.

Although the decision of a court of appeals denying a request for permission to file a second or successive section 2255 motion is not appealable or reviewable by the Supreme Court on *certiorari*, *see* § 2244(b)(3)(E), the AEDPA did not repeal the Supreme Court's authority to entertain original habeas corpus petitions under 28 U.S.C. §§ 2241 and 2242. *See Felker*, 518 U.S. at 660–61, 116 S. Ct. at 2338–39. Therefore, if a court of appeals denies authorization to file a second or successive section 2255 motion, a petition for writ of habeas corpus in the original jurisdiction of the Supreme Court may be filed. The chances of it being granted, however, are very slim.

§ 19.25. Standards governing original writs to the Supreme Court.

The standards governing the Supreme Court's consideration of an original habeas corpus petition are unclear. The Court has stated that the restrictions on second or successive motions contained in section 2255(h) "inform" its consideration of an original habeas petition, *Felker*, 518 U.S. at 663, 116 S. Ct. at 2339, but other considerations are also relevant. The Court's own rules governing the grant of an original habeas petition note that "[t]his writ is rarely granted," and require a petitioner to show that "exceptional circumstances warrant the exercise of the Court's discretionary powers, and that adequate relief cannot be obtained in any other form or from any other court." Supreme Court Rule 20.4(a). Since the enactment of the AEDPA in 1996, the Supreme Court has not yet found any circumstances sufficiently "exceptional" to warrant consideration of an original petition.

§ 19.26. There is a "rule of five" for original habeas petitions.

Once an original habeas corpus petition is filed, it appears that a "rule of five" is required before the Justices will hear oral argument on the petition. *See, e.g., In re Tarver*, 528 U.S. 1152, 120 S. Ct. 1235, 145 L. Ed. 2d 1123 (2000) (Mem.); *In re Wright*, 529 U.S. 1001, 120 S. Ct. 1266, 146 L. Ed. 2d 215 (2000) (Mem). In *Tarver* and *Wright*, the Court's memorandum orders denied petitions for writ of habeas corpus in the Court's original jurisdiction, despite listing four Justices who were in favor of oral argument. These orders appear to signal that, unlike a *certiorari* petition where only four votes are required for the Court to hear the case, no argument will be held on an original habeas petition without the votes of five justices.

Part VII:

Appendix: Text of Section 2255 and the Rules Governing § 2255 Proceedings

Appendix

Contents

I. Title 28, United States Code § 2255 (2008)

§ 2255. Federal custody; remedies on motion attacking sentence.

(a) A prisoner in custody under sentence of a court established by Act of Congress claiming the right to be released upon the ground that the sentence was imposed in violation of the Constitution or laws of the United States, or that the court was without jurisdiction to impose such sentence, or that the sentence was in excess of the maximum authorized by law, or is otherwise subject to collateral attack, may move the court which imposed the sentence to vacate, set aside or correct the sentence.

(b) Unless the motion and the files and records of the case conclusively show that the prisoner is entitled to no relief, the court shall cause notice thereof to be served upon the United States attorney, grant a prompt hearing thereon, determine the issues and make findings of fact and conclusions of law with respect thereto. If the court finds that the judgment was rendered without jurisdiction, or that the sentence imposed was not authorized by law or otherwise open to collateral attack, or that there has been such a denial or infringement of the constitutional rights of the prisoner as to render the judgment vulnerable to collateral attack, the court shall vacate and set the judgment aside and shall discharge the prisoner or resentence him or grant a new trial or correct the sentence as may appear appropriate.

(c) A court may entertain and determine such motion without requiring the production of the prisoner at the hearing.

(d) An appeal may be taken to the court of appeals from the order entered on the motion as from a final judgment on application for a writ of habeas corpus.

(e) An application for a writ of habeas corpus in behalf of a prisoner who is authorized to apply for relief by motion pursuant to this section, shall not be entertained if it appears that the applicant has failed to apply for relief, by motion, to the court which sentenced him, or that such court has denied him relief, unless it also appears that the remedy by motion is inadequate or ineffective to test the legality of his detention.

(f) A 1-year period of limitation shall apply to a motion under this section. The limitation period shall run from the latest of—

- **(1)** the date on which the judgment of conviction becomes final;
- **(2)** the date on which the impediment to making a motion created by governmental action in violation of the Constitution or laws of the United States is removed, if the movant was prevented from making a motion by such governmental action;
- **(3)** the date on which the right asserted was initially recognized by the Supreme Court, if that right has been newly recognized by the Supreme Court and made retroactively applicable to cases on collateral review; or
- **(4)** the date on which the facts supporting the claim or claims presented could have been discovered through the exercise of due diligence.

(g) Except as provided in section 408 of the Controlled Substances Act, in all proceedings brought under this section, and any subsequent proceedings on review, the court may appoint counsel, except as provided by a rule promulgated by the Supreme Court pursuant to statutory authority. Appointment of counsel under this section shall be governed by section 3006A of title 18.

(h) A second or successive motion must be certified as provided in section 2244 by a panel of the appropriate court of appeals to contain—

- **(1)** newly discovered evidence that, if proven and viewed in light of the evidence as a whole, would be sufficient to establish by clear and convincing evidence that no reasonable factfinder would have found the movant guilty of the offense; or
- **(2)** a new rule of constitutional law, made retroactive to cases on collateral review by the Supreme Court, that was previously unavailable.

(June 25, 1948, c. 646, 62 Stat. 967; May 24, 1949, c. 139, § 114, 63 Stat. 105; Apr. 24, 1996, Pub. L. 104-132, Title I, § 105, 110 Stat. 1220; Jan. 7, 2008, Pub. L. 110-177, Title V, § 511, 121 Stat. 2545.)

II. Rules Governing § 2255 Proceedings in the U.S. District Courts (and appended Model Form) 2008

Rule

Appendix of Forms

Rule 1. Scope

These rules govern a motion filed in a U.S. district court under 28 U.S.C. § 2255 by:

(a) a person in custody under a judgment of that court who seeks a determination that:

  (1) the judgment violates the Constitution or laws of the United States;

  (2) the court lacked jurisdiction to enter the judgment;

  (3) the sentence exceeded the maximum allowed by law; or

  (4) the judgment or sentence is otherwise subject to collateral review; and

(b) a person in custody under a judgment of a state court or another federal court, and subject to future custody under a judgment of the district court, who seeks a determination that:

  (1) future custody under a judgment of the district court would violate the Constitution or laws of the United States;

  (2) the district court lacked jurisdiction to enter the judgment;

(3) the district court's sentence exceeded the maximum allowed by law; or

(4) the district court's judgment or sentence is otherwise subject to collateral review.

(As amended Apr. 26, 2004, eff. Dec. 1, 2004.)

Advisory Committee Notes

1976 Adoption

The basic scope of this postconviction remedy is prescribed by 28 U.S.C. § 2255. Under these rules, the person seeking relief from federal custody files a motion to vacate, set aside, or correct sentence, rather than a petition for habeas corpus. This is consistent with the terminology used in section 2255 and indicates the difference between this remedy and federal habeas for a state prisoner. Also, habeas corpus is available to the person in federal custody if his "remedy by motion is inadequate or ineffective to test the legality of his detention."

Whereas sections 2241-2254 (dealing with federal habeas corpus for those in state custody) speak of the district court judge "issuing the writ" as the operative remedy, section 2255 provides that, if the judge finds the movant's assertions to be meritorious, he "shall discharge the prisoner or resentence him or grant a new trial or correct the sentence as may appear appropriate." This is possible because a motion under § 2255 is a further step in the movant's criminal case and not a separate civil action, as appears from the legislative history of section 2 of S. 20, 80th Congress, the provisions of which were incorporated by the same Congress in title 28 U.S.C. as § 2255. In reporting S. 20 favorably, the Senate Judiciary Committee said (Sen. Rep. 1526, 80th Cong. 2d Sess., p. 2):

The two main advantages of such motion remedy over the present habeas corpus are as follows:

First, habeas corpus is a separate civil action and not a further step in the criminal case in which petitioner is sentenced (Ex parte *Tom Tong*, 108 U.S. 556, 559 (1883)). It is not a determination of guilt or innocence of the charge upon which petitioner was sentenced. Where a prisoner sustains his right to discharge in habeas corpus, it is usually because some right—such as lack of counsel—has been denied that reflects no determination of his guilt or innocence but affects solely the fairness of his earlier criminal trial. Even under the broad power in the statute "to dispose of the party as law and justice require" (28 U.S.C.A., sec 461), the court or judge is by no means in the same advantageous position in habeas corpus to do justice as would be so if the matter were determined in the criminal proceeding (see *Medley*, petitioner, 134 U.S. 160, 174 (1890)). For instance, the judge (by habeas corpus) cannot grant a new trial in the criminal case. Since the motion remedy is in the criminal proceeding, this section 2 affords the opportunity and expressly gives the broad powers to set aside the judgment and to "discharge the prisoner or resentence him or grant a new trial or correct the sentence as may appear appropriate."

The fact that a motion under § 2255 is a further step in the movant's criminal case rather than a separate civil action has significance at several points in these rules. *See, e.g.*, advisory committee note to Rule 3 (re: no filing fee), advisory committee note to Rule 4 (re: availability of files, etc., relating to the judgment), advisory committee note to Rule 6 (re: availability of discovery under criminal procedure rules), advisory committee note to Rule 11 (re: no extension of time for appeal), and advisory committee note to Rule 12 (re: applicability of federal criminal rules). However, the fact that Congress has characterized the motion as a further step in the criminal proceedings does not mean that proceedings upon such a motion are of necessity governed by the legal principles that are applicable at a criminal trial regarding such matters as counsel, presence, confrontation, self-incrimination, and burden of proof.

The challenge of decisions such as the revocation of probation or parole are not appropriately dealt with under 28 U.S.C. § 2255, which is a continuation of the original criminal action. Other remedies, such as habeas corpus, are available in such situations.

Although Rule 1 indicates that these rules apply to a motion for a determination that the judgment was imposed "in violation of the . . . laws of the United States," the language of 28 U.S.C. § 2255, it is not the intent of these rules to define or limit what is encompassed within that phrase. See *Davis v. United States*, 417 U.S. 333 (1974), holding that it is not true "that every asserted error of law can be raised on a § 2255 motion," and that the appropriate inquiry is "whether the claimed error of law was 'a fundamental defect which inherently results in a complete miscarriage of justice,' and whether '[i]t . . . present[s] exceptional circumstances where the need for the remedy afforded by the writ of habeas corpus is apparent.'"

For a discussion of the "custody" requirement and the intended limited scope of this remedy, see advisory committee note to § 2254 Rule 1.

2004 Amendments

The language of Rule 1 has been amended as part of general restyling of the rules to make them more easily understood and to make style and terminology consistent throughout the rules. These changes are intended to be stylistic, and no substantive change is intended.

Rule 2. The Motion

(a) Applying for Relief. The application must be in the form of a motion to vacate, set aside, or correct the sentence.

(b) Form. The motion must:

  (1) specify all the grounds for relief available to the moving party;

  (2) state the facts supporting each ground;

  (3) state the relief requested;

  (4) be printed, typewritten, or legibly handwritten; and

  (5) be signed under penalty of perjury by the movant or by a person authorized to sign it for the movant.

(c) Standard Form. The motion must substantially follow either the form appended to these rules or a form prescribed by a local district-court rule. The clerk must make forms available to moving parties without charge.

(d) Separate Motions for Separate Judgments. A moving party who seeks relief from more than one judgment must file a separate motion covering each judgment.

(As amended Pub. L. 94-426, § 2(3), (4), Sept. 28, 1976, 90 Stat. 1334; Apr. 28, 1982, eff. Aug. 1, 1982; Apr. 26, 2004, eff. Dec. 1, 2004.)

Advisory Committee Notes

1976 Adoption

Under these rules the application for relief is in the form of a motion rather than a petition (see Rule 1 and advisory committee note). Therefore, there is no requirement that the movant name a respondent. This is consistent with 28 U.S.C. § 2255. The U.S. Attorney for the district in which the judgment under attack was entered is the proper party to oppose the motion because the federal government is the movant's adversary of record.

If the movant is attacking a federal judgment that will subject him to future custody, he must be in present custody (see Rule 1 and advisory committee note) as the result of a state or federal governmental action. He need not alter the nature of the motion by trying to include the government officer who presently has official custody of him as a pseudo-respondent, or third-party plaintiff, or other fabrication. The court hearing his motion attacking the future custody can exercise jurisdiction over those having him in present custody without the use of artificial pleading devices.

There is currently a split among the courts as to whether a person currently in state custody may use a § 2255 motion to obtain relief from a federal judgment under which he will be subjected to custody in the future. Negative, see *Newton v. United States*, 329 F. Supp. 90 (S.D. Texas

1971); affirmative, see *Desmond v. The United States Board of Parole*, 397 F.2d 386 (1st Cir. 1968), *cert. denied*, 393 U.S. 919 (1968); and *Paalino v. United States*, 314 F.Supp. 875 (C.D. Cal. 1970). It is intended that these rules settle the matter in favor of the prisoner's being able to file a § 2255 motion for relief under those circumstances. The proper district in which to file such a motion is the one in which the court that rendered the sentence under attack is situated.

Under Rule 35, Federal Rules of Criminal Procedure, the court may correct an illegal sentence or a sentence imposed in an illegal manner, or may reduce the sentence. This remedy should be used, rather than a motion under these § 2255 rules, whenever applicable, but there is some overlap between the two proceedings that has caused the courts difficulty.

The movant should not be barred from an appropriate remedy because she has mis-styled her motion. See *United States v. Morgan*, 346 U.S. 502, 505 (1954). The court should construe it as whichever one is proper under the circumstances and decide it on its merits. For a § 2255 motion construed as a Rule 35 motion, see *Heflin v. United States*, 358 U.S. 415 (1959); and *United States v. Coke*, 404 F.2d 836 (2d Cir. 1968). For writ of error *coram nobis* treated as a Rule 35 motion, see *Hawkins v. United States*, 324 F.Supp. 223 (E.D. Texas, Tyler Division 1971). For a Rule 35 motion treated as a § 2255 motion, see *Moss v. United States*, 263 F.2d 615 (5th Cir. 1959); *Jones v. United States*, 400 F.2d 892 (8th Cir. 1968), *cert. denied*, 394 U.S. 991 (1969); and *United States v. Brown*, 413 F.2d 878 (9th Cir. 1969), *cert. denied*, 397 U.S. 947 (1970).

One area of difference between § 2255 and Rule 35 motions is that for the latter there is no requirement that the movant be "in custody." *Heflin v. United States*, 358 U.S. 415, 418, 422 (1959); *Duggins v. United States*, 240 F.2d 479, 483 (6th Cir. 1957). Compare with Rule 1 and advisory committee note for § 2255 motions. The importance of this distinction has decreased since *Peyton v. Rowe*, 391 U.S. 54 (1968), but it might still make a difference in particular situations.

A Rule 35 motion is used to attack the sentence imposed, not the basis for the sentence. The court in *Gilinsky v. United States*, 335 F.2d 914, 916 (9th Cir. 1964), stated, "a Rule 35 motion presupposes a valid conviction. . . . [C]ollateral attack on errors allegedly committed at trial is not permissible under Rule 35." By illustration the court noted at page 917: "a Rule 35 proceeding contemplates the correction of a sentence of a court having jurisdiction. . . . [J]urisdictional defects . . . involve a collateral attack, they must ordinarily be presented under 28 U.S.C. § 2255." In *United States v. Semet*, 295 F. Supp. 1084 (E.D. Okla. 1968), the prisoner moved under Rule 35 and § 2255 to invalidate the sentence he was serving on the grounds of his failure to understand the charge to which he pleaded guilty. The court said:

> As regards Defendant's Motion under Rule 35, said Motion must be denied as its [sic] presupposes a valid conviction of the offense with which he was charged and may be used only to attack the sentence. It may not be used to examine errors occurring prior to the imposition of sentence.
>
> **295 F. Supp. at 1085**

See also: *Moss v. United States*, 263 F.2d at 616; *Duggins v. United States*, 240 F.2d at 484; *Migdal v. United States*, 298 F.2d 513, 514 (9th Cir. 1961); *Jones v. United States*, 400 F.2d at 894; *United States v. Coke*, 404 F.2d at 847; and *United States v. Brown*, 413 F.2d at 879.

A major difficulty in deciding whether Rule 35 or § 2255 is the proper remedy is the uncertainty as to what is meant by an "illegal sentence." The Supreme Court dealt with this issue in *Hill v. United States*, 368 U.S. 424 (1962). The prisoner brought a § 2255 motion to vacate sentence on the ground that he had not been given a Fed.R.Crim.P. 32(a) opportunity to make a statement in his own behalf at the time of sentencing. The majority held this was not an error subject to collateral attack under § 2255. The five-member majority considered the motion as one brought pursuant to Rule 35, but denied relief, stating:

> [T]he narrow function of Rule 35 is to permit correction at any time of an illegal sentence, not to re-examine errors occurring at the trial or other proceedings prior to the imposition of sentence. The sentence in this case was not illegal. The punishment meted out was not in excess of that prescribed by the relevant statutes, multiple terms were not imposed for the same offense, nor were the terms of the sentence itself legally or constitutionally invalid in any other respect.
>
> **368 U.S. at 430**

The four dissenters felt the majority definition of "illegal" was too narrow.

> [Rule 35] provides for the correction of an "illegal sentence" without regard to the reasons why that sentence is illegal and contains not a single word to support the Court's conclusion that only a sentence illegal by reason of the punishment it imposes is "illegal" within the meaning of the Rule. I would have thought that a sentence imposed in an illegal manner—whether the amount or form of the punishment meted out constitutes an additional violation of law or not—would be recognized as an "illegal sentence" under any normal reading of the English language.
>
> **368 U.S. at 431–32**

The 1966 amendment of Rule 35 added language permitting correction of a sentence imposed in an "illegal manner." However, there is a 120-day time limit on a motion to do this, and the added language does not clarify the intent of the rule or its relation to § 2255.

The courts have been flexible in considering motions under circumstances in which relief might appear to be precluded by *Hill v. United States*. In *Peterson v. United States*, 432 F.2d 545 (8th Cir. 1970), the court was confronted with a motion for reduction of sentence by a prisoner claiming to have received a harsher sentence than his codefendants because he stood trial rather than plead guilty. He alleged that this violated his constitutional right to a jury trial. The court ruled that, even though it was past the 120-day time period for a motion to reduce sentence, the claim was still cognizable under Rule 35 as a motion to correct an illegal sentence.

The courts have made even greater use of § 2255 in these types of situations. In *United States v. Lewis*, 392 F.2d 440 (4th Cir. 1968), the prisoner moved under § 2255 and Rule 35 for relief from a sentence he claimed was the result of the judge's misunderstanding of the relevant sentencing law. The court held that he could not get relief under Rule 35 because it was past the 120 days for correction of a sentence imposed in an illegal manner and under *Hill v. United States* it was not an illegal sentence. However, § 2255 was applicable because of its "otherwise subject to collateral attack" language. The flaw was not a mere trial error relating to the finding of guilt, but a rare and unusual error that amounted to "exceptional circumstances" embraced in § 2255's words "collateral attack." See 368 U.S. at 444 for discussion of other cases allowing use of § 2255 to attack the sentence itself in similar circumstances, especially where the judge has sentenced out of a misapprehension of the law.

In *United States v. McCarthy*, 433 F.2d 591, 592 (1st Cir. 1970), the court allowed a prisoner who was past the time limit for a proper Rule 35 motion to use § 2255 to attack the sentence he received upon a plea of guilty on the ground that it was induced by an unfulfilled promise of the prosecutor to recommend leniency. The court specifically noted that under § 2255, this was a proper collateral attack on the sentence and there was no need to attack the conviction as well.

The court in *United States v. Malcolm*, 432 F.2d 809, 814, 818 (2d Cir. 1970), allowed a prisoner to challenge his sentence under § 2255 without attacking the conviction. It held Rule 35 inapplicable because the sentence was not illegal on its face, but the manner in which the sentence was imposed raised a question of the denial of due process in the sentencing itself, which was cognizable under § 2255.

The flexible approach taken by the courts in the above cases seems to be the reasonable way to handle these situations in which Rule 35 and

§ 2255 appear to overlap. For a further discussion of this problem, see C. Wright, Federal Practice and Procedure: Criminal §§ 581–587 (1969, Supp. 1975).

See the advisory committee note to Rule 2 of the § 2254 rules for further discussion of the purposes and intent of Rule 2 of these § 2255 rules.

1982 Amendment

Subdivision (b). The amendment takes into account 28 U.S.C. § 1746, enacted after adoption of the § 2255 rules. Section 1746 provides that in lieu of an affidavit, an unsworn statement may be given under penalty of perjury in substantially the following form if executed within the United States, its territories, possessions, or commonwealths: "I declare (or certify, verify, or state) under penalty of perjury that the foregoing is true and correct. Executed on (date). (Signature)." The statute is "intended to encompass prisoner litigation," and the statutory alternative is especially appropriate in such cases because a notary might not be readily available. *Carter v. Clark*, 616 F.2d 228 (5th Cir. 1980). The § 2255 forms have been revised accordingly.

2004 Amendments

The language of Rule 2 has been amended as part of general restyling of the rules to make them more easily understood and to make style and terminology consistent throughout the rules. These changes are intended to be stylistic, and no substantive change is intended, except as described here.

Revised Rule 2(b)(5) has been amended by removing the requirement that the motion be signed personally by the moving party. Thus, under the amended rule the motion may be signed by movant personally or by someone acting on behalf of the movant, assuming that the person is authorized to do so, for example, counsel for the movant. The Committee envisions that the courts would apply third-party, or "next-friend," standing analysis in deciding whether the signer was actually authorized to sign the motion on behalf of the movant. *See generally Whitmore v. Arkansas*, 495 U.S. 149 (1990) (discussion of requisites for "next friend" standing in habeas petitions). *See also* 28 U.S.C. § 2242 (application for state habeas corpus relief may be filed by the person who is seeking relief or by someone acting on behalf of that person).

The language in new Rule 2(c) has been changed to reflect that a moving party must substantially follow the standard form, which is appended to the rules, or a form provided by the court. The current rule, Rule 2(c), seems to indicate a preference for the standard "national" form. Under the amended rule, there is no stated preference. The Committee understood that the current practice in some courts is that if the moving party first files a motion using the national form, that courts may ask the moving party to supplement it with the local form.

Current Rule 2(d), which provided for returning an insufficient motion, has been deleted. The Committee believed that the approach in Federal Rule of Civil Procedure 5(e) was more appropriate for dealing with motions that do not conform to the form requirements of the rule. That Rule provides that the clerk may not refuse to accept a filing solely for the reason that it fails to comply with these rules or local rules. Before the adoption of a one-year statute of limitations in the Antiterrorism and Effective Death Penalty Act of 1996, 110 Stat. 1214, the moving party suffered no penalty, other than delay, if the motion was deemed insufficient. Now that a one-year statute of limitations applies to motions filed under § 2255, *see* 28 U.S.C. § 2244(d) (1), the court's dismissal of a motion because it is not in proper form may pose a significant penalty for a moving party, who may not be able to file another motion within the one-year limitations period. Now, under revised Rule 3(b), the clerk is required to file a motion, even though it may otherwise fail to comply with the provisions in revised Rule 2(b). The Committee believed that the better procedure was to accept the defective motion and require the moving party to submit a corrected motion that conforms to Rule 2(b).

Rule 3. Filing the Motion; Inmate Filing

(a) **Where to File; Copies.** An original and two copies of the motion must be filed with the clerk.

(b) **Filing and Service.** The clerk must file the motion and enter it on the criminal docket of the case in which the challenged judgment was entered. The clerk must then deliver or serve a copy of the motion on the United States attorney in that district, together with a notice of its filing.

(c) **Time to File.** The time for filing a motion is governed by 28 U.S.C. § 2255 para. 6.

(d) **Inmate Filing.** A paper filed by an inmate confined in an institution is timely if deposited in the institution's internal mailing system on or before the last day for filing. If an institution has a system designed for legal mail, the inmate must use that system to receive the benefit of this rule. Timely filing may be shown by a declaration in compliance with 28 U.S.C. § 1746 or by a notarized statement, either of which must set forth the date of deposit and state that first-class postage has been prepaid.

(As amended Apr. 26, 2004, eff. Dec. 1, 2004.)

Advisory Committee Notes

1976 Adoption

There is no filing fee required of a movant under these rules. This is a change from the practice of charging $15 and is done to recognize specifically the nature of a § 2255 motion as being a continuation of the criminal case whose judgment is under attack.

The long-standing practice of requiring a $15 filing fee has followed from 28 U.S.C. § 1914(a), whereby "parties instituting any civil action . . . pay a filing fee of $15, except that on an application for a writ of habeas corpus the filing fee shall be $5." This has been held to apply to a proceeding under § 2255 despite the rationale that such a proceeding is a motion and thus a continuation of the criminal action. (See note to Rule 1.)

> A motion under Section 2255 is a civil action and the clerk has no choice but to charge a $15.00 filing fee unless by leave of court it is filed in forma pauperis.
>
> ***McCune v. United States*, 406 F.2d 417, 419 (6th Cir. 1969).**

Although the motion has been considered to be a new civil action in the nature of habeas corpus for filing purposes, the reduced fee for habeas has been held not applicable. The Tenth Circuit considered the specific issue in *Martin v. United States*, 273 F.2d 775 (10th Cir. 1960), *cert. denied*, 365 U.S. 853 (1961), holding that the reduced fee was exclusive to habeas petitions.

> Counsel for Martin insists that, if a docket fee must be paid, the amount is $5 rather than $15 and bases his contention on the exception contained in 28 U.S.C. § 1914 that in habeas corpus the fee is $5. This reads into § 1914 language which is not there. While an application under § 2255 may afford the same relief as that previously obtainable by habeas corpus, it is not a petition for a writ of habeas corpus. A change in § 1914 must come from Congress.
>
> **273 F.2d at 778.**

Although for most situations, § 2255 is intended to provide to the federal prisoner a remedy equivalent to habeas corpus as used by state prisoners, there is a major distinction between the two. Calling a § 2255 request for relief a motion rather than a petition militates toward charging no new filing fee, not an increased one. In the absence of convincing evidence to the contrary, there is no reason to suppose that Congress did not mean what it said in making a § 2255 action a motion. Therefore, as in other motions filed in a criminal action, there is no requirement of a filing fee. It is appropriate that the present situation of docketing a § 2255 motion as a new action and charging a $15 filing fee be remedied by rule when the whole question of § 2255 motions is thoroughly thought through and organized.

Even though there is no need to have a *forma pauperis* affidavit to proceed with the action because there is no requirement of a fee for filing the motion, the affidavit remains attached to the form to be supplied by potential movants. Most such movants are indigent, and this is a convenient way of getting this into the official record so that the judge may appoint counsel, order the government to pay witness fees, allow docketing of an appeal, and grant any other rights to which an indigent is entitled in the course of a § 2255 motion, when appropriate to the particular situation, without the need for an indigency petition and adjudication at such later point in the proceeding. This should result in a streamlining of the process to allow quicker disposition of these motions.

For further discussion of this rule, see the advisory committee note to Rule 3 of the § 2254 rules.

2004 Amendments

The language of Rule 3 has been amended as part of general restyling of the rules to make them more easily understood and to make style and terminology consistent throughout the rules. These changes are intended to be stylistic, and no substantive change is intended, except as indicated here.

Revised Rule 3(b) is new and is intended to parallel Federal Rule of Civil Procedure 5(e), which provides that the clerk may not refuse to accept a filing solely for the reason that it fails to comply with these rules or local rules. Before the adoption of a one-year statute of limitations in the Antiterrorism and Effective Death Penalty Act of 1996, 110 Stat. 1214, the moving party suffered no penalty, other than delay, if the petition was deemed insufficient. That act, however, added a one-year statute of limitations to motions filed under § 2255, *see* 28 U.S.C. § 2244(d)(1). Thus, a court's dismissal of a defective motion may pose a significant penalty for a moving party who may not be able to file a corrected motion within the one-year limitation period. The Committee believed that the better procedure was to accept the defective motion and require the moving party to submit a corrected motion that conforms to Rule 2. Thus, revised Rule 3(b) requires the clerk to file a motion, even though it may otherwise fail to comply with Rule 2.

Revised Rule 3(c), which sets out a specific reference to 28 U.S.C. § 2255, ¶ 6, is new and has been added to put moving parties on notice that a one-year statute of limitations applies to motions filed under these Rules. Although the rule does not address the issue, every circuit that has addressed the issue has taken the position that equitable tolling of the statute of limitations is available in appropriate circumstances. *See, e.g., Dunlap v. United States*, 250 F.3d 1001, 1004–07 (6th Cir. 2001); *Moore v. United States*, 173 F.3d 1131, 1133–35 (8th Cir. 1999); *Sandvik v. United States*, 177 F.3d 1269, 1270–72 (11th Cir. 1999). The Supreme Court has not addressed the question directly. *See Duncan v. Walker*, 533 U.S. 167, 181 (2001) ("We . . . have no occasion to address the question that Justice Stevens raises concerning the availability of equitable tolling.").

Rule 3(d) is new and provides guidance on determining whether a motion from an inmate is considered to have been filed in a timely fashion. The new provision parallels Federal Rule of Appellate Procedure 25(a)(2)(C).

Rule 4. Preliminary Review

(a) Referral to a Judge. The clerk must promptly forward the motion to the judge who conducted the trial and imposed sentence or, if the judge who imposed sentence was not the trial judge, to the judge who conducted the proceedings being challenged. If the appropriate judge is not available, the clerk must forward the motion to a judge under the court's assignment procedure.

(b) Initial Consideration by the Judge. The judge who receives the motion must promptly examine it. If it plainly appears from the motion, any attached exhibits, and the record of prior proceedings that the moving party is not entitled to relief, the judge must dismiss the motion and direct the clerk to notify the moving party. If the motion is not dismissed, the judge must order the United States attorney to file an answer, motion, or other response within a fixed time, or to take other action the judge may order.

(As amended Apr. 26, 2004, eff. Dec. 1, 2004.)

Advisory Committee Notes

1976 Adoption

Rule 4 outlines the procedure for assigning the motion to a specific judge of the district court and the options available to the judge and the government after the motion is properly filed.

The long-standing majority practice in assigning motions made pursuant to § 2255 has been for the trial judge to determine the merits of the motion. In cases where the § 2255 motion is directed against the sentence, the merits have traditionally been decided by the judge who imposed sentence. The reasoning for this was first noted in *Carvell v. United States*, 173 F.2d 348–49 (4th Cir. 1949):

> Complaint is made that the judge who tried the case passed upon the motion. Not only was there no impropriety in this, but it is highly desirable in such cases that the motions be passed on by the judge who is familiar with the facts and circumstances surrounding the trial, and is consequently not likely to be misled by false allegations as to what occurred.

This case, and its reasoning, has been almost unanimously endorsed by other courts dealing with the issue.

Commentators have been critical of having the motion decided by the trial judge. See Developments in the Law–Federal Habeas Corpus, 83 Harv. L. Rev. 1038, 1206–08 (1970).

> [T]he trial judge may have become so involved with the decision that it will be difficult for him to review it objectively. Nothing in the legislative history suggests that "court" refers to a specific judge, and the procedural advantages of section 2255 are available whether or not the trial judge presides at the hearing.
>
> The theory that Congress intended the trial judge to preside at a section 2255 hearing apparently originated in *Carvell v. United States*, 173 F.2d 348 (4th Cir. 1949) (per curiam), where the panel of judges included Chief Judge Parker of the Fourth Circuit, chairman of the Judicial Conference committee which drafted section 2255. But the legislative history does not indicate that Congress wanted the trial judge to preside. Indeed the advantages of section 2255 can all be achieved if the case is heard in the sentencing district, regardless of which judge hears it. According to the Senate committee report the purpose of the bill was to make the proceeding a part of the criminal action so the court could resentence the applicant, or grant him a new trial. (A judge presiding over a habeas corpus action does not have these powers.) In addition, Congress did not want the cases heard in the district of confinement because that tended to concentrate the burden on a few districts, and made it difficult for witnesses and records to be produced.
>
> **83 Harv. L. Rev. at 1207–08**

The Court of Appeals for the First Circuit has held that a judge other than the trial judge should rule on the 2255 motion. *See Halliday v. United States*, 380 F.2d 270 (1st Cir. 1967).

There is a procedure by which the movant can have a judge other than the trial judge decide his motion in courts adhering to the majority rule. He can file an affidavit alleging bias in order to disqualify the trial judge. And there are circumstances in which the trial judge will, on his own, disqualify himself. See, *e.g., Webster v. United States*, 330 F.Supp. 1080 (1972). However, there has been some questioning of the effectiveness of this procedure. See Developments in the Law–Federal Habeas Corpus, 83 Harv. L. Rev. 1038, 1200–07 (1970).

Subdivision (a) adopts the majority rule and provides that the trial judge, or sentencing judge if different and appropriate for the particular motion, will decide the motion made pursuant to these rules, recognizing that, under some circumstances, he may want to disqualify himself. A movant is not without remedy if he feels this is unfair to him. He can file an affidavit of bias. And there is the right to appellate review if the trial judge refuses to grant his motion. Because the trial judge is thoroughly familiar with the case, there is obvious administrative advantage in giving him the first opportunity to decide whether there are grounds for granting the motion.

Because the motion is part of the criminal action in which the judgment to which it is directed was entered, the files, records, transcripts, and correspondence relating to that judgment are automatically available to the judge in his consideration of the motion. He no longer need order them incorporated for that purpose.

Rule 4 has its basis in § 2255 (rather than 28 U.S.C. § 2243 in the corresponding habeas corpus rule), which does not have a specific time limitation as to when the answer must be made. Also, under § 2255, the U.S. Attorney for the district is the party served with the notice and a copy of the motion and required to answer (when appropriate). Subdivision (b) continues this practice because there is no respondent involved in the motion (unlike habeas) and the U.S. Attorney, as prosecutor in the case in question, is the most appropriate one to defend the judgment and oppose the motion.

The judge has discretion to require an answer or other appropriate response from the U.S. Attorney. See advisory committee note to Rule 4 of the § 2254 rules.

2004 Amendments

The language of Rule 4 has been amended as part of general restyling of the rules to make them more easily understood and to make style and terminology consistent throughout the rules. These changes are intended to be stylistic and no substantive change is intended.

The amended rule reflects that the response to a Section 2255 motion may be a motion to dismiss or some other response.

Rule 5. The Answer and the Reply

(a) **When Required.** The respondent is not required to answer the motion unless a judge so orders.

(b) **Contents.** The answer must address the allegations in the motion. In addition, it must state whether the moving party has used any other federal remedies, including any prior post-conviction motions under these rules or any previous rules, and whether the moving party received an evidentiary hearing.

(c) **Records of Prior Proceedings.** If the answer refers to briefs or transcripts of the prior proceedings that are not available in the court's records, the judge must order the government to furnish them within a reasonable time that will not unduly delay the proceedings.

(d) **Reply.** The moving party may submit a reply to the respondent's answer or other pleading within a time fixed by the judge.

(As amended Apr. 26, 2004, eff. Dec. 1, 2004.)

Advisory Committee Notes

1976 Adoption

Unlike the habeas corpus statutes (see 28 U.S.C. §§ 2243, 2248), § 2255 does not specifically call for a return or answer by the U.S. Attorney or set any time limits as to when one must be submitted. The general practice, however, if the motion is not summarily dismissed, is for the government to file an answer to the motion as well as counter-affidavits, when appropriate. Rule 4 provides for an answer to the motion by the U.S. Attorney, and Rule 5 indicates what its contents should be.

There is no requirement that the movant exhaust her remedies prior to seeking relief under § 2255. However, the courts have held that such a motion is inappropriate if the movant is simultaneously appealing the decision.

> We are of the view that there is no jurisdictional bar to the District Court's entertaining a Section 2255 motion during the pendency of a direct appeal but that the orderly administration of criminal law precludes considering such a motion absent extraordinary circumstances.
>
> *Womack v. United States*, 395 F.2d 630, 631 (D.C.Cir. 1968).

Also *see Masters v. Eide*, 353 F.2d 517 (8th Cir. 1965). The answer may thus cut short consideration of the motion if it discloses the taking of an appeal that was omitted from the form motion filed by the movant.

There is nothing in § 2255 that corresponds to the § 2248 requirement of a traverse to the answer. Numerous cases have held that the government's answer and affidavits are not conclusive against the movant, and, if they raise disputed issues of fact, a hearing must be held. *Machibroda v. United States*, 368 U.S. 487, 494, 495 (1962); *United States v. Salerno*, 290 F.2d 105, 106 (2d Cir. 1961); *Romero v. United States*, 327 F.2d 711,

712 (5th Cir. 1964); *Scott v. United States*, 349 F.2d 641, 642, 643 (6th Cir. 1965); *Schiebelhut v. United States*, 357 F.2d 743, 745 (6th Cir. 1966); and *Del Piano v. United States*, 362 F.2d 931, 932, 933 (3d Cir. 1966). None of these cases make any mention of a traverse by the movant to the government's answer. As under Rule 5 of the § 2254 rules, there is no intention here that such a traverse be required, except under special circumstances. See advisory committee note to Rule 9.

Subdivision (b) provides for the government to supplement its answers with appropriate copies of transcripts or briefs if for some reason the judge does not already have them under her control. This is because the government will in all probability have easier access to such papers than the movant, and it will conserve the court's time to have the government produce them rather than the movant, who would in most instances have to apply *in forma pauperis* for the government to supply them for her anyway.

For further discussion, see the advisory committee note to Rule 5 of the § 2254 rules.

2004 Amendments

The language of Rule 5 has been amended as part of general restyling of the rules to make them more easily understood and to make style and terminology consistent throughout the rules. These changes are intended to be stylistic, and no substantive change is intended.

Revised Rule 5(a), which provides that the respondent is not required to file an answer to the motion, unless a judge so orders, is taken from current Rule 3(b). The revised rule does not address the practice in some districts, where the respondent files a pre-answer motion to dismiss the motion. But revised Rule 4(b) contemplates that practice and has been changed to reflect the view that if the court does not dismiss the motion, it may require (or permit) the respondent to file a motion.

Finally, revised Rule 5(d) adopts the practice in some jurisdictions giving the movant an opportunity to file a reply to the respondent's answer. Rather than using terms such as "traverse," see 28 U.S.C. § 2248, to identify the movant's response to the answer, the rule uses the more general term "reply." The Rule prescribes that the court set the time for such responses, and in lieu of setting specific time limits in each case, the court may decide to include such time limits in its local rules.

Rule 6. Discovery

(a) **Leave of Court Required.** A judge may, for good cause, authorize a party to conduct discovery under the Federal Rules of Criminal Procedure or Civil Procedure, or in accordance with the practices and principles of law. If necessary for effective discovery, the judge must appoint an attorney for a moving party who qualifies to have counsel appointed under 18 U.S.C. § 3006A.

(b) Requesting Discovery. A party requesting discovery must provide reasons for the request. The request must also include any proposed interrogatories and requests for admission, and must specify any requested documents.

(c) Deposition Expenses. If the government is granted leave to take a deposition, the judge may require the government to pay the travel expenses, subsistence expenses, and fees of the moving party's attorney to attend the deposition.

(As amended Apr. 26, 2004, eff. Dec. 1, 2004.)

Advisory Committee Notes

1976 Adoption

This rule differs from the corresponding discovery rule under the § 2254 rules in that it includes the processes of discovery available under the Federal Rules of Criminal Procedure as well as the civil. This is because of the nature of a § 2255 motion as a continuing part of the criminal proceeding (see advisory committee note to Rule 1) as well as a remedy analogous to habeas corpus by state prisoners.

See the advisory committee note to rule 6 of the § 2254 rules. The discussion there is fully applicable to discovery under these rules for § 2255 motions.

2004 Amendments

The language of Rule 6 has been amended as part of general restyling of the rules to make them more easily understood and to make style and terminology consistent throughout the rules. These changes are intended to be stylistic, and no substantive change is intended, except as indicated here.

Although current Rule 6(b) contains no requirement that the parties provide reasons for the requested discovery, the revised rule does so and also includes a requirement that the request be accompanied by any proposed interrogatories and requests for admission, and must specify any requested documents. The Committee believes that the revised rule makes explicit what has been implicit in current practice.

Rule 7. Expanding the Record

(a) In General. If the motion is not dismissed, the judge may direct the parties to expand the record by submitting additional materials relating to the motion. The judge may require that these materials be authenticated.

(b) **Types of Materials.** The materials that may be required include letters predating the filing of the motion, documents, exhibits, and answers under oath to written interrogatories propounded by the judge. Affidavits also may be submitted and considered as part of the record.

(c) **Review by the Opposing Party.** The judge must give the party against whom the additional materials are offered an opportunity to admit or deny their correctness.

(As amended Apr. 26, 2004, eff. Dec. 1, 2004.)

Advisory Committee Notes

1976 Adoption

It is less likely that the court will feel the need to expand the record in a § 2255 proceeding than in a habeas corpus proceeding, because the trial (or sentencing) judge is the one hearing the motion (see Rule 4) and should already have a complete file on the case in his possession. However, Rule 7 provides a convenient method for supplementing his file if the case warrants it.

See the advisory committee note to Rule 7 of the § 2254 rules for a full discussion of reasons and procedures for expanding the record.

2004 Amendments

The language of Rule 7 has been amended as part of general restyling of the rules to make them more easily understood and to make style and terminology consistent throughout the rules. These changes are intended to be stylistic and no substantive change is intended.

Revised Rule 7(a) is not intended to restrict the court's authority to expand the record through means other than requiring the parties themselves to provide the information.

The language in current Rule 7(d), which deals with authentication of materials in the expanded record, has been moved to revised Rule 7(a).

Rule 8. Evidentiary Hearing

(a) **Determining Whether to Hold a Hearing.** If the motion is not dismissed, the judge must review the answer, any transcripts and records of prior proceedings, and any materials submitted under Rule 7 to determine whether an evidentiary hearing is warranted.

(b) **Reference to a Magistrate Judge.** A judge may, under 28 U.S.C. § 636(b), refer the motion to a magistrate judge to conduct hearings and to file proposed findings of fact and recommendations for disposition. When they are filed, the clerk must promptly serve copies of the proposed findings and recommendations on all parties. Within 10 days after being served, a party may file objections as provided by local court rule. The judge must determine *de novo* any proposed finding or recommendation to which objection is made. The judge may accept, reject, or modify any proposed finding or recommendation.

(c) Appointing Counsel; Time of Hearing. If an evidentiary hearing is warranted, the judge must appoint an attorney to represent a moving party who qualifies to have counsel appointed under 18 U.S.C. § 3006A. The judge must conduct the hearing as soon as practicable after giving the attorneys adequate time to investigate and prepare. These rules do not limit the appointment of counsel under § 3006A at any stage of the proceeding.

(d) Producing a Statement. Federal Rule of Criminal Procedure 26.2(a)–(d) and (f) applies at a hearing under this rule. If a party does not comply with a Rule 26.2(a) order to produce a witness's statement, the court must not consider that witness's testimony.

(As amended Pub. L. 94-426, § 2(6), Sept. 28, 1976, 90 Stat. 1335; Pub. L. 94-577, § 2(a) (2), (b) (2), Oct. 21, 1976, 90 Stat. 2730, 2731; Apr. 22, 1993, eff. Dec. 1, 1993; Apr. 26, 2004, eff. Dec. 1, 2004.)

Advisory Committee Notes

1976 Adoption

The standards for § 2255 hearings are essentially the same as for evidentiary hearings under a habeas petition, except that the previous federal fact-finding proceeding is in issue rather than the state's. Also, § 2255 does not set specific time limits for holding the hearing, as does § 2243 for a habeas action. With these minor differences in mind, see the advisory committee note to Rule 8 of § 2254 rules, which is applicable to Rule 8 of these § 2255 rules.

1993 Amendment

The amendment to Rule 8 is one of a series of parallel amendments to Federal Rules of Criminal Procedure 32, 32.1, and 46, which extend the scope of Rule 26.2 (Production of Witness Statements) to proceedings other than the trial itself. The amendments are grounded on the compelling need for accurate and credible information in making decisions concerning the defendant's liberty. See the advisory committee note to Rule 26.2(g). A few courts have recognized the authority of a judicial officer to order production of prior statements by a witness at a Section 2255 hearing, see, e.g., *United States v. White*, 342 F.2d 379, 382, n.4 (4th Cir. 1959). The amendment to Rule 8 grants explicit authority to do so. The amendment is not intended to require production of a witness's statement before the witness actually presents oral testimony.

2004 Amendments

The language of Rule 8 has been amended as part of general restyling of the rules to make them more easily understood and to make style and terminology consistent throughout the rules. These changes are intended to be stylistic and no substantive change is intended, except as described here.

The requirement in current Rule 8(b)(2) that a copy of the magistrate judge's findings must be promptly mailed to all parties has been changed in revised Rule 8(b) to require that copies of those findings be served on all parties. As used in this rule, "service" means service consistent with Federal Rule of Civil Procedure 5(b), which allows mailing the copies.

Rule 9. Second or Successive Motions

Before presenting a second or successive motion, the moving party must obtain an order from the appropriate court of appeals authorizing the district court to consider the motion, as required by 28 U.S.C. § 2255, para. 8.

(As amended Pub. L. 94-426, § 2(9), (10), Sept. 28, 1976, 90 Stat. 1335; Apr. 26, 2004, eff. Dec. 1, 2004.)

Advisory Committee Notes

1976 Adoption

Unlike the statutory provisions on habeas corpus (28 U.S.C. §§ 2241–2254), § 2255 specifically provides that "a motion for such relief may be made at any time" [emphasis added]. Subdivision (a) provides that delayed motions may be barred from consideration if the government has been prejudiced in its ability to respond to the motion by the delay and the movant's failure to seek relief earlier is not excusable within the terms of the rule. Case law, dealing with this issue, is in conflict.

Some courts have held that the literal language of § 2255 precludes any possible time bar to a motion brought under it. In *Heflin v. United States*, 358 U.S. 415 (1959), the concurring opinion noted:

> The statute [28 U.S.C. § 2255] further provides: "A motion . . . may be made at any time." This . . . simply means that, as in

> habeas corpus, there is no statute of limitations, no res judicata, and that the doctrine of laches is inapplicable.
>
> **358 U.S. at 420**

McKinney v. United States, 208 F.2d 844 (D.C. Cir. 1953) reversed the district court's dismissal of a § 2255 motion for being too late, the court stating:

> McKinney's present application for relief comes late in the day: he has served some fifteen years in prison. But tardiness is irrelevant where a constitutional issue is raised and where the prisoner is still confined.
>
> **208 F.2d at 846, 847**

In accord, see *Juelich v. United States*, 300 F.2d 381, 383 (5th Cir. 1962); *Conners v. United States*, 431 F.2d 1207, 1208 (9th Cir. 1970); *Sturrup v. United States*, 218 F. Supp. 279, 281 (E.D.N. Car. 1963); and *Banks v. United States*, 319 F. Supp. 649, 652 (S.D.N.Y. 1970).

It has also been held that delay in filing a § 2255 motion does not bar the movant because of lack of reasonable diligence in pressing the claim.

> The statute [28 U.S.C. § 2255], when it states that the motion may be made at any time, excludes the addition of a showing of diligence in delayed filings. A number of courts have considered contentions similar to those made here and have concluded that there are no time limitations. This result excludes the requirement of diligence which is in reality a time limitation.
>
> **Haier v. United States, 334 F.2d 441, 442 (10th Cir. 1964)**

Other courts have recognized that delay may have a negative effect on the movant. In *Raines v. United States*, 423 F.2d 526 (4th Cir. 1970), the court stated:

> [B]oth petitioners' silence for extended periods, one for 28 months and the other for nine years, serves to render their allegations less believable. "Although a delay in filing a section 2255 motion is not a controlling element . . . it may merit some consideration. . . ."
>
> **423 F.2d at 531**

In *Aiken v. United States*, 191 F.Supp. 43, 50 (M.D.N. Car. 1961), *aff'd* 296 F.2d 604 (4th Cir. 1961), the court said: "While motions under 28 U.S.C. § 2255 may be made at any time, the lapse of time affects the good faith and credibility of the moving party." For similar conclusions, see: *Parker v. United States*, 358 F.2d 50, 54 n. 4 (7th Cir. 1965), *cert. denied*, 386 U.S. 916 (1967); *Le Clair v. United States*, 241 F.Supp. 819, 824 (N.D. Ind. 1965); *Malone v. United States*, 299 F.2d 254, 256 (6th Cir. 1962), *cert. denied*, 371 U.S. 863 (1962); *Howell v. United States*, 442 F.2d 265, 274 (7th Cir. 1971); and *United States v. Wiggins*, 184 F. Supp. 673, 676 (D.C. Cir. 1960).

There have been holdings by some courts that a delay in filing a § 2255 motion operates to increase the burden of proof that the movant must meet to obtain relief. The reasons for this, as expressed in *United States v. Bostic*, 206 F. Supp. 855 (D.C. Cir. 1962), are equitable in nature.

> Obviously, the burden of proof on a motion to vacate a sentence under 28 U.S.C. § 2255 is on the moving party. . . . The burden is particularly heavy if the issue is one of fact and a long time has elapsed since the trial of the case. While neither the statute of limitations nor laches can bar the assertion of a constitutional right, nevertheless, the passage of time may make it impracticable to retry a case if the motion is granted and a new trial is ordered. No doubt, at times such a motion is a product of an afterthought. Long delay may raise a question of good faith.
>
> **206 F. Supp. at 856–57**

See also *United States v. Wiggins*, 184 F.Supp. at 676.

A requirement that the movant display reasonable diligence in filing a § 2255 motion has been adopted by some courts dealing with delayed motions. The court in *United States v. Moore*, 166 F.2d 102 (7th Cir. 1948), *cert. denied*, 334 U.S. 849 (1948), did this, again for equitable reasons.

> [W]e agree with the District Court that the petitioner has too long slept upon his rights. . . . [A]pparently there is no limitation of time within which . . . a motion to vacate may be filed, except that an applicant must show reasonable diligence in presenting his claim. . . .
>
> The reasons which support the rule requiring diligence seem obvious. . . . Law enforcement officials change, witnesses die, memories grow dim. The prosecuting tribunal is put to a disadvantage if an unexpected retrial should be necessary after long passage of time.
>
> **166 F.2d at 105**

In accord see *Desmond v. United States*, 333 F.2d 378, 381 (1st Cir. 1964), on remand, 345 F.2d 225 (1st Cir. 1965).

One of the major arguments advanced by the courts that would penalize a movant who waits an unduly long time before filing a § 2255 motion is that such delay is highly prejudicial to the prosecution. In *Desmond v. United States*, writing of a § 2255 motion alleging denial of effective appeal because of deception by movant's own counsel, the court said:

> [A]pplications for relief such as this must be made promptly. It will not do for a prisoner to wait until government witnesses have become unavailable as by death, serious illness or absence from the country, or until the memory of available government witnesses has faded. It will not even do for a prisoner to wait any longer than is reasonably necessary to prepare appropriate moving papers, however inartistic, after discovery of the deception practiced upon him by his attorney.
>
> **333 F.2d at 381**

In a similar vein are *United States v. Moore* and *United States v. Bostic*, *supra*, and *United States v. Wiggins*, 184 F.Supp. at 676.

Subdivision (a) provides a flexible, equitable time limitation based on laches to prevent movants from withholding their claims so as to prejudice the government both in meeting the allegations of the motion and in any possible retrial. It includes a reasonable diligence requirement for ascertaining possible grounds for relief. If the delay is found to be excusable, or nonprejudicial to the government, the time bar is inoperative.

Subdivision (b) is consistent with the language of § 2255 and relevant case law.

The annexed form is intended to serve the same purpose as the comparable one included in the § 2254 rules.

For further discussion applicable to this rule, see the advisory committee note to Rule 9 of the § 2254 rules.

2004 Amendments

The language of Rule 9 has been amended as part of general restyling of the rules to make them more easily understood and to make style and terminology consistent throughout the rules. These changes are intended to be stylistic, and no substantive change is intended, except as indicated here.

First, current Rule 9(a) has been deleted as unnecessary in light of the applicable one-year statute of limitations for § 2255 motions, added as part of the Antiterrorism and Effective Death Penalty Act of 1996, 28 U.S.C. § 2255, ¶ 6.

Second, the remainder of revised Rule 9 reflects provisions in the Antiterrorism and Effective Death Penalty Act of 1996, 28 U.S.C. § 2255, ¶ 8, which now require a moving party to obtain approval from the appropriate court of appeals before filing a second or successive motion.

Finally, the title of the rule has been changed to reflect the fact that the revised version addresses only the topic of second or successive motions.

Rule 10. Powers of a Magistrate Judge

A magistrate judge may perform the duties of a district judge under these rules, as authorized by 28 U.S.C. § 636.

(As amended Pub. L. 94-426, § 2(12), Sept. 28, 1976, 90 Stat. 1335; Apr. 30, 1979, eff. Aug. 1, 1979; Apr. 26, 2004, eff. Dec. 1, 2004.)

Advisory Committee Notes

1976 Adoption

See the advisory committee note to Rule 10 of the § 2254 rules for a discussion fully applicable here as well.

1979 Amendment

This amendment conforms the rule to 18 U.S.C. § 636. See the advisory committee note to Rule 10 of the Rules Governing Section 2254 Cases in the United States District Courts.

2004 Amendments

The language of Rule 10 has been amended as part of general restyling of the rules to make them more easily understood and to make style and terminology consistent throughout the rules. These changes are intended to be stylistic and no substantive change is intended.

Rule 11. Time to Appeal

Federal Rule of Appellate Procedure 4(a) governs the time to appeal an order entered under these rules. These rules do not extend the time to appeal the original judgment of conviction.

(As amended Apr. 30, 1979, eff. Aug. 1, 1979; Apr. 26, 2004, eff. Dec. 1, 2004.)

Advisory Committee Notes

1976 Adoption

Rule 11 is intended to make clear that, although a § 2255 action is a continuation of the criminal case, the bringing of a § 2255 action does not extend the time.

1979 Amendment

Prior to the promulgation of the Rules Governing § 2255 Proceedings, the courts consistently held that the time for appeal in a section 2255 case is as provided in Fed.R.App.P. 4(a), that is, 60 days when the government is a party, rather than as provided in appellate rule 4(b), which says that the time is 10 days in criminal cases. This result has often been explained on the ground that rule 4(a) has to do with civil cases and that "proceedings under section 2255 are civil in nature." *E.g., Rothman v. United States*, 508 F.2d 648 (3d Cir. 1975). Because the new section 2255 rules are based upon the premise "that a motion under § 2255 is a further step in the movant's criminal case rather than a separate civil action," see advisory committee note to Rule 1, the question has arisen whether the new rules have the effect of shortening the time for appeal to that provided in appellate rule 4(b). A sentence has been added to Rule 11 in order to make it clear that this is not the case.

Even though section 2255 proceedings are a further step in the criminal case, the added sentence correctly states current law. In *United States v. Hayman*, 342 U.S. 205 (1952), the Supreme Court noted that such appeals "are governed by the civil rules applicable to appeals from final judgments in habeas corpus actions." In support, the Court cited *Mercado v. United States*, 183 F.2d 486 (1st Cir. 1950), a case rejecting the argument that because § 2255 proceedings are criminal in nature the time for appeal is only ten days. The *Mercado* court concluded that the situation was governed by that part of 28 U.S.C. § 2255 that reads: "An appeal may be taken to the court of appeals from the order entered on the motion as from a final judgment on application for a writ of habeas corpus." Thus, because appellate rule 4(a) is applicable in habeas cases, it likewise governs in § 2255 cases even though they are criminal in nature.

2004 Amendments

The language of Rule 11 has been amended as part of general restyling of the rules to make them more easily understood and to make style and terminology consistent throughout the rules. These changes are intended to be stylistic, and no substantive change is intended.

Rule 12. Applicability of the Federal Rules of Civil Procedure and the Federal Rules of Criminal Procedure

The Federal Rules of Civil Procedure and the Federal Rules of Criminal Procedure, to the extent that they are not inconsistent with any statutory provisions or these rules, may be applied to a proceeding under these rules.

(As amended Apr. 26, 2004, eff. Dec. 1, 2004.)

Advisory Committee Notes

1976 Adoption

This rule differs from rule 11 of the § 2254 rules in that it includes the Federal Rules of Criminal Procedure as well as the civil. This is because of the nature of a § 2255 motion as a continuing part of the criminal proceeding (see advisory committee note to Rule 1) as well as a remedy analogous to habeas corpus by state prisoners.

Because § 2255 has been considered analogous to habeas as respects the restrictions in Fed.R.Civ.P. 81(a) (2) (*see Sullivan v. United States*, 198 F.Supp. 624 (S.D.N.Y. 1961), Rule 12 is needed. For discussion, see the advisory committee note to Rule 11 of the § 2254 rules.

2004 Amendments

The language of Rule 12 has been amended as part of general restyling of the rules to make them more easily understood and to make style and terminology consistent throughout the rules. These changes are intended to be stylistic, and no substantive change is intended.

Appendix of Forms

Motion to Vacate, Set Aside, or Correct a Sentence by a Person in Federal Custody

(Motion Under 28 U.S.C. § 2255)

Instructions

1. To use this form, you must be a person who is serving a sentence under a judgment against you in a federal court. You are asking for relief from the conviction or the sentence. This form is your motion for relief.
2. You must file the form in the United States district court that entered the judgment that you are challenging. If you want to challenge a federal judgment that imposed a sentence to be served in the future, you should file the motion in the federal court that entered that judgment.
3. Make sure the form is typed or neatly written.
4. You must tell the truth and sign the form. If you make a false statement of a material fact, you may be prosecuted for perjury.
5. Answer all the questions. You do not need to cite law. You may submit additional pages if necessary. If you do not fill out the form properly, you will be asked to submit additional or correct information. If you want to submit a brief or arguments, you must submit them in a separate memorandum.
6. If you cannot pay for the costs of this motion (such as costs for an attorney or transcripts), you may ask to proceed in forma pauperis (as a poor person). To do that, you must fill out the last page of this form. Also, you must submit a certificate signed by an officer at the institution where you are confined showing the amount of money that the institution is holding for you.
7. In this motion, you may challenge the judgment entered by only one court. If you want to challenge a judgment entered by a different judge or division (either in the same district or in a different district), you must file a separate motion.
8. When you have completed the form, send the original and two copies to the Clerk of the United States District Court at this address:

   Clerk, United States District Court for ________________

   Address

   City, State Zip Code______________________________
9. **<u>CAUTION</u>: You must include in this motion all the grounds for relief from the conviction or sentence that you challenge. And you must state the facts that support each ground. If you**

fail to set forth all the grounds in this motion, you may be barred from presenting additional grounds at a later date.

10. <u>**CAPITAL CASES**</u>**: If you are under a sentence of death, you are entitled to the assistance of counsel and should request the appointment of counsel.**

Motion Under 28 U.S.C. § 2255 to Vacate, Set Aside, or Correct Sentence by a Person in Federal Custody

United States District Court	District:
Name (under which you were convicted):	Docket or Case No.:
Place of Confinement:	Prisoner No.:
UNITED STATES OF AMERICA v.	Movant (*include* name under which you were convicted)

MOTION

1. (a) Name and location of court that entered the judgment of conviction you are challenging: ______________________
____
____
____
____
____
____

(b) Criminal docket or case number (if you know): __________
____

2. (a) Date of the judgment of conviction (if you know): ________
____

(b) Date of sentencing: ______________________
____

3. Length of sentence: ______________________
____

4. Nature of crime (all counts): ______________________
____

____
____
____
____
____
____
____
____

5. (a) What was your plea? (Check one)
(1) Not guilty [ ] (2) Guilty [ ] (3) Nolo contendere (no contest) [ ]
(b) If you entered a guilty plea to one count or indictment, and a not guilty plea to another count or indictment, what did you plead guilty to and what did you plead not guilty to? _______
____
____
____
____
____
____
____

6. If you went to trial, what kind of trial did you have? (Check one)
Jury [ ] Judge only [ ]
7. Did you testify at a pretrial hearing, trial, or post-trial hearing?
Yes [ ] No [ ]
8. Did you appeal from the judgment of conviction?
Yes [ ] No [ ]
9. If you did appeal, answer the following:
(a) Name of court: ______________________________
____
(b) Docket or case number (if you know): ______________
____
(c) Result: ____________________________________
____
(d) Date of result (if you know): __________________
____
(e) Citation to the case (if you know): ______________
____
(f) Grounds raised: ______________________________
____
____
____
____

(g) Did you file a petition for certiorari in the United States Supreme Court? Yes [ ] No [ ]
If "Yes," answer the following:
(1) Docket or case number (if you know): ___
(2) Result: ___
(3) Date of result (if you know): ___
(4) Citation to the case (if you know): ___
(5) Grounds raised: ___

10. Other than the direct appeals listed above, have you previously filed any other motions, petitions, or applications concerning this judgment of conviction in any court?
Yes [ ] No [ ]

11. If your answer to Question 10 was "Yes," give the following information:
    (a) (1) Name of court: ______________________________
    ____
    (2) Docket or case number (if you know): ______________
    ____
    (3) Date of filing (if you know): ____________________
    ____
    (4) Nature of the proceeding: ______________________
    ____
    (5) Grounds raised: ______________________________
    ____
    ____
    ____
    ____
    ____
    ____
    ____
    ____
    ____
    ____
    ____
    ____
    ____
    (6) Did you receive a hearing where evidence was given on your motion, petition, or application?
    Yes [ ] No [ ]
    (7) Result: ______________________________
    ____
    (8) Date of result (if you know):____________________
    ____
    (b) If you filed any second motion, petition, or application, give the same information:
    (1) Name of court: ______________________________
    ____
    (2) Docket or case number (if you know): ___________
    ____
    (3) Date of filing (if you know): __________________
    ____
    (4) Nature of the proceeding: ____________________
    ____

(5) Grounds raised: ______________________________

____

____

____

____

____

____

____

____

____

____

____

____

____

____

____

____

(6) Did you receive a hearing where evidence was given on your motion, petition, or application?
Yes [ ] No [ ]

(7) Result: ______________________________

____

(8) Date of result (if you know): ______________________________

____

(c) Did you appeal to a federal appellate court having jurisdiction over the action taken on your motion, petition, or application?
(1) First petition: Yes [ ] No [ ]
(2) Second petition: Yes [ ] No [ ]

(d) If you did not appeal from the action on any motion, petition, or application, explain briefly why you did not: ______________

____

____

____

____

____

12. For this motion, state every ground on which you claim that you are being held in violation of the Constitution, laws, or treaties of the United States. Attach additional pages if you have more than four grounds. State the *facts* supporting each ground.

GROUND ONE: ______________________________

____

____

____

(a) Supporting facts (Do not argue or cite law. Just state the specific facts that support your claim.):

____

____

____

____

____

____

____

____

____

____

____

____

____

____

____

____

____

____

____

(b) **Direct Appeal of Ground One:**

(1) If you appealed from the judgment of conviction, did you raise this issue?

Yes [ ]   No [ ]

(2) If you did not raise this issue in your direct appeal, explain why:

____

____

____

____

(c) **Post-Conviction Proceedings:**

(1) Did you raise this issue in any post-conviction motion, petition, or application?

Yes [ ]   No [ ]

(2) If your answer to Question (c)(1) is "Yes," state:

Type of motion or petition: ______________________________

____

Name and location of the court where the motion or petition was filed: ______________________________
____
____

Docket or case number (if you know): ______________
____

Date of the court's decision: ______________________
____

Result (attach a copy of the court's opinion or order, if available): ______________________________
____
____
____
____
____
____

(3) Did you receive a hearing on your motion, petition, or application?
Yes [ ] No [ ]

(4) Did you appeal from the denial of your motion, petition, or application?
Yes [ ] No [ ]

(5) If your answer to Question (c)(4) is "Yes," did you raise this issue in the appeal?
Yes [ ] No [ ]

(6) If your answer to Question (c)(4) is "Yes," state:
Name and location of the court where the appeal was filed: ______________________________
____
____
____
____

Docket or case number (if you know): ______________
____

Date of the court's decision: ______________________
____

Result (attach a copy of the court's opinion or order, if available): ______________________________
____
____
____
____
____
____

(7) If your answer to Question (c)(4) or Question (c)(5) is "No," explain why you did not appeal or raise this issue:

____

____

____

____

____

____

GROUND TWO: ____

____

____

____

(a) Supporting facts (Do not argue or cite law. Just state the specific facts that support your claim.): ______________________

____

____

____

____

____

____

____

____

____

____

____

____

____

____

____

____

____

____

(b) **Direct Appeal of Ground Two:**

(1) If you appealed from the judgment of conviction, did you raise this issue?

Yes [ ] No [ ]

(2) If you did not raise this issue in your direct appeal, explain why:______________________________

____

____

____

____

____

(c) Post-Conviction Proceedings:

(1) Did you raise this issue in any post-conviction motion, petition, or application?
Yes [ ] No [ ]

(2) If your answer to Question (c)(1) is "Yes," state:
Type of motion or petition: ______________________

____

Name and location of the court where the motion or petition was filed: ______________________

____

____

Docket or case number (if you know): ______________________

____

Date of the court's decision: ______________________

____

Result (attach a copy of the court's opinion or order, if available): ______________________

____

____

____

____

____

(3) Did you receive a hearing on your motion, petition, or application?
Yes [ ] No [ ]

(4) Did you appeal from the denial of your motion, petition, or application?
Yes [ ] No [ ]

(5) If your answer to Question (c)(4) is "Yes," did you raise this issue in the appeal?
Yes [ ] No [ ]

(6) If your answer to Question (c)(4) is "Yes," state:
Name and location of the court where the appeal was filed: ______________________

____

____

____

____

Docket or case number (if you know): ______________________

____

Date of the court's decision: ______________________

____

Result (attach a copy of the court's opinion or order, if available): ______________________________

(7) If your answer to Question (c)(4) or Question (c)(5) is "No," explain why you did not appeal or raise this issue:

____

GROUND THREE: ______________________________

(a) Supporting facts (Do not argue or cite law. Just state the specific facts that support your claim.): ______________________________

(b) **Direct Appeal of Ground Three:**

(1) If you appealed from the judgment of conviction, did you raise this issue?

Yes [ ] No [ ]

(2) If you did not raise this issue in your direct appeal, explain why: ______________________________

____

____

____

____

____

____

(c) **Post-Conviction Proceedings:**

(1) Did you raise this issue in any post-conviction motion, petition, or application?

Yes [ ] No [ ]

(2) If your answer to Question (c)(1) is "Yes," state:

Type of motion or petition: ______________________________

____

Name and location of the court where the motion or petition was filed: ______________________________

____

____

____

____

Docket or case number (if you know): ______________________________

____

Date of the court's decision: ______________________________

____

Result (attach a copy of the court's opinion or order, if available): ______________________________

____

____

____

____

____

____

(3) Did you receive a hearing on your motion, petition, or application?

Yes [ ] No [ ]

(4) Did you appeal from the denial of your motion, petition, or application?

Yes [ ] No [ ]

(5) If your answer to Question (c)(4) is "Yes," did you raise this issue in the appeal?
Yes [ ] No [ ]

(6) If your answer to Question (c)(4) is "Yes," state:
Name and location of the court where the appeal was filed: ____________________

Docket or case number (if you know): ____________________

Date of the court's decision: ____________________

Result (attach a copy of the court's opinion or order, if available): ____________________

(7) If your answer to Question (c)(4) or Question (c)(5) is "No," explain why you did not appeal or raise this issue:

____

GROUND FOUR: ____________________

(a) Supporting facts (Do not argue or cite law. Just state the specific facts that support your claim.):

____

(b) **Direct Appeal of Ground Four**:

(1) If you appealed from the judgment of conviction, did you raise this issue?

Yes [ ] No [ ]

(2) If you did not raise this issue in your direct appeal, explain why:

(c) **Post-Conviction Proceedings**:

(1) Did you raise this issue in any post-conviction motion, petition, or application?

Yes [ ] No [ ]

(2) If your answer to Question (c)(1) is "Yes," state:

Type of motion or petition:

Name and location of the court where the motion or petition was filed:

Docket or case number (if you know):

Date of the court's decision:

Result (attach a copy of the court's opinion or order, if available):

(3) Did you receive a hearing on your motion, petition, or application?
Yes [ ] No [ ]

(4) Did you appeal from the denial of your motion, petition, or application?
Yes [ ] No [ ]

(5) If your answer to Question (c)(4) is "Yes," did you raise this issue in the appeal?
Yes [ ] No [ ]

(6) If your answer to Question (c)(4) is "Yes," state:
Name and location of the court where the appeal was filed: ______________________________
____
____
____
____

Docket or case number (if you know): ______________
____

Date of the court's decision: ______________________
____

Result (attach a copy of the court's opinion or order, if available): ______________________________
____
____
____
____
____
____

(7) If your answer to Question (c)(4) or Question (c)(5) is "No," explain why you did not appeal or raise this issue:
____
____
____
____
____
____

13. Is there any ground in this motion that you have *not* previously presented in some federal court? If so, which ground or grounds have not been presented, and state your reasons for not presenting them: ______________________________
____
____
____

14. Do you have any motion, petition, or appeal *now pending* (filed and not decided yet) in any court for the judgment you are challenging? Yes [ ] No [ ]

    If "Yes," state the name and location of the court, the docket or case number, the type of proceeding, and the issues raised.

15. Give the name and address, if known, of each attorney who represented you in the following stages of the judgment you are challenging:
    (a) At preliminary hearing:
    (b) At arraignment and plea:
    (c) At trial:
    (d) At sentencing:
    (e) On appeal:

(f) In any post-conviction proceeding: ____________________

____

____

____

(g) On appeal from any ruling against you in a post-conviction proceeding: ____________________

16. Were you sentenced on more than one count of an indictment, or on more than one indictment, in the same court and at the same time? Yes [ ] No [ ]

17. Do you have any future sentence to serve after you complete the sentence for the judgment that you are challenging?
Yes [ ] No [ ]
(a) If so, give name and location of court that imposed the other sentence you will serve in the future: ____________________

____

____

____

____

(b) Give the date the other sentence was imposed: ____________________

____

(c) Give the length of the other sentence: ____________________

____

(d) Have you filed, or do you plan to file, any motion, petition, or application that challenges the judgment or sentence to be served in the future? Yes [ ] No [ ]

18. **TIMELINESS OF MOTION**: If your judgment of conviction became final over one year ago, you must explain why the one-year statute of limitations as contained in 28 U.S.C. § 2255 does not bar your motion.* ____________________

____

____

* The Antiterrorism and Effective Death Penalty Act of 1996 ("AEDPA") as contained in 28 U.S.C. § 2255, paragraph 6, provides in part that:

A one-year period of limitation shall apply to a motion under this section. The limitation period shall run from the latest of

(1) the date on which the judgment of conviction became final;
(2) the date on which the impediment to making a motion created by governmental action in violation of the Constitution or laws of the United States is removed, if the movant was prevented from making such a motion by such governmental action;
(3) the date on which the right asserted was initially recognized by the Supreme Court, if that right has been newly recognized by the Supreme Court and made retroactively applicable to cases on collateral review; or
(4) the date on which the facts supporting the claim or claims presented could have been discovered through the exercise of due diligence.

Therefore, movant asks that the Court grant the following relief: ____

or any other relief to which movant may be entitled.

Signature of Attorney (if any)

I declare (or certify, verify, or state) under penalty of perjury that the foregoing is true and correct and that this Motion Under 28 U.S.C. § 2255 was placed in the prison mailing system on ______________________ ____________ (month, date, year).
Executed (signed) on __________ (date).

____
Signature of Movant

If the person signing is not movant, state relationship to movant and explain why movant is not signing this motion. ____________________
____
____
____
____
____
____

[INSERT APPROPRIATE COURT]
IN FORMA PAUPERIS DECLARATION

United States **v.** ______________________________ **(Movant)**	**DECLARATION IN SUPPORT OF REQUEST TO PROCEED** IN FORMA PAUPERIS

I, ______________________________, declare that I am the movant in the above entitled case; that in support of my motion to proceed without being required to prepay fees, costs or give security therefor, I state that because of my poverty, I am unable to pay the costs of said proceeding or to give security therefor; that I believe I am entitled to relief.

1. Are you presently employed? Yes [ ] No [ ]
   a. If the answer is "yes," state the amount of your salary or wages per month, and give the name and address of your employer.
      ____
      ____
      ____
      ____

b. If the answer is "no," state the date of last employment and the amount of the salary or wages per month which you received.

____

____

____

____

2. Have you received within the past twelve months any money from any of the following sources?
   a. Business, profession or form of self-employment? Yes [ ] No [ ]
   b. Rent payments, interest or dividends? Yes [ ] No [ ]
   c. Pensions, annuities or life insurance payments? Yes [ ] No [ ]
   d. Gifts or inheritances? Yes [ ] No [ ]
   e. Any other sources? Yes [ ] No [ ]

   If the answer to any of the above is "yes," describe each source of money and state the amount received from each during the past twelve months.

____

____

____

____

____

____

3. Do you own any cash, or do you have money in a checking or savings account?
   Yes [ ] No [ ] (Include any funds in prison accounts)

   If the answer is "yes," state the total value of the items owned.

____

____

____

____

____

____

4. Do you own real estate, stocks, bonds, notes, automobiles, or other valuable property (excluding ordinary household furnishings and clothing)?
   Yes [ ] No [ ]

   If the answer is "yes," describe the property and state its approximate value.

____

____

____

____

5. List the persons who are dependent upon you for support, state your relationship to those persons, and indicate how much you contribute toward their support.

____

____

____

____

I declare (or certify, verify, or state) under penalty of perjury that the foregoing is true and correct. Executed on ____________ (date).

____

Signature of Movant

CERTIFICATE

I hereby certify that the movant herein has the sum of $________ on account to his credit at the __________ institution where he is confined. I further certify that movant likewise has the following securities to his credit according to the records of said ____________ institution:

____

____

____

____

____

____

____

____

____

Authorized Officer of Institution

Table of Cases

C

D

J

K

L

M

N

O

P

Q

R

S

T

U

Y

Z

Index

T